Teaching Reading in Kindergarten

A Structured Approach to Daily Reading
That Helps Every Child Become a Confident, Capable Reader

Randee Bergen

■SCHOLASTIC

New York • Toronto • London • Auckland • Sydney
Mexico City • New Delhi • Hong Kong • Buenos Aires

Dedication

This book is dedicated to Shirlie M. Lohof
a beloved friend, wife, mother, volunteer, and teaching assistant gone too soon.

"I have learned more with this job than with any other I've had in my life. I'm not talking about how to run the copy machine or even about how to better work with kids. I'm talking about realizing the potential of five-year-olds. I never knew that we could—that we should—expect so much from them, and that they'd be able to do it."

Acknowledgments

To each and every kindergarten student who has passed through my classroom, I thank you for what you brought to the learning situation, for sharing your unique ways of constructing knowledge, and for everything that you taught me about how young children learn to read. You all left a lasting effect. And to Joanna Davis-Swing and Sarah Glasscock, editors extraordinaire, who so patiently and expertly guided me in organizing and presenting this wealth of knowledge and experience. Last, to my readers—may you discover the true capabilities of kindergartners and do everything in your means to provide them the gift and love of literacy.

■ ■ ■ ■ ■ ■

Cover design: Lindsey Dekker
Cover photograph: Kelly Sparks, Smiles in There Photography
Interior photographs: Randee Bergen; Kelly Sparks, Smiles in There Photography
Illustrations © Scholastic Inc.; Manuel Rivera, Paige Billin-Frye, Maxie Chambliss, Steve Cox, and Sue Dennen; Camila Bertoco, from The Noun Project
Interior design: Sarah Morrow
Development Editor: Joanna Davis-Swing
Editor: Sarah Glasscock
Copy Editor: Lynne Wilson

ISBN: 978-0-545-52943-3
Copyright © 2013 by Randee Bergen
All rights reserved.
Printed in the U.S.A.

1 2 3 4 5 6 7 8 9 10   40   20 19 18 17 16 15 14 13

CONTENTS

Free Downloadable Teacher Resources

Go to **http://teacherexpress.scholastic.com/teachingreadingK** to download
a pdf with the following resources:

- *Sample Kindergarten Yearlong Plan*
- *Letter Formation Cues for Lowercase and Uppercase Letters*
- *Ideas for Introducing and Teaching Letter Sounds and Names*
- *Cards for Teaching Letter Chunks*
- *10 Emergent Reader Templates*

How to Maximize Student Learning

Two key premises compelled me to write this book.

- Kindergarten is steadily becoming more academic in nature, and school districts, teachers, parents, and even kindergarten students themselves are expecting more challenging and purposeful literacy instruction—and thus more learning—to occur during the first year of formal schooling. This expectation has created, and will continue to generate, the need for professional development for kindergarten teachers that, up to now, has not been easily fulfilled. As Regie Routman sums up so impeccably: "We need to get down to the essence of what we believe and what we do to ensure our students become excellent readers who choose to read. If we don't know how to teach reading and move students forward, we must take responsibility for learning how. We must jumpstart our own professional development" (2003, p. 42).

- The second premise arises from the first. Once you begin to implement a system of regular, explicit, and individualized reading instruction, it surely will not be long until you discover, as have I over the past decade, that your kindergarten students can do a whole lot more than they have traditionally been expected or permitted to do. Establishing what these students, as a whole, can actually achieve should revolutionize expectations at the kindergarten level and change dramatically the ways in which we can help all children maximize their reading development during the kindergarten year. As I stated in my first book, *Teaching Writing in*

Kindergarten: A Structured Approach to Daily Writing That Helps Every Child Become a Confident, Capable Writer (2008), by raising our expectations and strategically nurturing the growth of students' early literacy skills, we may, ultimately, redefine what constitutes best practice at the kindergarten level.

Kindergarten teachers have been conditioned to expect the following level of reading achievement for their students: kindergartners should learn the names and sounds of most of the letters, recognize a prescribed number of sight words, develop a basic concept of print, and demonstrate emergent-reading Level 3/C skills. The chart below shows a reading level correlation chart for kindergarten through grade 8.

Reading Level Correlation Chart

Grade Level	Reading Recovery	Fountas-Pinnell Guided Reading	DRA	Basal Equivalent	Lexile Ranges Aligned to CCR Expectations*
Kindergarten	A, B	A	A	Readiness	N/A
	1		1		
	2	B	2	PrePrimer 1	
	3	C	3		
Grade 1	4		4	PrePrimer 2	N/A
	5	D	6		
	6				
	7	E	8	PrePrimer 3	
	8				
	9	F	10	Primer	
	10				
	11	G	12		
	12				
	13	H	14	Grade 1	
	14				
	15	I	16		
	16				

Grade Level	Reading Recovery	Fountas-Pinnell Guided Reading	DRA	Basal Equivalent	Lexile Ranges Aligned to CCR Expectations*
Grade 2	18	J, K	20	Grade 2	450–790
	20	L, M	28		
Grade 3	22	N	30	Grade 3	
			34		
	24	O, P	38		
Grade 4	26	Q, R, S	40	Grade 4	770–980
Grade 5	28	T, U, V	44	Grade 5	
Grade 6	30	W, X, Y		Grade 6	955–1155
Grade 7	32	Z		Grade 7	
Grade 8	34	Z		Grade 8	

* College and Career Readiness (CCR)

The assumption that a Level 3/C is equivalent to an end-of-kindergarten reading level forms the basis of these expectations for kindergarten students. It is also at the heart of any misconception about kindergarten students and their true capabilities when it comes to learning to read. Despite the history and depiction of kindergarten in this nation, and in light of the changes that are facing us, I propose that kindergarten teachers take charge of their own professional development in order to become better teachers of literacy. In the process of becoming direct and explicit teachers of reading at the kindergarten level, we will become honest observers of the true nature of students and their learning potential. It is time to change our expectations and our teaching to better match the veritable capabilities of kindergarten students.

Rather than striving to get most students to a Level 3/C reading level, I suggest that we make every effort to get our *lowest-achieving* students to that level, and that we expect and teach the *majority* of our students to read beyond that mark. Until now, there has not been a comprehensive resource that teachers could easily get their hands on that shows just how one might go about teaching reading in the kindergarten setting. *Teaching Reading in Kindergarten* will empower kindergarten teachers across the nation to start the process of taking responsibility for their own professional development.

Research Supports Increased Expectations

Many research studies have concluded that children who learn to read earlier tend to be proficient and voracious readers throughout school and life (Early Childhood Longitudinal Study by the National Center for Education Statistics as reported by McGill-Franzen, 2006; Connie Juel in 1988; Delores Durkin in 1966 and 1974–1975; Stainthorp and Hughes in 2004; and, Richard Allington's series of studies reported in 2006). The most powerful research, however, is that conducted by neuroscientist and professor of pediatrics at the Yale Center for the Study of Learning and Attention, Sally Shaywitz (2003).

Richard Gentry (2006) puts in plain words the implications of the brain scan work completed by Shaywitz: Facilitating reading development in kindergartners will actually reduce the number of students who need future intervention and/or are eventually identified as having a learning disability. A neurological glitch that occurs during fetal development can trigger a learning disability. A promising aspect of Shaywitz's work is that preliminary studies involving children who are just learning to read indicate that, with the proper instruction, the brain can repair itself. But this fix requires early instruction and intervention, when the brain is plastic and malleable for rerouting neural systems. According to Gentry, Shaywitz's work shows that this rerouting and repair is best achieved around the ages of five and six.

John Abbott, too, speaks of the effects of a stimulating and challenging learning environment (1997). Traditionalists believe that humans are born with a set amount of intelligence that cannot be altered. However, recent research on the human brain is providing a growing understanding of its workings and changing the way intelligence is defined. Researchers now view the brain as a unique living organism that grows and reshapes itself in response to challenges.

Early reading instruction promotes intelligence and makes it possible to reroute neural systems and prevent this learning disability. Early teaching and intervention is necessary, and the place for this is the kindergarten classroom. Kindergarten teachers can more readily establish a culture of learning and the behavior expectations that are necessary for the ultimate in teaching and learning. We are in a position to explicitly teach and develop in our students, early in life, behaviors and attitudes that contribute to a more concentrated and deeper type of learning. These behaviors and attitudes then become habit and carry forward to succeeding grade levels. Such learning habits include attending to and fully engaging in instruction, developing the practice of self-monitoring, and continually challenging oneself to work up to one's potential. Launching a culture of learning that teaches and calls for such learning behaviors is more possible in the kindergarten setting than in any other grade level because students at this age are more open to whatever it is we are going to expect from them.

Kindergartners, collectively, are remarkably amenable to instruction. This seems to be true despite their backgrounds or variations in natural ability to learn. They are eager to acquire knowledge and new skills, and most do so almost effortlessly—so learning to read is not considered hard work but instead an enjoyable and stimulating process. And, since it is an inherent characteristic of almost all students at this age to want to please adults, it makes sense to expect more from them—without pushing too hard—in order to create the opportunity to fully discover just how much each student is capable of doing. Nurturing kindergartners in the full development of their reading skills establishes a foundation in literacy and a confidence within them that will serve them well for the rest of their lives.

About This Book

In this book, I provide you with the means for contemplating and implementing changes in your schedule, materials and text choices, management ideas, and instructional methods that will make reading at a higher level a real possibility for your kindergarten students.

Before undertaking a daily reading program in your kindergarten classroom, you'll want to take the time to understand the basic premise of this program and to see the big picture. The guiding principles of this approach (page 9) and the yearlong plan for its implementation (page 10) outline the goals and expectations, as well as the scope and sequence, for teaching reading in kindergarten. An overview of a yearlong plan is on page 12. The specific routines, procedures, strategies, and timelines for implementation are thoroughly discussed in

Chapters 1–8.

This computer mouse icon indicates which material in this book is downloadable, including charts and templates for emergent readers. You'll find these materials online at **http://teacherexpress.scholastic.com/ teachingreadingK**.

Is It Developmentally Appropriate?

In education, the term "developmentally appropriate" represents the concept that the suitability of an approach matches the approximate cognitive and behavioral stages of a child. Today's kindergarten students are not only different from kindergartners in the past, they are also more significantly different from each other than they used to be. To be developmentally appropriate, a teaching approach should focus on individualized, differentiated instruction so it meets the specific needs of each student. All students—no matter their background or prior experience with print—can and will benefit from receiving the same explicit and solid instruction detailed in this book. According to Marie Clay (2001), about 10–20 percent of all children will seriously struggle with learning to read. Herein lies the beauty of this new way of teaching reading in kindergarten: You can facilitate the reading development of students who are ready and, at the same time, develop the skills of those who need a little more time and intervention.

Guiding Principles for Teaching Reading in Kindergarten

As I have developed and refined this approach to teaching kindergarten students to read, the following beliefs and practices have become the foundation of my instruction. They are the keys to maximizing your teaching and helping students become confident and independent readers.

1. Make every effort to help struggling students learn to read at a Level 3/C, but expect and teach the majority of students to read beyond that mark.

2. Establish and remain committed to a balanced literacy approach that includes read-alouds, shared reading, small-group and individualized instruction, and true independent reading.

3. Use preplanned, whole-group engagements to teach "in front of" students' reading experiences and individualized instruction to teach "into" a child's experiences.

4. Procure a variety of high-quality texts that complement a balanced approach to teaching literacy, including read-alouds, shared-reading texts, quality leveled books, and a wide assortment of texts for independent reading.

5. For the first six weeks of the school year, provide direct and explicit instruction to develop concepts of print and the notion of reading. Establish three rotating centers: Teacher Center (direct instruction), Assistant Center (guided practice), and Independent Center (independent practice).

6. After the first six weeks, move from small-group instruction to individualized instruction in order to maximize reading development.

7. Provide highly structured routines, expectations, and the explicit teaching of key strategies to support students in becoming independent readers.

8. Teach students at each one's individual skill level and encourage them to progress at their own rate with no ceiling of opportunity. Employ modeling, scaffolding, prompting, backing off, and reinforcement to support student learning.

9. Move students steadily along the continuum of learning, using Vygotsky's (1978) zone of proximal development in combination with Bruner and Sherwood's (1975) concept of scaffolding. Recognize what students are on the verge of doing independently tomorrow if given just a bit of support from you today.

10. Keep parents informed about and involved in their child's process of learning to read by sharing expectations and strategies and sending home appropriately leveled books.

The Yearlong Plan

August–September*

For the first six weeks of school, shared reading and small-group instruction serve as a way to introduce the whole notion of reading, concepts of print, and the skill of voice-print match.

- Establish a daily schedule and classroom routines, including three daily centers, that support a balanced approach to teaching literacy.

- Introduce the notion of reading, concepts of print, and voice-print match during shared reading and shared writing.

- Acquire and create books and texts that enhance your instructional needs.

- Create opportunities for students to practice voice-print match during small-group instruction.

- Incorporate phonemic awareness and phonics activities daily.

- Introduce and have students practice reading and writing basic sight words.

October and Beyond

After about six weeks, individualized instruction replaces small-group instruction, and established structures and strategies help students move into independent reading.

- Acquire high-quality, leveled texts for guided-reading instruction. Understand how books are leveled and which strategic reading behaviors and processes must be taught for students to access the various levels.

- Put appropriately-leveled books into a zipping bag for each student as he or she meets with you on a regular basis for individualized reading instruction.

- Establish expectations for and explicitly instruct students in how to independently read the books in their book bag.

- Send home appropriately-leveled books with students, along with tips for parents on how to support their child in the emergent stage of reading.

- Employ the five main teaching actions when working alongside students—modeling, scaffolding, prompting, backing off, and reinforcing.

- Focus on five critical strategies—learning behaviors, word analysis, predicting and crosschecking, fix-ups, and relevant comments and questions.

- Continue introducing sight words. Assist students in recognizing them and learning to spell them.

- Conduct assessments to monitor students' acquisition of letter names, letter sounds, and sight words.

- Provide intervention for those students struggling with letter names, letter sounds, and sight words.

- Use interactive read-aloud, along with the five critical strategies, to develop comprehension.

January

Students' reading skills have developed to the point that they are ready and can be responsible for true independent reading time.

- Continue with the above.

- Establish expectations for and explicitly instruct students in how to choose just-right books and productively engage in true independent reading time.

* *This yearlong plan is based on a mid-August through May school year. If you begin teaching in September, simply adjust your plan forward by two weeks.*

Yearlong Plan Overview

Week	Date	Theme
1	8/20	Busy Bee, Rules
2	8/27	First Names/Me
3	9/3	Birthdays
4	9/10	Bus
5	9/17	Color Words
6	9/24	Safety
7	9/25	Scarecrows
8	10/8	Apples
9	10/15	Fall/Leaves
10	10/22	Bats
11	10/29	Halloween
12	11/5	Voting, Little Red Hen
13	11/12	Little Red Hen
14	11/19	Thanksgiving
15	11/26	Family, Houses
16	12/3	Opposites
17	12/10	Gingerbread Man
18	12/17	Christmas
19	1/7	New Year's, Last Names
20	1/14	Winter
21	1/21	Martin Luther King, Jr.
22	1/28	Pledge, Patriotic Songs
23	2/4	100th Day of School
24	2/11	Valentine's Day, Friends
25	2/18	USA
26	2/25	Questions, Dr. Seuss
27	3/3	Ducks
28	3/17	Spring, Easter
29	3/24	Spring, Wind, Rain
30	3/31	Plants
31	4/7	Caterpillars & Butterflies
32	4/14	Teeth
33	4/21	Earth Day, Earth's Animals
34	4/28	Farm, Baby Animals
35	5/5	Mother's Day
36	5/12	Watermelon
37	5/19	Pizza

CHAPTER 1

Getting Started

Regie Routman talks about "teaching with a sense of urgency." Teaching should be driven by the desire to make every moment in the classroom count. As professionals, we need to be aware of how we are utilizing every moment and opportunity we have to teach, know the skills and strategies that need to be taught, and optimize our materials and activities and the contexts in which we use them. Boushey and Moser from *The Daily Five* agree: "Creating urgency in learning establishes a culture where every moment of learning and practicing counts for students and teachers. It is not anxiety that teachers and students feel when they are teaching and learning with a sense of urgency, but a responsibility to take ownership for their own teaching and learning" (2006, p. 22).

The first step in maximizing students' learning in kindergarten, or any grade level for that matter, then, is to teach immediately, teach with intent and urgency, and teach with your end goal in mind at all times.

In kindergarten, that end goal is to get all students reading at least Level 3/C text, with most students reading beyond that level. To teach to this goal, it is necessary to do the following:

- Establish the time and expectations for a balanced approach to teaching reading.

- Create a yearlong plan.

- Arrange your classroom.

- Gather texts.
- Set up routines.

Establishing Daily Reading Time

From the first day of school, focus on getting started on the important academic work that occurs within the framework of the classroom routines and that, inherently, creates community within the classroom.

A BALANCED LITERACY APPROACH

A balanced reading program includes a range of literacy activities and a responsive teacher who knows how to structure literacy interactions that move children to higher levels of responsibility and understanding. In *One Child at a Time*, Pat Johnson succinctly explains the balanced approach:

> *A balanced literacy approach does not mean an eclectic program with pieces from every method of teaching reading. Balance refers to having a balance in your program of* whose responsibility it is to do the reading work. *In other words, how much responsibility for figuring out the words and comprehending the meaning is the job of the teacher and how much of that job belongs to the students? Each of the four contexts for reading—read-aloud time, shared reading, guided reading, and independent reading—provide different amounts of teacher support and different amounts of student responsibility* (2006, pp. 20–21).

The contexts of teaching reading that make up a balanced approach—read-aloud, shared reading, guided reading (usually referred to in this book as small-group or individualized reading instruction), and independent reading—appear in the daily schedules on the next pages and are discussed throughout the book. Unfortunately, not all of these teaching contexts are being implemented in kindergarten classrooms. For example, one-on-one or small-group instruction does not happen in many kindergarten classrooms because teachers feel their students are not yet ready to benefit from such instruction or because— especially with half-day programs—they think there isn't enough time to conduct small-group instruction. In some cases, a context isn't being implemented effectively. For example, although time might be allotted for independent reading, if students are not receiving explicit, individualized instruction with appropriate texts, then they probably end up just looking at books and not actually reading them during independent reading time. Again, this book will address those concerns.

Daily Schedule

These half- and full-day schedules provide a window into the amount of time in any given instructional day that should be devoted to explicit literacy instruction. As you teach, feel free to modify your schedule in order to find the best ways to plug in the various components you want to include.

Half-Day Kindergarten Schedule

Monday, Tuesday, Thursday, Friday

8:45	First bell rings.
8:50	Tardy bell rings.
8:45–9:15	Writing
9:15–9:30	Name Game (phonemic awareness, phonics)
9:30–10:00	Specials
10:00–10:30	Math (2 days a week) Computer lab (2 days a week)
10:30–10:40	Recess
10:40–10:45	Drinks
10:45–11:00	Whole-group reading (shared or read-aloud)
11:00–11:45	Centers*
11:45–11:50	Shared writing or debriefing
11:50	Dismissal

Wednesday

8:45	First bell rings.
8:50	Tardy bell rings.
8:45–9:15	Math and writing
9:15–9:30	Name Game
9:30–9:45	Whole-group reading (shared or read-aloud)
9:45–9:55	Recess
9:55–10:00	Drinks
10:00–10:45	Centers*
10:45–10:50	Shared writing or debriefing
10:50	Dismissal *early release for professional growth time*

Full-Day Kindergarten Schedule M–F

8:20	First bell rings. (Tardy bell rings at 8:25.)	12:00–12:25	Shared reading
8:20–8:50	Writing	12:25–12:55	Down time/independent reading/individual or group interventions
8:50–9:05	Name Game (phonemic awareness, phonics)	12:55–1:15	Read-aloud
9:05–9:50	Morning centers*	1:15–1:35	Afternoon recess
9:55–10:20	Specials	1:35–1:40	Drinks
10:20–10:35	Morning recess	1:40–2:20	Calendar/whole-group math instruction
10:35–10:40	Drinks	2:20–3:05	Afternoon centers*
10:40–11:05	Whole-group reading (shared or read-aloud)	3:05–3:10	Shared writing or debriefing
11:05–11:10	Hand washing	3:10	Dismissal
11:10–12:00	Lunch/lunch recess		

* includes individual or small-group reading instruction and independent reading*

The essential elements of the daily schedule are the following:

- Whole-group time for read-aloud and shared reading
- Center time that makes it possible for you to meet with students in small groups or individually while others work and/or read independently
- Time devoted to the isolated study of phonemic awareness and phonics
- Writing time

WHOLE-GROUP READING TIME

The time established for whole-group reading on the sample daily schedules is generally filled with shared reading or interactive read-aloud, two of the four important components of a balanced approach to teaching literacy.

- Shared reading is a staple activity in kindergarten. The teacher reads from a specifically selected big book or chart while students look at the text and follow along. This can also now be done using a document camera with regular-size books and text. During this activity, the teacher may introduce print conventions, teach sight words, and develop key strategies and comprehension skills. Learn more about optimizing shared-reading time in Chapter 2.

- Read-aloud, on the other hand, requires that students listen to—more than look at—text while the teacher reads, demonstrates how fluent reading sounds, shares illustrations, and encourages talk that strengthens comprehension of the text. This is discussed at length in Chapter 8.

With both of these types of whole-class instruction, it is the teacher's responsibility to do the reading work. Students are encouraged and expected to listen, observe, and think about the text and the instructional points, and to join in at their comfort level during shared reading.

CENTERS

Learning centers are generally defined as designated areas in the classroom where students go to engage in various activities that facilitate language development, build peer relationships, or teach skills or knowledge. In order to support a balanced approach to teaching reading and provide the time needed for individual instruction, I recommend setting up three different centers that small groups revolve through:

- *Teacher Center*: In the first six weeks, small groups of students work with you. After that, small groups continue to visit the Teacher Center, but you pull individuals from the group to provide tailored instruction while the others read on their own.

- *Assistant Center*: An assistant or parent works with small groups who are doing activities that require supervision or immediate feedback.

- *Independent Center*: Small groups read or work independently on activities.

As you will learn in Chapter 3, this approach to running centers complements a variety of activities, requires very little planning or preparation, allows closure on all activities for all students by the end of the day, greatly minimizes the amount of time that has to be devoted to physically moving students through the centers, and makes clean-up easy. Most important, it permits you to conduct small-group or individualized reading instruction without having to put a lot of effort into managing the rest of the class.

PHONEMIC AWARENESS AND PHONICS

Kindergarten students must become familiar with the individual sounds in our language and learn to manipulate them in different ways. This includes hearing and isolating sounds (i.e., becoming aware of the individual phonemes of our language) as well as associating the correct letters with each sound. For intense phonemic awareness and phonics instruction, I use the Name Game. This game involves the complete analysis of students' first names and, later in the year, last names, including all the letters, sounds, blends, chunks, various possible sounds for vowels, and other fascinating discussions that stem from such examination. The Name Game activity is a principal component to teaching a deeper foundation in reading and writing. A description of how to introduce the Name Game on the first day of school appears in Chapter 2, and Chapter 3 includes an in-depth discussion of its use in teaching phonemic awareness and phonics.

WRITING TIME

Learning to write is closely linked with learning to read and is vital to a student's success in reading. An effective kindergarten writing program is just as important to the teaching of reading as the actual reading instruction itself. I have incorporated brief explanations about teaching writing in various sections in this book. My methods for teaching writing are explained in full detail in my book, *Teaching Writing in Kindergarten: A Structured Approach to Daily Writing that Helps Every Child Become a Confident, Capable Writer.*

Rounding Out a Full Day of Kindergarten

It's important to understand that students in a full-day setting are getting twice as much instruction and learning time as their half-day or part-time counterparts and should, therefore, be achieving at significantly higher levels than what is traditionally expected of half-day students.

Some full-day kindergarten programs view the first half of the day as time for structured learning activities and the afternoon as time for free choice and exploration activities. This approach does not benefit students, academically, as much as it could. I highly recommend using the additional time to enrich and enhance what you are doing instructionally. Afternoons offer more time for shared reading, writing, read-alouds, one-on-one instruction, the sharing of student writing, and word work.

Yearlong Planning

Once you have established a daily schedule, the next task is to consider how best to fill in these daily time slots. I recommend creating a yearlong plan designed around weekly thematic units to help you sequence the instruction and activities, and the accompanying materials and texts in a way that will support your long-range goals for your students.

Teaching With a Thematic Approach

The backbone of a kindergarten yearlong plan is typically, but not necessarily, weekly thematic units. Teaching with a thematic approach means planning activities around a central topic. In *Guided Reading: Good First Teaching for All Children* (1996), Fountas and Pinnell share how themes create an overarching web of meaning that helps children connect various reading and writing activities in a purposeful way. In *The Reading Workshop: Creating Space for Readers* (2001), Frank Serafini explains that reading books randomly affords students few, if any, opportunities to make connections across different titles; the connections that range across themes seem to be the most significant for children in understanding literature.

A yearlong plan overview, like the one on page 12, functions as the basic framework for what you plan to do throughout the school year. It begins as an outline but can, like the complete plan available in Teacher Express, grow into a rich and intricately woven tapestry of short- and long-term goals, instructional reminders, learning activities, and related books and materials. Yearlong planning takes vision. You must know where you want your students to be by the end of the year and what it is going to take to get them there. Committing a yearlong plan to paper serves many purposes; the most important of which is to ensure that your teaching moves along in a steady, systematic manner from the first day of school to the last.

A yearlong plan is a dynamic document. It should be continually modified and updated. Having a well-sequenced yearlong plan will allow you to more easily make adjustments in your instruction and pacing because the placement of the activities, strategies, and skills can fluctuate within a particular section of the plan.

BUILDING WEEKLY THEMES

Once the backbone of your yearlong plan, the thematic units, is in place, begin gathering books, materials, and learning activities that relate to each theme. Here are some tips for doing that:

- Think about sight words that you could introduce during each unit, then find books and activities that incorporate the teaching of these sight words and the theme.

- Search the Internet for thematic unit ideas or kindergarten activities.

- Browse through teacher supply catalogs, especially those organized by thematic unit.

- Find a key piece of literature and use its theme, characters, and teaching points to create additional texts or design related learning activities.

- Check publishers' catalogs.

- Search online book stores by entering a certain theme or topic, check the pages of books to ensure compatibility with your students' needs, and look for used books in good condition.

- Search the public library for read-alouds, big books, and other shared-reading texts. (This allows you to test the effectiveness of certain titles before purchasing your own copies.)

- Exchange ideas with your grade-level partners or other kindergarten teachers in the district.

- Create your own books when you cannot find or afford exactly what you need.

- Develop activities or modify activities you've used in the past.

Download the yearlong plan at **http://teacherexpress. scholastic.com/ teachingreadingK**.

Gathering books, ideas, and materials will be an ongoing process as you continually update your plan. The yearlong plan available on Teacher Express was written, tweaked, adjusted, and modified over a three-year period with the support of my past teammate, Mary Arends, in Littleton, Colorado. Though it grew into a five-page plan, we still never considered it to be a complete and finished document. It changed weekly as we carefully considered the implementation and effectiveness of each theme's related activities and the timing of the introduction of and focus on certain skills and strategies.

Kindergarten Yearlong Plan

WEEK	THEME/ WORDS/ CHUNKS	BOOKS/CHARTS	ACTIVITIES
Aug. 23 *5 days*	Busy Bee, Rules *I*	Busy Bee chart; Miss Bindergarten Gets Ready for Kindergarten; Copy Cat's Animal Noises; First Day Jitters; I is for One; Panda Kindergarten; A Place Called Kindergarten; A School Day; Splat the Cat	Back-to-School scavenger hunt: individual assessments; introduce rules/ROAR; playground rules; recognize first name; copy first name correctly; #s 1–9 w/# poems; graph # of letters in first names; start voice-print match; start learning letters in name; count school days; explain Wednesday folders; model thinking aloud about text; introduce "Say Something"; free explore manipulatives; I paper book; make busy bees; Name Game (pass busy bee on stick; say "Busy Bee, Busy Bee, can you say your name for me?"); no calendar until September; giant Busy Bee notes
Aug. 30 *5 days*	First Names *me om*	Me chart; Spend Time With Me; The ABC Book (w/writing); The Monster at the End of This Book; Meet the Barkers; My Mouth Is a Volcano (blurting)	Continue copying/writing names correctly; continue learning letters in name; #s with # poems; free explore manipulatives; snip scraps; "just a dot, not a lot" gluing; Me game (hold up a name card, student says, "That's me, m-e!"); I Like paper book; I Am paper book; I Am class book with photos/names of classmates; voice-print match; learn alphabet song; practice pointing to letters while singing; giant Busy Bee notes; arrange school bus ride (First Student 241–1570); building blocks; put up calendar together; introduce days-of-the-week song
Sept. 6 *4 days*	Birthdays *o, red*	Cakes; Happy Birthday song chart; It's My Birthday; Bingo chart; r-e-d song and chart; 1 1, Cinnamon Bun chant; 1 2, Buckle My Shoe	Bingo song and clapping patterns; continue writing names; learn letters in names; discuss/ graph birthdays; months-of-the-year song and dance; put calendar up together; finger patterns to show #s; 1 2, Buckle . . sequence cards; match fingers to # cards; voice-print match; days-of-the-week song; Red Stuff paper book; The Color Book paper book, A Good Book paper book, It's My Birthday paper book; giant Busy Bee notes; send note for bus ride; practice touch and count/move and count; introduce magnetic letters; birthday cake color word sheet; "things that are red" sheet

TEACHING READING IN KINDERGARTEN © 2013 by Randee Bergen, Scholastic Teaching Resources ■ Yearlong Plan 1

▉ PROCURING READING MATERIAL

The efficacy of your reading instruction—read-aloud, shared reading, small-group and individual work at the teacher table during centers, and independent reading—relies upon the appropriateness of the books and other reading materials you have available for students. All texts must be representative of the appropriate reading level for the time of year they are being used and integrated and sequenced within an overall instructional plan. It is important to know which books best suit each of the components of the balanced literacy approach and also to understand the characteristics of each level of text. More information about the latter appears in Chapter 5.

Reading Materials for a Balanced Literacy Approach

To successfully implement a balanced literacy approach in your kindergarten classroom, you must have a sufficient number and variety of quality reading materials for each activity. The chart below, adapted from Fountas and Pinnell (1996, p. 27), provides an overview.

Four Types of Reading in Kindergarten With Varying Levels of Responsibility	Reading Materials
Read-Aloud: Teacher purposefully chooses and reads a book or other text to students. Students actively listen and only occasionally look at or read a minimal amount of the text.	Picture books or poetry books chosen for: • relevancy of the topic • repeated use of a particular sight word(s) • building of vocabulary and concepts • facilitation of conversation and strategies aimed at aiding comprehension.
Shared Reading: Teacher purposefully chooses and reads emergent-level texts with enlarged print.	Purchased or teacher-created large-print books and charts chosen for: • study of concepts of print and practice in voice-print match • repeated use of a particular sight word(s) • building of vocabulary and concepts • modeling and practice of various reading strategies • relevance of topic (possibly)
Small-Group or Individualized Instruction: Teacher purposefully chooses texts at students' instructional level. Students do most of the reading with support from the teacher as needed.	Purchased or teacher-created small books of varying reading levels carefully chosen to: • sufficiently support and challenge individual students at their particular reading levels
Independent Reading: Students choose from a selection of appropriate texts. They read individually or with partners, but with little or no assistance from adults.	• shared-reading books and charts (already introduced and practiced with the teacher) • books created by the class • a wide selection of books organized loosely by reading levels in tubs or areas

SELECTING AND ORGANIZING READING MATERIALS

The selection of instructional reading materials demands special consideration. First, if you do not have the reading material you need for all the different instructional modes in the balanced-literacy approach, then you most likely will not sufficiently employ each mode of instruction. As Allington put it, "the ease and productivity of teaching will be affected." Likewise, if you have plenty of reading material but the selections are not at the appropriate level or do not correspond well to your instructional scope and sequence, then students will not benefit as much as they could because the materials are not complementing your instruction.

You can begin by thoughtfully analyzing the books you currently possess and sorting each by instructional category. After you complete this process, then you can begin to slowly and steadily procure additional reading materials. And, if you are in the same boat as most teachers—you cannot find exactly what you were hoping for or do not have the money to purchase what you need—then you'll want to consider creating some reading materials.

If you do not have a complete yearlong plan based on weekly thematic units at this time, I highly recommend starting a simple chart that lists some ideas you have for instructional units, the approximate time you plan to teach them, and your objectives for each unit. This chart could be organized by month, season, or grading period. Having this organizational tool will make gathering and organizing texts much easier. It will also help you notice where the holes might be in read-aloud books or shared-reading materials for certain units.

Consider, too, whether other kindergarten teachers might want to join you in this endeavor. You do not necessarily have to teach the same units or follow an identical sequence in a yearlong plan, but it might benefit everyone to come together and explore the number of different texts you have, collectively, and are willing to share.

As you acquire and incorporate titles into a yearlong plan or chart, it can be helpful to jot down some information about each one, including the following:

- purpose (e.g., read-aloud or shared reading)

- reason for use (e.g., thematic unit concept, reading strategy, general vocabulary, sight word vocabulary)

- type of text (e.g., picture book, big book, poetry chart, song chart, teacher-made book, anthology)

- location (e.g., Mr. G's room, school big-book storage area, public library, need to purchase)

- timing (e.g., first week of the yearlong plan, near the 100th day of school, correct sequence of titles—I have a note to read *My Lucky Day* after reading *Wolf's Chicken Stew* to enhance students' connections between the texts and reinforce vocabulary and concepts from the first story.)

- priority level (e.g., definitely read or only if time allows)

Obviously, listing all of the above information for every title would take up too much space. And, it isn't necessary. For each title, I record only the information I am not sure I can easily recall—perhaps because I am not familiar with a title or because I remember pondering the purpose of a title the previous year. You probably know many books so well that it won't be necessary to include any information besides the title in your yearlong plan or chart.

▦ DEVELOPING WEEKLY PLANS

The yearlong plan will become a framework for daily planning, which is made easier and more beneficial by developing intermediary weekly plans. The literacy materials and other related activities listed on the yearlong plan for any given week should be sequenced in the best possible manner to promote continuity, connections, and deeper learning. Completing a weekly plan rather than a daily plan will help ensure the best possible progression. Typical weekly plans derived from a yearlong plan appear on the next pages. Notice how the template of the weekly plan helps limit the amount of writing that is required. When you create weekly plans in advance, you can share them with parents, your instructional assistant, and other colleagues with whom you collaborate, such as grade-level partners, the ELL teacher, the speech and language specialist, or even the music teacher.

Communicating With Parents

Your weekly plans include important information for parents. I encourage parents to use this document to stay abreast not only of upcoming events but also of how they can support their children on a daily basis. I demonstrate at a parent night or fall parent-teacher conferences how they can use the weekly plans to ask their child specific questions about the day, follow up on and practice certain skills, or discuss the writing topic in advance so students will have more ideas during writing time.

Adhering to a yearlong plan and the subsequent weekly plans will assist you in establishing and maintaining a consistent instructional pulse in your classroom. Without creating and adhering to a plan, you won't know the necessary sequential steps to take to maximize reading development. When you don't have a plan, it is all too easy to let the discussion about a book go on and on, stretch recess a little bit longer, and put things off.

Classroom Arrangement and Routines

Classroom management is best described as the orchestration of the learning environment and how a teacher goes about creating, implementing, and maintaining a setting that substantially enhances instruction and maximizes students' ability to learn and be successful. An immeasurable diversity of management systems and styles can be effective and greatly enhance teaching. In fact, there are as many ways of positively managing a classroom as there are teachers, for each teacher has his or her own personality, priorities, space and parameters in which to work, and creative ideas on how best to put it all together.

Sample Half-Day Weekly Kindergarten Plans

Monday 10/11	Tuesday 10/12	Wednesday 10/13	Thursday 10/14	Friday 10/15
8:45–9:15: Writing Weekend news	8:45–9:15: Writing 10 apples up on top	8:45–9:15: Writing Apples	8:45–9:15: Writing Apple food	8:45–9:15: Writing Apple tree seasons
9:15–9:30: Name Game	9:15–9:30: Name Game	9:15–9:30: Name Game	9:15–9:30: Name Game	9:15–9:30: Name Game
9:30–10:00: Music	9:30–10:00: P.E.	9:30–9:45: WG Rdg. 10 Apples chart	9:30–10:00: Music	9:30–10:00: P.E.
10:00–10:30: Math color 10 apples and cut out as many as can	10:00–10:30: Comp. draw 10 apples, write numbers on them	9:45–10:00: Recess	10:00–10:30: Comp. type numbers to 20 with space between	10:00–10:30: Math count apples; color apples to match
10:30–10:45: Recess	10:30–10:45: Recess	10:00–10:45: Centers glue apples up on top in correct number order; make page for book	10:30–10:45: Recess	10:30–10:45: Recess
10:45–11:00: WG Rdg. *Ten Apples Up on Top!*	10:45–11:00: WG Rdg. *Apples*		10:45–11:00: WG Rdg. *The Seasons of Arnold's Apple Tree*	10:45–11:00: WG Rdg *Johnny Appleseed*
11:00–11:45: Centers * rdg w/Ms. Bergen * taste 3 apple colors, pick favorite * building blocks	11:00–11:45: Centers * rdg w/Ms. Bergen * take-home books * story on tape/CD	Don't forget— Early Release Wednesday	11:00–11:45: Centers * rdg w/Ms. Bergen * *Apples* paper book * read color words; color apples correctly	11:00–11:45: Centers * rdg w/Ms. Bergen * color/read *Apples* * story on tape/CD
11:50: Dismissal	11:50: Dismissal	10:50: Dismissal	11:50: Dismissal	11:50: Dismissal

Take-Home Books Note to Parents: Please help your child read his/her take-home books every day. Children should have their books in their backpacks on Tuesday so they can exchange them for new ones. Thank you!

Sight Words to Practice: *I, me, am, a, red, the, stop, see, is, it, go, can, red, up, like*

DAILY ROUTINES

Daily routines are an important aspect of classroom management. A daily routine should be just that—routine, consistent, the same every day. Routines make it possible for you and your students to move about the room in an organized and efficient manner. They also make it possible for you to provide students the opportunity to be confident and responsible with their behavior choices, and create a setting in which you can spend more time on actual quality instruction than on explaining and giving directions. Routines give children conceptual models of acceptable standards that they can use to evaluate their performance, both academic and behavioral. When these concepts are internalized, students are then free to focus on the real issue of learning.

The daily schedule establishes a routine in my classroom, and each component has its own consistent activities and expectations. My routines work for me and my style; you will want to establish routines that work for you. As you read on, there will be many examples of routines in my classroom that you may want to consider, or tweak, for your own class.

CLASSROOM ARRANGEMENT

Your classroom meeting area is essential for a variety of reasons. First, it is much easier to teach explicitly and model when students are huddled close to you. I prefer speaking in a quiet voice and find that students attend better when they have to strain ever so slightly to

Sample Full-Day Weekly Kindergarten Plans

Monday 10/11	Tuesday 10/12	Wednesday 10/13	Thursday 10/14	Friday 10/15
8:20: Writing Weekend news	8:45: Writing 10 apples up on top	8:45: Writing Apple tree seasons	8:45: Writing Apple food	8:45: Writing Johnny Appleseed
8:50: Name Game	8:50: Name Game	8:50: Name Game	8:50: Name Game	8:50: Name Game
9:05: Centers * rdg w/Ms. Bergen * taste three apple colors, pick favorite * building blocks	9:05: Centers * rdg w/Ms. Bergen * take-home books * story on tape/CD	9:05: Centers * rdg w/Ms. Bergen * practice sight words * apple puzzles	9:05: Centers *rdg w/Ms. Bergen * *Apples* paper book * read color words; color apples correctly	9:05: Centers * rdg w/Ms. Bergen * color/read *Apples* * story on tape/CD
9:55: Music	9:55: P.E.	9:55: Computer Lab	9:55: Music	9:55: P.E.
10:20: Recess	10:20: Recess	10:20: Recess	10:20: Recess	10:20: Recess
10:40: Shared Rdg *Ten Apples Up on Top!*	10:40: Shared Rdg *Apples; Seasons of Arnold's Apple Tree*	10:40: Shared Rdg 10 Apples chart	10:40: Shared Rdg *Johnny Appleseed* book	10:40: Shared Rdg Johnny Appleseed chart
11:10: Lunch	11:10: Lunch	11:10: Lunch	11:10: Lunch	11:10: Lunch
12:00: Shared Reading ➜ review already introduced books, songs, and charts				
12:25: Down Time, Independent Reading Time, Individual and Small-Group Interventions				
12:55: Read Aloud ➜ *Junie B. Jones and Her Big Fat Mouth*				
1:15: Recess	1:15: Recess	1:15: Recess	1:15: Recess	1:15: Recess
1:40: WG Math color/cut out apples	1:40: WG Math glue apples in # order	1:40: WG Math read apples class book	1:40: WG Math write #s to 20	1:40: WG Math sort and count apples
2:20: Centers * rdg w/Ms. Bergen * write sentence about favorite apple color * dramatic play	2:20: Centers * rdg w/Ms. Bergen * practice new take-home books * story on tape/CD	2:20: Centers * rdg w/Ms. Bergen * walk w/apples (beanbags) up on top * sequence # cards	2:20: Centers * rdg w/Ms. Bergen * Johnny Appleseed hats * story on tape/CD	2:20: Centers * rdg w/Ms. Bergen * torn-paper apple art * apple puzzles
3:10: Dismissal	3:10: Dismissal	3:10: Dismissal	3:10: Dismissal	3:10: Dismissal

hear me. Speaking often in a soft tone, rather than projecting my voice to students spread across the classroom, ultimately encourages everyone to use low voices as well. It is easier, too, to get students' attention and maintain it when I can make direct and close eye contact with each and every one of them.

Student Seating

I have found tables to be more appropriate and useful than desks in my classroom. Kindergarten students need to move around from place to place within the classroom, for instance, when they move through centers. Desks indicate possession of the space they occupy; I, however, want students to feel welcome to sit anywhere and to avoid the hassles that typically arise when a child is in someone else's assigned space. Kindergarten students do not need to be responsible for their own school supplies or have them handy at all times; in fact, sitting at a desk full of markers, glue, and other interesting items can be a real distraction. Nor do they have classroom work and personal belongings that older students usually keep in their desks. It makes sense, then, to store students' supplies in a central area, and use tables. If you do have desks in your classroom, try pushing several of them together to form a tabletop. It helps to turn the desks so that the open part is on the inside and inaccessible. In my classroom, nametags are not attached to any tables, desks, or chairs; this helps alleviate the notion that students have their own spot.

Classroom Library

Many classrooms have a designated reading area, complete with couches, rugs, beanbags, lamps, and baskets of books categorized by reading level, genre, or subject matter. And you

may, at this moment, be trying to quash your dread as you wonder where your reading corner will be, how you're going to get baskets of books, and how you're ever going to keep them organized.

Your classroom does not necessarily have to have a certain area designated as the reading area or the library (notice there is not one on the map of my classroom). More important, in a kindergarten classroom, baskets of books do not have to be set out and available to students at all times. Students can become

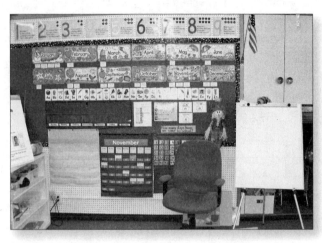

Wall of visual aids in the classroom meeting area

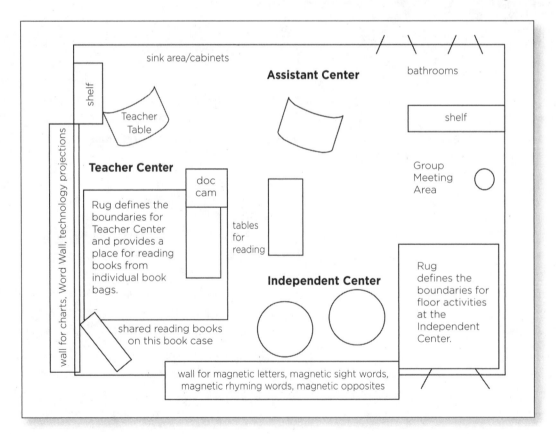

overwhelmed by having too many books visible and available, especially if an appropriate text is too hard to locate or a selected text is too difficult to read, rendering their choices pointless.

Teacher Table

The teacher table is another important instructional area in my classroom. Some teachers move about the classroom to instruct students. This works, and is vital, for many learning activities, such as teaching writing or observing and assessing students during math workshop. However, for reading instruction, it seems most appropriate to have a specific spot where I can sit and students can come for explicit small-group or individualized reading instruction.

I strategically place my teacher table in a spot that allows me to face the rest of the classroom so I can keep an eye on students at the other centers. Though I may be teaching a small group or just one child, I am, of course, in charge of supervising all students, and occasionally, teaching students from afar who are working elsewhere in the room. My teacher table is oriented so that when students sit at it, their backs are to the rest of the class. This means their eyes will be on me, and they will be more focused on my instruction. A shelf near my teacher table houses the books that I use during small-group or individual reading instruction. I am the only one who has access to these books, so I keep them directly behind my table.

Independent Reading Area

In close proximity to my teacher table is the independent reading area. The boundaries of this area are defined by a large wall. Students may sit on the floor, on beanbags, or at tables to read on their own or with partners. They may read their individual books, shared-reading titles that we have already read together as a class, and charts that have been introduced, all of which are kept in this area. (I hang charts on the boundary wall.) I position my teacher table so I can supervise and hear everyone in the Independent Reading Area and guide them in their reading when necessary. Another reason to be close to this spot is so I can call students in this area to my table for reading instruction without disrupting the rest of the class.

Students reading in the Independent Reading Area

Word Wall

Designate one wall in your classroom as the Word Wall. It should be prominent and accessible so you and your students can refer to it often. When choosing a location, think about where you usually are during teaching and writing time. It's helpful if the Word Wall is low so students can physically touch the words; however, if it's too low, students may not be able to see around one another to find the words they need. I display words above the appropriate letters of the alphabet as shown below, putting the letters, a representative picture for each letter, and the words that begin with that letter together in the same place. The sooner you start introducing sight words and posting them on the Word Wall, the sooner students will begin to recognize the concept of a word and identify, read, and spell individual words. Make sure students watch you attach a word to the Word Wall so they know it is there, and you can hold them accountable for finding that word when it is needed.

Print on the Walls of the Classroom

Too much environmental print can be overwhelming and inaccessible to students, so don't display too much print on your walls at the beginning of the year. Your walls will fill up as you explicitly teach to certain reading materials and then make them visible and available to students to notice, refer to, and practice reading.

■ MATERIAL PREPARATION

In addition to sheets of paper, pencils, and pointers, you'll need to prepare the materials discussed below.

Name Cards

One of the first goals to accomplish in the first week or two of school is having students recognize their first names in print. Before the first day of school, prepare a large, laminated name card for each student. Commercial name cards that have a top line, bottom line, and dotted middle line are available. Be sure to write the names the way you want your students to write them, with a correctly formed capital letter followed by correctly formed lowercase letters. If you are going to use letter cues, such as the ones shown on Teacher Express, form the letters precisely the way you will be teaching students to form them. Since students will transport the name cards around the classroom, the cards will not be attached to tables or

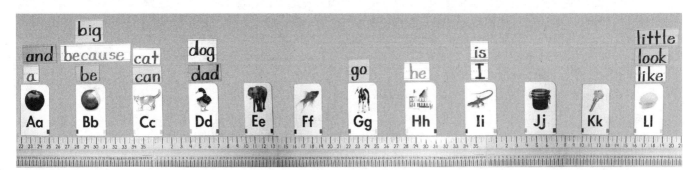

By December, this Word Wall from a half-day kindergarten class includes 34 sight words.

desks. In addition to name recognition, you can use these name cards for attendance, analysis of name spelling, and writing first names.

Place the name cards in a pocket chart or on tables or desks, so students can pick them up when they enter the classroom. Teach students to look for their name card when they first enter the classroom and pick it up and move it to another location to indicate that they are present that day. If a student is unfamiliar with his or her name, show the student the name card and point out one or two salient features to notice; for example, that the name is a long one, starts with an *S*, or has two *e*'s in the middle.

Picture Alphabets

Display two or three picture alphabets in your classroom, one in each of the specific areas where you will teach or where you will send children to work or learn. I prefer picture alphabet flashcards, which are about 3 inches wide and 5 inches tall. I display one set of picture alphabet cards in the whole-group meeting area. When I am seated in my rolling chair, I can roll over to the alphabet and point to the letter and corresponding picture to help students make a connection between the letter and its sound. I hang another set of picture alphabet flashcards on the opposite wall of the classroom, which serves as the foundation of the class Word Wall. At the beginning of the year, the wall is blank; but as I introduce sight words, I attach the word above the letter flashcard that it begins with. This assists students in associating the letter, sound, picture, and word.

Conclusion

It's always nice to read a professional book during the summer and go into a new school year with a solid plan on how to start and a checklist of things to do to make the plan materialize. We know, however, that reality is not so neat and tidy, and that often we change directions or decide to try new approaches after the school year is in full swing. I urge you to do the latter— if you're reading this while school is already in session—and get started now, doing whatever you can, to support kindergartners in getting a good start on their reading development. This is their kindergarten year, and no child should have to wait.

CHAPTER 2

The First Six Weeks:
Whole-Group Shared Reading

Regardless of which assessments you conduct at the beginning of the school year and the student needs that are revealed, the following set of early reading concepts and skills should unfailingly be taught to all students at the beginning of the year:

- Attention to print

- Notion of what reading is

- Voice-print match

Every single student requires, and will profit from, explicit instruction in and practice with these concepts and skills. And all kindergarten students can benefit from explicit reading instruction from the get-go. I recommend starting right away and explicitly teaching the skills they need to know to be on the verge of learning to read. These skills are not letter names and sounds, but attention to print, an understanding of what reading is, and voice-print match. Instead of waiting for students to begin noticing particular words or details of print, point these things out to them and then encourage them to take note of such things on their own. Don't wait for students to emulate voice-print match, which could take most of the school year for some students; demonstrate it during shared reading and then use the venue of small-group or individualized instruction to allow them the opportunity to practice it for themselves and to receive immediate feedback on their attempts. If the ultimate goal is to get children to use independent reading strategies successfully, then we should get started immediately on teaching these skills.

What exactly is explicit instruction?

Explicit instruction is direct and intentional teaching. It allows students to know what is of primary importance and what is expected of them, and it involves explanations that make a task visible and clear. By showing students the strategies, mental processes, and behaviors that make a task doable and a text accessible, explicit instruction guides students to exhibit the type of learning behaviors teachers need from them. Teaching explicitly will make a huge impact on learning.

Attention to Print

Print is everywhere. Students encounter it not only at school, but also at home and in the community. As soon as students become aware that print is intentional and meaningful, they can begin to learn about it and from it, either incidentally or via deliberate teaching. That is why it is vital to draw their attention to print and teach them to discriminate certain facets of it as soon as possible. You can start students on this path as early as the first week of school using name cards, picture alphabets, and the Word Wall.

USING STUDENTS' NAMES

The easiest and most captivating way to draw students' attention to print is through the frequent reading, writing, and discussion of their first names. Children love to see their name in print and are intrigued to learn about the features that make their name uniquely theirs. Of nearly equal interest to them are the names of their peers.

Reading First Names

Every kindergarten student needs to learn to recognize his or her name in print. A student's first name will most likely be his or her first sight word. More than that, name recognition and the realization that it always appears the same is the basis of students' concept of what constitutes a word. As they read their name, they will slowly begin to realize the following:

- It has a certain number of letters.

- The letters are always in the same order.

- No other name looks like their name.

Initially, children tend to recognize their name as a whole instead of as a specific sequence of letters, usually by zeroing in on one or two prominent features, such as its length, shape of the beginning letter, or configuration of the entire group of letters. Kindergarten students are also capable of dissecting their name and understanding how each letter/letter combination and sound contributes to its total make-up. And they are fascinated with the intricacies of how their name is spelled. Our goal is to take students beyond recognition of their own name; we want them to analyze how the letters are functioning, how their peers' names are spelled, and how the spelling of names can be generalized to other words they see in print and to the spelling they do in their own writing.

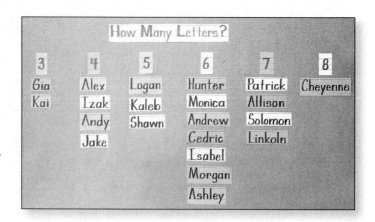

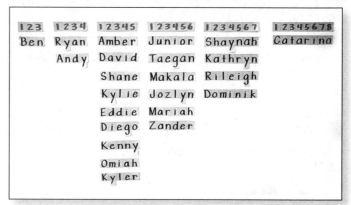

Samples of name graphs

The Name Game

The Name Game (Bergen, 2008) is a highly effective, daily instructional activity that draws students' attention to the analysis of the spelling of their own and their peers' names. It introduces a whole host of important beginning literacy concepts, literacy-related vocabulary, and skills, including sound segmentation (the ability to hear and separate the individual phonemes that constitute words), letter names, letter sounds, letter chunks and blends, correct letter size and formation, position and sequence of letters in words, capital letters versus lowercase letters, silent letters, and spelling generalizations. Students love the Name Game because it begins as a guessing game, and it follows a regular routine, which means they quickly learn how to participate in and benefit from it. The Name Game is a visually stimulating activity as well as an exercise in auditory discrimination. Students learn to crosscheck the information they hear with the letters they see.

I rely so much upon students' names and the associated Name Game activities to teach concepts about print and phonemic awareness and phonics that one of the first things I do at the beginning of the year is study the letters, phonemes, digraphs, chunks, small words, and spelling rules represented in the first and last names on my class list. There are always unique names on the class list and names that do not follow commonly accepted phonics rules. These names prove to be very useful in helping kids remember phonics concepts; it is as if the letters' noncompliance—their misbehavior—makes them more memorable. I create a Name Graph that shows the number of letters in each student's first name and display it in the whole-group area.

Busy Bee: A Student Helper

An ongoing theme and mascot in my classroom is the Busy Bee. Students tend to refer to the Name Game as the Busy Bee Game since it results in the unveiling of the Busy Bee, my special helper for the day. You will notice many references to the Busy Bee and bees in general throughout this book since they have, over the years, become such an integral part of my classroom and instruction. Any classroom theme or mascot could be used in ways similar to how I apply the Busy Bee.

Use the Name Game to count the letters in a name and choose a helper: Within the first few days of school, I introduce the Name Game to students, but first I do a preliminary lesson that explores the number of letters in each student's name. The object is to introduce the term "letter" and for students to realize that names (words) are comprised of different numbers of letters. Initially, most students will not remember how many letters are in their name, so I keep the Name Graph handy (see page 32) or post a list of names. As discussed in Chapter 1, student name cards should always be easily accessible.

To initiate the activity, gather children around you on the floor. Explain that they are going to play a guessing game called the Name Game to discover who the special helper for the day will be. Announce, "This student has *six* letters in his or her name." Then draw six lines on the board or chart paper and encourage children to try to guess the letters that make up the name. When a student makes a correct guess, write the letter on the appropriate line. When the letter is not in the name, write it in another area of the board or chart paper. Students will see you write the letter that matches the guess, form the letter correctly, and be able to refer to this pool of letters for future guesses. Always use lowercase letters except for the first letter in the name.

Initially, most students will randomly guess letters; others will want to join the game but will not know any letter names. Encourage them to raise their hands and then sing the Alphabet Song to give them some ideas or suggest letters in their own name. If a student is at a complete loss, you might say, "Would you like to guess the letter *m*?" Also, begin to teach strategies to help students guess the name; for example, if the name has six letters, draw their attention to the Name Graph or show them how to count the letters on other students' name cards or on the class list to find a name that has six letters. Or, if they know that the name ends in *t*, tell them to find names that end with that letter.

In addition to teaching letter names, you can extend the Name Game to work on sound segmentation, letter sounds, and chunking letters. Once students have determined who the special helper for the day is, ask that child to stand in front of the class and help you lead a variety of extension activities. Information on how to use the Name Game to promote phonemic awareness and to teach phonics appears in Chapter 4.

WRITING FIRST NAMES

Learning to write their names correctly will further focus students' attention on print and greatly enhance their initial concepts about it. The physical act of writing—of learning how to make controlled marks on a piece of paper that closely resemble the letters on their name card—will help students develop their understanding of the concepts of directionality (writing always goes in a line from left to right) and spelling (the same letters are used every time in the same order).

Each day, for the first six weeks of school, I give students a plain sheet of paper for a half-hour of writing instruction. The first thing they must do is sit down and copy their name, as well as they can, from their name card onto the sheet of paper. My classroom assistant and I circulate and explicitly teach students as needed and to the precise level of their understanding and ability. Our comments progress from explaining what "copy" means, to directionality and letter sequence, to proper letter size and formation. The following examples of explicit teaching result in students really looking at and becoming aware of the letters in their first names:

- "You have to look at your name card; that is why I made it for you. Start here, with the first letter. This is D. Try to make a D on your paper. Try to copy it so yours looks just like this one."

- "Oh, you already know how to write your name. That's really good. But, you wrote your name with capital letters, and I want you to learn how to write your name like it is on your name card. Remember when I said to look at your name card and try to copy your name just the way you see it?"

- "Don't forget that you have to put the letters in a line, right next to each other. Look at your name card. See how the A is first, and the m is next to it, and then the i is next? Your letters should be in a line, just like these. Try it again, this way."

- "Oh! Be careful! I can tell that you're about to write an o, but you're starting at the bottom. Remember, the letter o starts at the top and we circle backwards."

- "Do you see this little stick on the side of the m? I will show you how to make that. Watch. When we write m, we say, *'Down, trace it up, bump, bump.'* Now you try it, and I'll say it with you. Make sure your pencil does exactly what your mouth is saying."

- "Your letters are very neat, and I can read your name. I noticed, though, that all your letters are the same size. Look at your name card. See how the letters in your name are different sizes? They go, 'tall, short, short, short, hang down.' Let's see if you can make the *K* tall, these letters short, and then make the *y* hang down."

LEARNING THE NAMES OF THE LETTERS

Learning to write their first name leads kindergarten students to another essential skill: knowing the names of the letters. As they listen to you repeatedly talk about the sequence and formation of each letter in their name, students will begin to pick up on the names of those letters. For the most part, this happens implicitly; however, it is imperative to make it explicit, too, by sometimes clearly stating each letter's name and your expectation that students try to remember what it is called. Focusing on their first names will help students establish a small base of known letters. Chapter 4 provides additional ideas for teaching all the letter names and sounds.

Modeling, over and over and over again, in whole-group instruction and with students one-on-one, how to use letter-formation cues to properly write letters will ensure that nearly everyone develops neat and controlled handwriting from the beginning. The use of letter cues to demonstrate proper handwriting is an example of very explicit teaching. The cues take the mystery out of how an adult, like you, can write all the letters so quickly and neatly without even trying hard or making mistakes. Here is an example of how I might explicitly model writing the letter *e*:

With the whole class: "I'm about to make the letter *e*. Remember, when we write an *e* we say, 'straight across and around.' Watch me and say it with me as I write. See if my pen does exactly what our mouths tell it to do. Ready? 'Straight across and around.' Look, my *e* turned out perfectly!"

With an individual: "Now, you say 'straight across and around' and write an *e* by yourself. Make your hand do exactly what your mouth tells it to do."

When I teach handwriting like this—saying letter formation cues every chance I get—students begin to rely on and memorize those cues. Soon, my room is abuzz with students using the cues on their own as they write. It is a joyful and purposeful noise that always makes my assistant and me exchange smiles. Also, the letter cues will assist students in attending to, recognizing, and memorizing letters. I cannot tell you how many times I have heard a student say something like, "Hey, there's one of those things that goes 'down with a dot,'" or "Oh, I know this letter. It's 'make a *c*, up, down.' Oh yeah, that's *a*!" When I hear comments like these, I know students are really beginning to examine the print around them.

Download letter formation cues for lowercase and uppercase letters at **http://teacherexpress.scholastic.com/teachingreadingK.**

Letter Formation Cues for Lowercase and Uppercase Letters

The cues listed below serve as short prompts or reminders for students. Use them as they are or tailor them to match your teaching style, curriculum, and student needs. Encourage students to verbalize the cues as they form letters, especially those letters that are difficult to make or often turn out reversed.

a	Make a c, up, down
b	Start at the top, straight down, circle around
c	Curve up and around and touch the ground
d	Make a c, go all the way up, and trace it down
e	Straight across and around
f	Curve up and around, down, and cross it
g	Make a c, go up, trace it down, down with a hook
h	Start at the top, go down, trace it up with a bump
i	Straight down, dot in the sky
j	Straight down, down with a hook, dot in the sky
k	Start at the top, straight down, little sideways v at the bottom
l	Start at the top, straight down to the ground
m	Go down, trace it up, bump, bump
n	Go down, trace it up, bump
o	Start at the top, circle back, close it perfectly
p	Straight down, down, trace it up, and circle around
q	Make a c, go up, straight down, down with a tail
r	Go down, trace it up with a curve
s	Forward c, backward c

Tip: Since the formation of many letters begins with the letter *c*, teach the letter *c* as early as possible.

Tip: Having students start at the top rather than the skyline works with both unlined and lined paper, whereas starting at the skyline might be confusing on unlined paper.

Tip: Having students make a *t* first helps prevent *h* and *d* reversals. Be sure students understand that once means to go over part of a line that was already made.

Tip: Mentioning the little sideways *v* will prevent lowercase *k* from turning out to be a capital K.

Tip: Although lowercase *n* does not start at the top (as in where the skyline is), reminding students to start up high inverts the action of starting *n* at the bottom and circling forward.

TEACHING READING IN KINDERGARTEN © 2013 by Randee Bergen, Scholastic Teaching Resources ■ Letter Formation 1

COMPONENTS OF PRINT: EYE-CATCHERS AND ATTENTION-GETTERS

I have discovered, over the years, that certain components of print really catch the eye of young students. Once these components are pointed out, students will be on the lookout for them.

Double Letters: The first is double letters, where the same letter occurs side by side in a word or name. As I mentioned earlier, the mascot in my classroom is the Busy Bee, and I introduce and teach the word *bee* in the first week of school. Because I have learned that kindergarten students are fascinated with double letters, I always point out that the word *bee* has two letters right next to each other that are exactly the same. I remind students that the repeating letter is called *e* and explain that when two letters that are the same are next to each other like this, they are called *double letters* because *double* means "two." If any students have double letters in their name, I bring it up at this time.

The visual aspect of double letters will attract students' attention, but so will the analysis of the sounds they can hear in names or words with double letters. If, for example, a name like Kenna comes up during Name Game, the breakdown of the sounds in the name will illuminate that, although there are two *n*'s, only one *n* sound can be heard. It is fascinating for students to learn—through visual and auditory analysis—that we pronounce the name /k/, /ĕ/, /n/, /ŭ/ and not /k/, /ĕ/, /n/, /n/, /ŭ/. They find it humorous when I provide an example, such as, "Does your mom ever say, "/k/, /e/, /n/, /n/, /ŭ/, did you clean your room?"

Silent Letters: Students are equally intrigued with silent letters that appear in words, especially in their own names. It would seem counterintuitive to draw students' attention to silent letters instead of focusing on the prominent sounds in words and names; however, when you use Name Game, there is no evading the difficult sounds, strange letter combinations, and interesting spellings of certain names. During the game, every name is analyzed and discussed, including the parts that do not really seem to make sense. (This is how I discovered students' incessant curiosity, from year to year and class to class, with double letters and silent letters.) Students are fascinated that a student with, for example, the name *Jake* is called /j/, /ā/, /k/ and not /j/, /a/, /k/, /ē/, especially when the visual of how his name is spelled is provided.

Jake's Name Game

Misbehaving Letters: A portion of Name Game is devoted to analyzing whether each letter in a name is behaving (making the sound it is supposed to make) or misbehaving (making the "wrong" sound, the sound of another letter). During the game, we examine each letter. If it behaves, I draw a star underneath it. A letter that misbehaves does not get a star; instead, it receives a notation about which letter sound it is making. Students love the fact that letters can be naughty and, because of this, are motivated to find out which letters are acting up.

Other Features of Print: In addition to letters themselves, students can be drawn to other features of print, such as the question mark. Kindergarten students hardly know what a question is, and teaching the difference between a statement and a question so early in the year is not the objective when I point out the question mark symbol and name it. From my experience, just knowing the name of this symbol causes students to look for and notice it in print. The same is true with all symbols, so I point them out and provide the correct terms as soon as I can.

White Space: Once you introduce the space between words—either during reading instruction or writing instruction—students will become aware of the white space between words in almost all the print they see. They'll notice, too, that in some texts the space is actually a color! When I remind students to leave a space between their name cards when they place them in the pocket chart, they sometimes measure and adjust the amount of space they leave between the names, realizing now that names (words) cannot be hooked together.

NOTICING PRINT IN THE CLASSROOM

Print, including charts and words on the Word Wall, is more meaningful and effective if you hang it together with students at the point of introduction and discussion. As I mentioned earlier, when school starts, picture alphabets should already be hanging on the classroom wall because you'll need to refer to them starting on the first day.

Concepts About Print

As students engage in pre-reading activities, such as being read to, whether at home during the preschool years or at school when they begin kindergarten, they develop certain concepts about print. These concepts about print (CAP), first recognized, cataloged, and coined by New Zealand educator and researcher Marie Clay, include the following:

- Holding a book and turning the pages
- Realizing that the print carries the message
- Understanding the difference between letters, words, and punctuation

These concepts are the fundamental understandings that support reading acquisition. It is imperative that you be aware of the individual concepts of print and how, traditionally, these concepts have been assessed (see the chart on the next page); however, I am not suggesting that you isolate and explicitly teach each concept of print, and then assess it. The concepts of print should be addressed, somewhat implicitly, as you talk about, model, think out loud, and support students with their reading. Nearly all kindergarten students will pick up on the concepts of print merely by participating in a literacy-rich classroom, and it will be evident, within the context of daily instruction, which concepts students understand and which ones you may eventually need to teach more explicitly.

Concepts About Print

Concept	How to Assess*
Front of the book	Hand a book in the vertical position to student (spine toward student). Say, "Show me the front of this book."
Print, not picture, carries the message	Open the book to the first page with a picture and print. Say, "Can you show me where to start reading?" Student should point to first word.
Directionality	Turn to the second page. Say, "Which way should I go?" Student should move finger from left to right.
Return sweep	On the first page with more than one line of text, point to the end of a line and say, "Where do I go when I get to here?" Student should point to the beginning of the next line.
Voice-print match	On a page with five or six words, say, "Point to the words on this page while I read them." Student's pointing should match the words as you say them.
Concept of word	Ask, "How many words are on this page?" Student should accurately count the words.
Concept of letter	Point to a word. Say, "How many letters are in this word?" Student should accurately count the letters.
Concept of first and last	Say, "Can you show me the first word (or letter) on this page? Can you show me the last word (or letter) on this page?" Student should point to either first word or first letter and then last word or last letter.
Left page before right page	Turn to a place in the book where print appears on both the left- and right-hand pages. Ask, "Where do I start reading?" Student should indicate the left-hand page.
Question mark	Point to a question mark. Say, "What does this mean?" Student should call it a question mark or say a question is being asked.
Period	Point to a period. Say, "What is this for?" Student should call it a period or say it means the idea or sentence is finished and you stop.

* *You will need a Level 3/C or Level 4/D book that has print and accompanying illustrations on each page. The student does not need to be able to read the book. There should be text and a picture on both the left and right pages when the book is opened. One of the pages must have at least two lines of text. It is helpful if there is a page that has a capital letter somewhere in addition to the beginning of the sentence. There should be at least one question mark in the story.*

Voice-Print Match

Voice-print match is a crucial skill for kindergarten students to master during the first six weeks of the school year. What is voice-print match? It is the ability to focus on one word after another and the understanding that our mouth must say just one word (and the correct word) for each word that is seen and/or pointed to while reading. Of all the concepts of print listed on the chart, voice-print match stands out as being more of a skill than just a concept. This makes it probably the most difficult concept on the chart to learn. It will require explicit instruction and plenty of guided practice. On the other hand, most kindergarten students will pick up on it quite easily if given frequent opportunities to practice it for themselves rather than just watching it being modeled, and if there is the expectation that they do it with precision.

MODELING AND PRACTICING VOICE-PRINT MATCH DURING SHARED READING

Kindergarten students can start learning about voice-print match on the first day of school. Your main venue for introducing this skill will be whole-group, shared-reading time. You'll demonstrate how to point to words and read—pointing to the words is what, in students' eyes, makes reading different from talking—and then let students come before the class and give it a try. Here are the steps for planning and carrying out a lesson on teaching voice-print matching.

Choose a Level 1/A or 2/B big book: Select a book that contains eight or fewer pages. The print in the book must be large enough to be seen by the entire class. Each page should have the same language pattern, with just one word changing per page; each page, except perhaps the last, should have three to five words; and the illustrations should provide readers with information about the novel word on each page.

Display the book: Gather the class in the meeting area and put the book on the tray of an easel or hold it in your lap.

Read the title: Since the title of a Level 1/A or 2/B book is often longer and more complex than the sentences within it, do not spend too much time on the title. Just quickly say, "The title of this book is . . ." or "This book is called . . ." and then read and point to each word with a pointer.

Explain the purpose of the lesson: Turn to the first page of text. Look at your students and explain that you are about to start teaching them how to read. Tell them—explicitly—that they must listen to everything you say and that they must look at the words and pictures you point to:

"I am going to point to each word and read this page to you. Listen, with your ears, to what my mouth is saying. Watch, with your eyes, what my stick is pointing to. I will be checking to see if you listen and watch."

Do not slip into the all-too-common frame of mind that since it's the first week of school it's okay, and to be expected really, that some kids will not be able to pay attention. Expect all students to give you their full attention.

Model reading the book: With your pointer, touch *beneath* each word with a slight tapping sound. Jump (don't slide) your pointer from one word to the next. Pause between each word to emphasize that you are saying one word with each tap. Pausing and tapping will make your reading sound choppy and unnatural, but it's important to do this for the first several weeks of instruction in voice-print match.

When you finish reading the page, immediately glance at and try to make eye contact with each student. Remark on the way in which they watched and listened while you read the page. Remind them that this is how students learn. This will reiterate to them that you really do expect to have their full attention. For the first few months of school, and as needed thereafter, the basics of *how to learn* need to be imbedded into everything you do.

Repeat this process for each page. Intermingle your emphasis on how to pay attention and learn with how to point to a word and say it at the same time. You can say, for example, "Watch really carefully now. Watch how right when I point to a word you can hear my mouth say that one word."

Introduce a network of strategies: Although voice-print match is the primary instructional focus in the shared reading you do during the first six weeks of school, it is crucial to introduce other strategies to students as well. These critical strategies, which will help lay a strong foundation for all kindergarten students, are explained at length in Chapter 7.

Read the book together: As you model reading the book, several students may pick up on the repeating language pattern and want to join in. Tell them that this is your turn—you need to continue modeling voice-print match, and students need to continue watching you—and they'll get to read the book with you in just a minute. After you've finished, reread the book, this time encouraging all students to join in. Insist that they keep their eyes on your pointer and do not let their voices get behind or ahead of the pace at which you are reading.

Engaging All Students

I want *all* students to be engaged, not just the student who gets a turn in front of the class or is chosen to answer a question or contribute an idea. I develop this constant cognitive engagement by telling students, "Even if it's not your turn, it can still seem like it's your turn. Think in your mind what you would do (say) and then see if that's the way the other person is doing (saying) it or if you would do (say) it another way. This will help make it seem like it's your turn."

Let students try pointing to the words: Let some students come forward and experience the feeling of pointing to words and reading. Almost everyone will want a chance, so have each student read just one page. Students should be successful with their first, and each subsequent, attempt at voice-print match, so provide varying and sufficient supports for each student to succeed.

The expectations, actions, and language that you can use to support students in developing their voice-print match during shared reading include the following:

- "Stand beside the easel. Keep your arm straight and use the pointer to point to the book. If you stand in front of the book, your classmates won't be able to see your good reading." If you do not ensure that all students can see, then they will, of course, quit attending visually.

- "Is everyone on the floor ready? Are you watching and listening just like before? Don't forget—look at our pointers." Both you and the student should have your own pointer. I give students a short pointer that is about a foot long. Lack of coordination and control can create a safety issue and the shorter pointer helps prevent unintentional poking.

- "Okay, I'm going to point and read first. Then you're going to copy me. Watch carefully. My turn." Point beneath each word with a tapping sound and jump (don't slide) your pointer from one word to the next. Pause between each word to emphasize how many words are on the page. When you're finished, say, "Now it's your turn. Try to do it just like I did."

Taking Turns

Students need to learn that there are times during instruction when they should watch you demonstrate and times when they get to join in and practice what is being taught. I help them distinguish between listening, watching, and trying it for themselves by saying, "my turn" or "your turn." Saying "my turn" is another way of getting students to listen and watch when you really need them to exhibit these important learning behaviors.

Ensuring student success: If the student has been watching carefully and is able to coordinate tapping beneath a word and jumping to the next, then he or she will probably be pretty successful on the first attempt. If not, immediately take the student's hand and help him or her point to the words. Guide the student to experience the steady, controlled rhythm of tapping and jumping from one word to the next. The tapping sound will provide helpful auditory input. Then let the student try it independently. Do it together again, if necessary, and then end the student's turn there, on a positive note.

By the second or third day of school, you can give verbal reminders, like the ones below, instead of going immediately to hand-over-hand physical assistance:

- Remember, when we point to words, we always keep things under control. Watch my stick and listen to it. It's always slow and steady and under control. Try it that way."

- "Look at the words when you point to them. I saw you looking at me. Remember, reading is looking at the words and saying them correctly. If you don't look at the words, then you're not reading; you're talking." Students tend to look at their teacher for confirmation. We don't want to encourage this; we want them to validate their reading on their own.

- "You're saying the words too quickly. You can only say one word at a time. Listen to how I read it. Try to make your voice sound just like mine."

- "Make your stick touch under the word. We don't want to cover the word. Our eyes need to be able to see the word." Establishing this expectation will pay off when students start visually attending to and analyzing words.

- "We make the pointer jump from one word to the next. We don't slide it. I want to hear that quiet tapping sound."

You might be concerned about whether your kindergarten students can be successful with this on the first day or during the first week of school. Students can flourish, or at least feel like they are, with almost any activity as long as we explicitly model how to do it and then provide the necessary scaffolds and support. Even if you have to guide the student's hand, take control of the movement of the pointer, or make your voice loud enough to mask a student's errors, he or she will feel success with the task. These errors can provide the makings for a wonderful teaching moment—perhaps one that wouldn't otherwise occur.

Reading Versus Talking

It is helpful to implant in students the notion of reading versus talking. Explain that if they do not look at the words, then they are telling the story and not reading it; they're talking, not reading. A consistent expectation that students always look at the words will pay off when they start to do repeated readings of the same book. Even if students memorize a book, as long as they are pointing to the words and really looking at them, they will notice aspects of the print that will move them forward in their reading development.

Using Charts to Model and Practice Voice-Print Match

Voice-print match can also be modeled and practiced with charts, especially if they have few words and obvious breaking points in the rhythm that will assistant students in staying on track. Model how to point to and read each word in a section or a line, using direct and explicit language, and then let students attempt it, using the echo reading method as you would with a book. Remember to point *beneath* the words, *tap* and *jump* your stick, and *exaggerate* saying each word correctly with the tap.

Practicing voice-print match on a chart is more difficult than it is in a shared-reading book. All the words on a chart are visible, compared to just a few words per page in a book, and students do not yet know concepts such as starting at the top, starting at the left, and finishing a phrase at the end of the line. This is exactly why it's important to practice voice-print match with charts as well as books: the sooner students learn these concepts about print, the better. Provide simple, explicit support, including guiding the pointer for the student, if need be. Repeat the "my turn"/"your turn" sequence for each line of the chart. Make a big deal about the student's reading. Then, ask the other students to applaud when the student has finished reading the last line of the chart. My students actually started applauding on their own, and I have noticed that this, more than my feedback, elicits satisfaction within the reader about his or her work.

Correcting Behavior

Although this rarely happens at the kindergarten level, occasionally students will giggle if a classmate incorrectly points to words. If this does occur, address it immediately. I usually say, "Oh, we never laugh when students try things. Of course she doesn't know how to do it perfectly. That's why she comes to school. That's why we all come to school." Or, "We can learn more if someone makes a mistake because then we get to talk about it and see how to make it better. So thank you very much for making that little mistake."

Acquiring and Organizing Shared-Reading Books and Charts

The purpose of shared reading is to introduce the notion of reading and teach strategic processing that will make text accessible to children. Whereas a read-aloud book may make it onto your yearlong plan for any number of reasons, a shared-reading text should be included mainly because its print is large enough to be seen by the whole group and it enhances a concept or skill that you want to explicitly teach.

- Materials used at the beginning of the school year should have a lower reading level, with three to five words per page, making it possible for students to clearly see the text and follow along as you point to and read the words. There may be a refrain or other repetitive text that helps children readily join in.

- Later in the school year, when most students have mastered voice-print match and are capable of independently reading emergent level text, the shared-reading material you choose should be at a higher reading level, with more words and lines of text per page, to increase its instructional value.

Therefore, when gathering and/or creating shared-reading materials, you will once again need to think about when you wish to use each title. Shared-reading material may take the form of big books, regular-sized books with extra-large print, shared writing done with the class, poetry or nursery rhyme charts, or other charts you make yourself. Be aware that some books that look like shared reading are not appropriate for that purpose at all. Many big books have far too much print on each page for kindergarten-aged children to look at and visually process. Often, the illustrations and word choice do not adequately support beginning readers. Big books with excessive text are still useful, however. They can be used as read-aloud books, where the focus is not on looking at and processing text.

TEACHER-MADE MATERIALS FOR SHARED READING

Good, quality shared-reading material—especially at Levels 1/A and 2/B—is difficult to find and, when it is in the form of big books, tends to be pricey. Therefore, I have taken the time to write my own books to use for shared reading at the beginning of the year. I determine the size of the book, the size of the print, and the length of sentences and the content in general. Additionally, I choose the topic, control the vocabulary, ensure that the illustrations provide adequate support, and introduce and emphasize sight words. I make these books medium-sized—large enough to be seen by everyone during instruction but small enough that students can handle them on their own.

When you realize a need for a specific type of shared-reading material, you are most likely already creating something in your mind. For me, it started with wanting shared-reading books that were big enough for the entire class to see and read together but small enough for them to then hold on their laps and manipulate on their own. I wanted my students to have access to these books and to be able to read them over and over again. (And it was very apparent that this is what they wanted as well.) I wanted these books to start out as shared-reading material but then become a part of the independent reading area. I also found myself thinking things like: "Boy, I sure do wish there was a book that featured the *oo* chunk." "It would be effective to have a shared-reading book with pictures of my students in it." "This week of my yearlong plan is heavy on read-alouds; I need more shared reading." "Wouldn't it be fun if the Busy Bee showed up in some of our classroom books?"

Here are some guidelines for creating your own big books for shared reading:

- Think about your yearlong plan and weekly themes. What are your shared-reading needs for the first week's theme? How can you introduce your first sight word? What do you need to round out and enhance the concepts and skills included in the rest of your yearlong plan?

- Choose a title carefully. Kindergarten students often abandon books with inaccessible titles, so keep the title as simple as possible. Students learn quickly that they do not need—and are not expected—to read the smaller print on the cover and title page of most books now, so using a smaller font for less essential information, such as author and illustrator, will cue them that it is okay to disregard these words and open the book and start reading. It is helpful to add some color, a single piece of clip art, a border, or some other identifying feature to the cover to assist students in distinguishing one book from another.

- Vary the size, shape, and orientation of books to make them more visually appealing to students, but use paper that is at least 8½ by 11 inches.

- Type just one sentence per page (two to five words). Use natural sounding language. For subsequent books, use longer sentences (but not so long that the majority of students can't track and make sense of the text with their eyes as it is read), more than one sentence per page, and more than one word change per page. The goal is to create books students can feel successful with but also to make each book slightly more challenging so students' reading skills continue to progress.

- Use a clear font, with a large size. Using two spaces between words will help students isolate and discriminate individual words.

- Intentionally choose and include a sight word you would like to introduce to students. As time goes on and you introduce more and more words, try to include these already-introduced words in subsequent books you write. Students rely on words that they recognize and can easily read to maintain accuracy with voice-print match and to successfully read short sentences. When I first read a shared-reading book that contains some sight words that I have introduced to the class, I'll point them out by saying, "Oh, we know this word. And we also know this word. These words are on our Word Wall. They'll make this page easy to read."

- Limit the book length to five to eight pages.

- Place text in the same position on each page (top or bottom). Level 3/C-type books can have text in both positions.

- Include an illustration on each page. Make sure that the art coincides with changes in words and adequately supports students in their attempts to read the book. If you cannot find a complementary picture or clip art for a certain set of words, then rewrite that page. Thousands of photos and artwork are available through free online clip art collections, or you can use photos of your students. Often, I work backwards, browsing through clip art collections to find items that are appealing and that my students will be able to relate to, and then write pages based on the art I have found.

- Incorporate a twist at the end. Students tend to reread books that have a twist at the end or something that will make them smile. You can see the excitement build in their voices, eyes, and body language as they near the end of such books, especially if they have heard or read it before and know what is coming. The surprise at the end, even if it is known, is often the incentive students need to work through the book. A simple twist I put on the last page of many of my teacher-created books is a reference to and a picture of the Busy Bee mascot in our classroom. When the Busy Bee appears in books, I say, "Hey! How did the Busy Bee get into this book? He must have flown right in. He *loves* books." Then, of course, I hear students say the same thing when they come to these pages on their own.

- Print the book in color, if applicable, and laminate it. The purpose behind making books is to not only have relevant, custom-designed instructional material but also

Bookshelf full of teacher-made shared-reading books

Brown Bear, Brown Bear is a simplified and slightly different version of the well-known classic by Bill Martin, Jr.

Spend Time With Me has three words per page and repeats the word me. Download a template for this book at **http://teacherexpress.scholastic.com/teachingreadingK.**

Download templates for What Is It?, Boo!, *and* Apples Up on Top! *at* **http://teacherexpress.scholastic.com/teachingreadingK**.

What Is It? *alternates between questions and statements. Students are encouraged to guess which possible gifts would fit inside each box. The words* is *and* it *are emphasized, as is the fact that sometimes these words appear with a capital letter at the beginning of a sentence.*

Boo! *introduces the* oo *chunk and contains the rhyming words* do, you, boo, *and* too.

The Busy Bee has found his way into the T-Shirts *book, motivating students to work their way through the text to find our mascot.*

Apples Up On Top!, *a teacher- and student-created version of the Theo. LeSieg classic, includes student names (with supporting picture clues) and repeating language with several sight words that were introduced to the class.*

to allow students to have access to and handle these books to their hearts' content. Print the cover and pages on stiffer paper, such as photo paper, and have the book professionally laminated and coil-bound so it will last for many years. The total cost is a fraction of what I would pay for a professionally published big book. If I create a book, such as *I Can See*, using pictures of students, or *Apples Up on Top!* (shown on page 47), with pages made

10 Apples *chart: This chart is an extension of the weekly apples theme, building upon a read-aloud, a shared-reading text, and several activities done during center time.*

Happy Birthday *song chart: Students are attracted to—and will read and reread and reread—any charts in which they can insert their name and the names of their peers.*

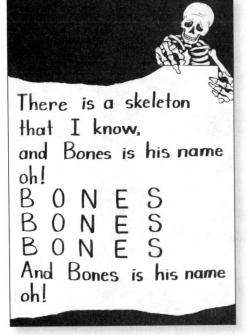

B-O-N-E-S *song chart: Students have already learned the* Bingo *song and the chart that goes with it, which serves as a scaffold when they learn to read this one.*

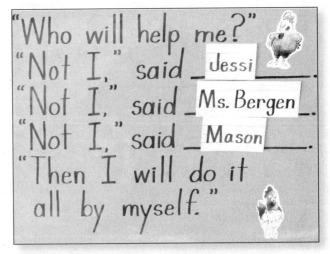

Students can attach magnetic names to the Who Will Help Me? *chart.*

by students, lamination is not necessary since the book will only be of interest to the current year's class.

You are welcome to copy and use the ideas for teacher-created books and charts that I've shared in this book as they are. Most likely, though, you will tweak them to match your specific instructional needs. Or, your imagination will be kindled and you'll start coming up with your own creations. Ultimately, it will be the success and empowerment that your creations provide for your students that motivate you to come up with even more shared-reading materials that are just right for their needs. If making books is not your cup of tea, be assured that there are many Level 3/C and higher big books that can be used for shared reading. Once you start to really teach reading in your kindergarten classroom, many of your students will progress beyond Level 3/C books, making it possible for you to use real books in this context sooner rather than later.

Creating Your Own Charts

- Use large rolls of colored butcher paper, readily found in most schools; poster board is too heavy and expensive.

- Handwrite your charts instead of creating them on the computer. To avoid making errors, carefully plan the placement of text and illustrations. Write the text on scratch paper first, thinking about the number of words that will fit on each line and the number of lines that will fit on the chart, and adjust the text as necessary.

- When you know the number of lines on your chart, measure the size of the paper and decide how far apart the lines can be. Three inches of space between lines, with lettering about 2¾ inches tall, is visually appropriate for kindergartners. You can go smaller if you need to fit more words per line or more lines on the chart, but lettering that is larger than 2¾ inches is hard for students to process since, after the initial introduction, they will usually stand in front of the chart when pointing to and reading it.

- Draw faint lines on the butcher paper to ensure that your lettering will be straight.

- Then use a thick, dark-colored marker to write the text on the butcher paper. You can always write the words in pencil first and then trace over them with a marker.

- If you do want to create the text on a computer and print it out, I recommend cutting the words apart and then gluing them on the butcher paper with extra space between the words. This will help students develop the concept of word and assist with voice-print match when they point to and read the chart.

- Add at least one picture. Doing so will help students discriminate one chart from the other, especially at the beginning of the year, when all print looks the same to them. You can draw illustrations (I, personally, need to copy a contour-line illustration), photocopy them from another source, or search clip art collections. You can also get creative with borders, interactive elements (for example, pictures that can be counted), and other materials, such as glitter. Be careful, however, to keep the area immediately around the

Attaching charts to hangers is an easy way to store them and to hang them in different areas of the room for a variety of instructional uses.

print free from distracting clutter. The words should be the focal point.

- Laminate the chart and then tape a hanger to the back.

Organizing and Storing Shared-Reading Material

The organization and storage of shared-reading materials can be a bit tricky. For one thing, shared-reading texts come in many different forms and sizes and are usually quite large since they need to be easily seen by all students. Big books are generally kept in one location—your classroom, another teacher's classroom, or a central spot like the library or school book room. Because the books I create are medium size, they fit in a cupboard or bin. I like to store them in the order in which I plan to use them, according to my yearlong plan.

Each chart I make, as well as those that I have purchased or inherited, is attached to a hanger so it can be easily displayed or stored. If I am going to introduce and use two charts of similar size at approximately the same time, then I may attach them

Making Connections

Obtain and create books and other reading material that share commonalities, such as characters, themes, and variations on (or sequels to) an original story. Making connections is an important part of reading, and we can help students do this by carefully selecting and sequencing the books we read to them. For example, several versions of the story of the Little Red Hen are available. Each has slight variations, perhaps in the steps taken to get some flour to bake the bread or which animals round out the list of characters. By reading several different versions, you can facilitate children's natural desire to search for connections and comparisons. Additionally, books such as *The Little Yellow Chicken* and *The Little Yellow Chicken Builds a House* by Joy Cowley, *Who Will Help?* adapted by Rozanne Lanczak Williams, and *The Little Red Hen Makes a Pizza* retold by Philemon Sturges, are twists on the original Little Red Hen story. And, to further showcase the high-frequency words and general theme of the story, I created the *Who Will Help Me?* chart, shown on page 48.

back-to-back to the same hanger. You can also use hangers with clips so you can interchange charts. The charts in my classroom hang from a dowel that spans two deep filing cabinets about three feet apart. This keeps the charts protected and out of sight until I am ready to present them. In previous classrooms, I have hung charts in a deep closet or from a compression shower curtain rod or clothes rack in an out-of-the-way spot. The wall on which charts are hung for student use can also double as a storage area. In this case, you would just need to establish the expectation that students read only the charts that are currently in front and visible.

MODELING AND PRACTICING VOICE-PRINT MATCH DURING SHARED WRITING

In my half-day kindergarten schedule, I set aside just 5 minutes each day for shared writing, but so much is accomplished. For shared writing, students watch and provide input as the teacher models how to write and how to read and reread the writing to ensure that it is making sense.

Writing the Busy Bee Note

I have discovered a unique type of shared writing that I believe contributes greatly to my students' budding reading skills. At the beginning of the year, our daily shared writing results in a giant note for the Busy Bee to take home and share with his or her family. Once again, since it is a fellow student who is helping with the teaching and the modeling of voice-print match, the other students tend to be highly engaged in the activity. The reason this shared writing is so powerful is that 1) we write virtually the same five-word sentence every day for 20 or more consecutive days until

Shared writing of the giant Busy Bee note

each student has gotten one of the giant notes to take home, and 2) the Busy Bee reads and rereads as the note is being written, so I know he or she will be able to successfully read the note at home.

The message we write every day on the Busy Bee note is shown above. Outlined below is the incredible amount of instruction, modeling, development of the concepts of print, and skills practice that can occur in 5 minutes. The comments in italics show how the instruction might be modified as the days go on and students gain knowledge about the process for writing the note.

Step 1: Count the number of words in the note.

Introduce the activity with, "Let's count and find out how many words we're going to write on

Isabela's note. Put up a fist like mine. A fist is zero. We always start with zero." Have students imitate you as you say the following:

Isabela (put up index finger)
is (put up middle finger)
the (put up ring finger)
Busy (put up pinky)
Bee (stick out thumb)
"Look, *five* fingers. We need to write *five* words in this sentence."

As the days pass and students become familiar with this activity, I replace step 1 with the following: "Who wants to tell us what sentence will be on Isabela's giant note? How many words will we write?"

Step 2: Write the first word.

"Let's go back to the first word—*Isabela.*" (Put up index finger.) "Isabela, can you spell your name?" I write the letters as Isabela spells her name. I might have to make the following correction: "Capital *I*; all names start with a capital letter" after Isabela tells me that her name starts with an *I*.

Step 3: Touch and read the first word.

"Okay, Isabela, touch this word and read it." Isabela touches her name with a pointer and says it. I compliment her pointing and reading.

As the days pass and the class becomes familiar with this activity, the student automatically points to and reads the words as I write them on the note, without prompting from me.

Step 4: Write the second word.

I turn to students on the floor. "Okay, now we're ready for the second word." I put my fist in the air and wait for students to do the same. "*Isabela*" (As my index finger goes up, I make sure students are mimicking me because they already understand that is what they are supposed to do.) "*is*" (My middle finger goes up.) "Watch me. I'm going to leave a space here because we can't hook *is* onto Isabela's name. Watch me write the word *is*. It's a short word. It has two letters, an *i* and an *s*," I say as I write the word *is*. I do not expect students to know which letter is an *i* and which is an *s*; that is not the point for today.

As the days pass and students become familiar with this activity, replace step 4: "Okay, let's read this together and figure out the next word. Isabela . . ." Students will call out is. *"You've seen me write* is *a lot. If you want to tell me how to spell it, go ahead."*

Step 5: Read the first two words.

"Okay, Isabela, watch me read this note so far. *Isabela is* . . ." I say, as I tap my pointer beneath each word. "Now it's your turn to read." The class is watching and paying close attention. It always helps to have a student point and read to maintain student attention; nevertheless, I make a comment that I will repeat often during the course of the year to ensure that the other students stay engaged: "Now, kids, your job is to watch Isabela closely and make sure she points and reads correctly."

Step 6: Write the third word.

"Now I'll write the next word. Watch me and copy me. *Isabela*" (index finger goes up) "*is*" (middle finger goes up) "*the*" (ring finger goes up). "Watch me write *the*." I quickly write the word *the* without talking about sounds, letters, or anything. Since this is the first day of school, the only thing I check for and insist upon is that students watch me write the word.

> *As the days pass and students become familiar with this activity, replace steps 6 and 7: "Who wants to spell* the *for me? We've already learned this word. We know it starts with the Bad Boys. The Busy Bee gets to read out loud, but you can read it in your head."*

You can download these cards at **http://teacherexpress.scholastic.com/teachingreadingK**.

Step 7: Read the third word.

"Now watch me read. Keep an eye on my pointer. *Isabela is the* . . . Your turn, Isabela. Can you point and read?" Isabela is able to match her voice to the three words as her pointer points to them. However, she, unknowingly, is pointing in a careless manner. "Watch me point," I say. I read the three words again, moving my pointer deliberately and tapping the chart paper as I touch beneath each word. "My pointer goes right under the words. I don't do wild pointing. I do careful pointing. Now you try." Isabela is observant and wants to do it right. This time she easily mimics the way I point to the words.

Step 8: Write the fourth word.

"We're almost done with our note. Watch me read it and help me figure out which word comes next." I tap beneath each word and read it, dragging out *the* in a way that encourages students to use the context to figure out the next word. "*Isabela is the . . .*" I then tap the empty spot where the next word should go. Students know which word comes next. Several call out, "Busy Bee!" "Yes, *Busy* is the next word." I count out the four words with my fingers. "Watch me write it." I write the word *busy*, point to and read all four words on the note, and then have Isabela read them.

As the days pass and students become more familiar with the concept of a word, you can explain that "Busy" and "Bee" are two separate words and that "Busy" must be written first and then "Bee."

Step 9: Write the last word.

"Just one more word to write. Help me figure it out." I point and read the words and then tap in the empty space where the next, and final, word should go. "*Isabela is the Busy . . .*" "Bee!" students say. "Let's check and make sure. Let's use our fingers." Together, the students and I put up a finger for each word, and double check to see if *Bee* is indeed the next word. After writing *Bee*, I read the note, tapping beneath each word.

As the days pass and students become familiar with this activity, they will, as you tap in the empty space where the next word goes, call out the word so you don't have to go through the process of putting up one finger for each word. Modeling this on a daily basis for 20-plus days will help students do this with their own writing as well as introduce the strategy of reading and rereading to ensure meaning.

Step 10: Read the entire note.

Isabela tries reading the note and demonstrates excellent voice-print match for the first day of school. I tear the note off the chart paper pad, fold it, and tell Isabela she gets to take the note home: "Now, when you get home, I want you to spread the note where there is room—on a table, the floor, wherever. I want you to get a pointer—a pencil or your finger—and point to the words as you read the note to someone in your family. You can read it to your mom, your grandma, your brother, your dog, or your teddy bear. Read it to everyone, if you want! But, watch out—they won't know that you already know how to point to words and read them. They'll probably think that they need to read the note to you. So, be sure to say, 'I will read this note to you and you watch me.' And then, after you read it, maybe you can hang the note up in your room so you can read it over and over and over again."

As the days pass and the students become familiar with this activity, replace step 10: "Now, Isabela, you know what to do, right? You remember about spreading the note out somewhere? Remember! Don't let anyone in your family read the note for you. You have to tell them that you know how to read it all by yourself. I hope you'll be able to hang it up in your bedroom!"

MODELING AND PRACTICING VOICE-PRINT MATCH DURING WRITING INSTRUCTION

As I mentioned previously, a kindergarten teacher cannot maximize students' reading development without also providing highly structured and individualized instruction in writing. Just as reading instruction begins with a six-week introduction to the notion of reading, writing instruction begins with a six-week introduction to the notion of writing. An important part of this whole-group instruction is teaching students that writing is talk put down on paper and that written words can be read by pointing to and reading them, just like the words in a book.

For the first six weeks of school, I model the steps for how to draw a simple picture and then write a one-word label or a short phrase or sentence to accompany it. Students copy each step onto their own sheet of paper. They absolutely love this process because the end result is always a recognizable picture and one to four words that they can point to and read. They become more confident in their ability to control a pencil, listening to me and copying, thinking about words and segmenting them into sounds, and reading back what they have written. My methods for teaching writing are explained at great length in my book, *Teaching Writing in Kindergarten: A Structured Approach to Daily Writing That Helps Every Child Become a Confident, Capable Writer.*

Conclusion

If students are to become literate, they must first become conscious of what reading is. They must realize that print is all around them, it can be interpreted, it is meaningful, and it is there for their benefit and delight. Early shared-reading and shared-writing experiences, along with opportunities to practice reading and writing, will help students discover and understand that reading and writing are fascinating, fulfilling, and achievable.

CHAPTER 3

The First Six Weeks: Small-Group Instruction

As you introduce the notion of reading, concepts of print, and voice-print matching via shared-reading time during the first six weeks of school, students should also get daily guided practice with these concepts and skills in a small-group instructional setting. This can be made possible by establishing the following centers and having students rotate through them:

- *Teacher Center:* Small groups receive reading instruction.

- *Assistant Center:* Small groups practice skills and concepts with a classroom assistant.

- *Independent Center:* Small groups practice skills and concepts independently.

The activities students do at each center should be purposeful so they advance academic growth, yet require minimal planning, preparation, and explanation. At the beginning of the year, you will, of course, have to give a detailed explanation of centers to students, including how groups rotate through and work at them, and you may sometimes plan special projects that will require specific directions. It is crucial that you do not get caught up in an instructional structure that 1) requires unwarranted planning and daily material preparation or 2) requires that the majority of your attention goes to managing the class and activities rather than your reading instruction at the Teacher Center.

This is basically a workshop approach that has been broken into shorter blocks of time that young learners can more easily manage. Each center has its own physical place in the classroom and all students go to all three places each day. The centers are set up in a way that lets students quickly learn how to meet the expectations and perform the tasks at each one, thus enabling them to self-monitor and take responsibility for their learning. With centers, kindergartners can be successful and reap the benefits of a workshop approach that was originally developed for older children.

Establishing Centers

By establishing and maintaining three distinct areas for the three types of centers, students' confusion about where they should be and where they should go next is dramatically reduced. They quickly learn the names and boundaries of the centers. The activities at the Assistant Center and the Independent Center vary from day to day, but the designated space for each center remains the same.

START CENTERS IMMEDIATELY

It is important to start centers on the first day of school, or at least during the first week, with you busy teaching at your center and your assistant working in his or her center on a daily basis. Students will learn, from the outset, that both of you are busy teaching, so they will quickly become independent workers and problem solvers. Also, if you plug yourself into the teacher-center activity on a daily basis right from the start, then you will never have to ponder how you are going to find the time to incorporate small-group reading (or, later, one-on-one reading) into the day.

GROUPING AND ROTATING STUDENTS THROUGH THE CENTERS

Students are not placed in pre-assigned groups. Every day, I send one-third to each center. I quickly call off students' names and tell them which center to go to. This requires no prior thought or planning, but I do, as I'm calling out names, balance the number of talkative students, slower workers, and positive role models per group.

The way in which students move from one center to the next is consistent. No matter where they begin, the groups move in a clockwise circular movement to the next center as shown on page 58.

Groups remain at each center for approximately 12–15 minutes. For the first month, I ring a bell that signals them to stop working, look at me, and listen to directions for moving to the next center: "If you are at my center, you are now going to Miss Lori's center" (the Assistant Center); "If you're with Miss Lori, she will tell you when you may go to the Independent Center" (in case she needs time to follow through with any students before sending them on); "If you're at the Independent Center, please come and show me your work" (if students completed written work at that center that day); or "If you're at the Independent Center, you're coming to my center."

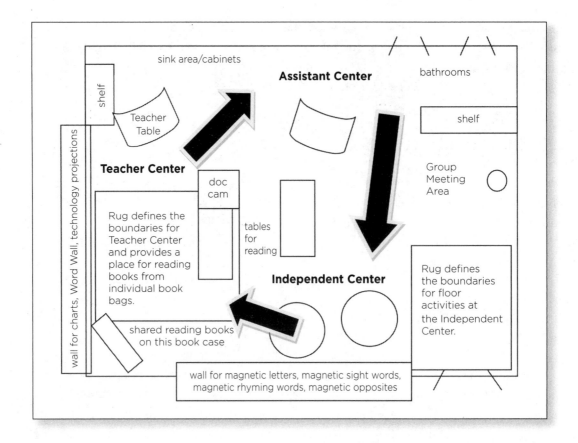

After a few weeks, students know what to do so I just ring the bell to signal the transition to the next center. The transition between centers takes but a moment. During this time, I watch students—focusing on the few who I know have not mastered the rotation system—to make sure they end up in the right place.

TEACHER CENTER

The Teacher Center in my classroom contains a kidney-shaped table with the books that I use for guided reading nearby. This center encompasses the Independent Reading Area with the rug that defines the boundaries, our shared-reading books, the long wall for hanging shared-reading charts that students practice reading, and tables where students and parent volunteers can sit and read. Students will not read independently until the second six weeks, but this area is established and included in the center rotation from the beginning.

During the first six weeks of school, I conduct guided reading with small groups of six to nine students at my center (one-third of my class, depending on class size). The first six weeks are, admittedly, hectic because not only am I trying to teach groups how to do voice-print match, but I am also teaching everyone the routines and expectations of the workshop. It all pays off though when, after six weeks, students understand the rotation through the centers, and I start working with students one-on-one or two-on-one at the Teacher Center.

ASSISTANT CENTER

The teaching, guided practice, or facilitation of any activity that requires adult supervision and/or immediate feedback occurs at the Assistant Center. Having a second center with an adult means that there is more opportunity for differentiation. In my classroom, the Assistant Center has a kidney-shaped table that is large enough to teach up to nine students if need be.

If you do not have a classroom assistant, this center could easily be turned into another center at which students work independently. Or, you could ask parent volunteers to take turns running the center. While having an assistant to provide quality teaching and immediate feedback for the students is a luxury, it is not a requirement for establishing a simple, three-center rotation workshop in kindergarten.

As the year goes on, you can establish a weekly schedule of activities for the Assistant Center wherein certain activities always happen on certain days. This makes planning easy, and it lessens the amount of explanation you'll need to give your assistant and, in turn, the explanation he or she needs to give students. Once a week, for example, my assistant will work with students on writing their first names in order to solidify proper letter formation and emphasize our expectation for neatness. Or I will often introduce a skill, concept, or math game during whole-group instruction and then have students practice it at the Assistant Center.

Planning Activities

I do not lock myself into a preplanned situation (i.e., I do not insist that every center be literacy-related or that there be one math center per day); rather, I plan the daily center activities according to which skills and concepts could best be practiced with an adult or tried out independently. The one exception, of course, is that I conduct reading instruction at my center every day from the very first day of school.

The center activities I plan during the first six weeks of school look somewhat different than those for the remainder of the school year since students begin with few skills they can apply to learning activities. And, because I will be teaching a group at my reading table, I don't want to create situations at other centers that will demand too much direction or oversight.

INDEPENDENT CENTER

What constitutes independent activity—that which does not require the oversight of an adult—will change as the school year progresses and students acquire more skills, mature, and learn to work better on their own and alongside their peers. For the first several weeks of school, kindergarten students need time to explore their learning environment and the materials and manipulatives that they will be expected to use later in a more structured manner, so I give them time to sort and build with pattern blocks, connecting cubes, and buttons. Some of the more traditional kindergarten center activities, such as building blocks, puzzles, and dramatic play can also be plugged in here. These can be easily done at tables or on the floor. Simple projects and pencil-and-paper seatwork that do not necessarily require the presence of an adult are also options.

In my classroom, the Independent Center has the following: two tables at which students can work; a place to store frequently-used materials at this center; large floor space for activities such as puzzles and building blocks; and an old heater along an entire wall that is perfect for housing a variety of magnets, such as rhyming pictures, opposites, sight words, lowercase letters, and pattern blocks.

A factor that contributes to the success of the Independent Center is to make sure students have something to do if they finish an activity prior to it being time to move on to the next center. For example, on some days, each of the students in the Independent Center listens to a different story on tape or CD, so they finish this task at different points in the 15-minute block of time. Since I do not want students interrupting me, the "if you get done early" activity is always the same: students may use the variety of magnets on the metal heater along the wall.

Since students are expected to stay at each center until a ringing bell signals them to move to the next center, this activity needs to be something within the boundaries of the center. Also, it should be a worthwhile, easy-to-manage, consistent activity that allows for some natural differentiation. Remember that students will need to receive directions for a novel "if you get done early" activity and that a unique activity might trigger them to rush through the original, more essential, activity.

Like the Teacher Center and the Assistant Center, activities for the Independent Center reoccur and, therefore, require very little planning and/or explaining. My students always listen to a story on tape or CD two days a week at the Independent Center. By midyear, they are able to handle, and benefit from, true independent reading time, and the Independent Center gradually morphs into a time and a place for independent reading.

Make the Independent Center Truly Independent

Almost any activity is going to run more smoothly with adult supervision, so it is tempting to assign parent volunteers or other professionals that come into your classroom to the Independent Center. However, it really is vital that students have a place where they can practice working on their own and learn to problem solve without the intervention of an adult. And expecting them to truly work independently will ensure that when they are expected to read independently at this center, they will be better prepared to do it in a productive manner.

Worksheets and Seatwork

On the days when students complete seatwork at the Independent Center, I check to see that the amount and quality of work they accomplished matches their ability to do it. It might be acceptable for some students to have very little work to show, while you might require others to complete everything. During transitions between centers, students line up at the Teacher Center, with their papers held in front of them. Checking goes quickly since I take just a quick glance at their work and do so with just one group at a time. I hold students accountable for what they were supposed to do at the Independent Center and may use recess time to have them write their name correctly, try something again, or get just a little bit more done.

Do try to keep worksheets and written seatwork to a minimum. It is time-consuming and expensive to prepare worksheets, not to mention to look over them and provide feedback to students. And worksheets rarely meet the learning needs of most students; they are too easy for some or too hard for others, causing either a lack of learning or frustration. On the other hand, students do need experience with completing written work and recording information in different formats, so do include some worksheet activities. Parents, too, can get a peek into their child's day and their work quality when you send worksheets home.

CLASSROOM MANAGEMENT DURING CENTERS TIME

This system requires very little classroom management on your part, so you can devote most of your time and attention to the group at your table or to the one or two students receiving reading instruction at your table. Share with your assistant your expectations that he or she manage the instruction and behavior of students at the Assistant Center. Establish that it is acceptable to ask students to take quick time-outs from the center if they disrupt the teaching or learning that is occurring there. I do sometimes intervene, if needed; however, once the classroom assistant (or parent volunteer) becomes competent at managing a small group, then you will only need to directly manage the students at your own center and the Independent Center.

If you have established a learning community in which students have the shared goal of becoming the best readers they can possibly be, then the community will end up taking care of many management issues. If you consistently teach with a sense of urgency and talk about the goal of everyone learning to read as well as he or she can, then you will create a culture within your classroom in which every moment of learning and practice counts for you and for every student. Your message will be that everyone must take ownership for his or her behavior and learning. In an environment such as this, students are rarely inclined to misbehave and dishonor the community.

Modeling and Practicing Voice-Print Match at the Teacher Center

Students are always eager to practice the voice-print match and early reading that I've been demonstrating and discussing during shared reading. Working with small groups at the Teacher Center gives students practice opportunities.

For the first six weeks, I spend about 12–15 minutes doing the following with each of the three small groups:

- Having students write their names on their own books that they get to keep (see below)

- Modeling voice-print match

- Talking about other concepts of print

- Providing opportunities to see sight words in context

- Giving all students the opportunity to practice pointing to words and reading their own books

- Offering immediate feedback and individualized instruction

To get so much accomplished in a short time requires fast-paced, intense instruction, to be sure, but it pays off. After the first six weeks, students will be able to read the earliest of emergent text somewhat independently, and that means I can start working with students individually or in pairs.

For the entire six-week period at the beginning of the school year, I use a set of homemade paper books for two consecutive days in a row. The first day is devoted to having students write their name on the cover of the book and a quick initial read-through. The second day is slightly more relaxed, at least for students. Here's an overview of how a two-day lesson progresses:

DAY 1

Write Names: Each student at my center receives a copy of the book I've created, a pencil, and his or her name card. I tell students to copy their name, as they see it on the name card, onto the line on the cover of the book. I point to the exact spot where they should start writing since most are not yet familiar with writing their names, let alone the concept of writing on a line. I provide hand-over-hand assistance to those who need it. Sometimes half of the time is devoted to name writing. At first, the goal is for students to write their name recognizably, but as the days go on, I talk to them more about proper letter height and formation, and each day I expect them to write their names a little bit better. Also, each day one or more students no longer needs to look at and copy from his or her name card, meaning that this portion of the center time is constantly decreasing in time.

Model Reading the Title: When students have written their names to my expectations, I remove the pencils and name cards so there are no distractions during the upcoming instruction. Then I focus their attention by saying the following:

"I am going to hold my book up like this so you can watch me, but you will keep your book on the table in front of you. I want you looking at my book right now. You will look at your book later. Watch my reading finger. I am going to read the title. My turn."

Using my index finger and a "witch finger," I read the title of the book, pointing beneath each word and using a jumping motion between words. If I notice that someone isn't watching, I say, "Oh, no, I need to do it again because not everyone was watching. When it's my turn, you *have* to watch." I do all of this quickly; the faster the instructional pace, the more likely I am to keep students' attention.

Saying "My turn" indicates to students that they should watch me and listen.

Practice Reading the Title: To reiterate what a title is, I say, "The name of this book is _____. What do you think this book will be about?" Then, I tell students that it is their turn to read the title: "Get your reading finger ready to point to the first word. I'm going to check and see if you are ready." Now is a good time to make sure each student is pointing underneath the word and not covering it up with their finger. I help students find their index finger and move fingers down or center them beneath the word, if needed. When everyone has his or her index finger under the first word of the title, I say, "Your turn. Read the title." This echo reading is particularly effective with these beginning books that have one sentence per page. Almost all students, regardless of prior experience or natural ability, are able to parrot back one sentence at a time. When it is students' turn to read, watch closely and assist as needed.

Witch Fingers

Other than books, very few props or materials are required to teach kindergarten students to read. However, one thing I do use in my classroom during the first six weeks of school is plastic witch fingers with bright red fingernails. They put the fun in pointing and do a fabulous job of drawing students' attention to the print. A brief lesson explaining that the fingers are for pointing and reading and not for poking is necessary. Any misuse can be kept to a minimum by being consistent with these expectations and the consequence of having the finger taken away. The novelty of the fingers wanes right about the same time as the comfort level of wearing them does, and most students outgrow their desire to use them just as they are mastering voice-print match. Witch fingers are available online or at costume shops.

Echo Read the Book: For each page, I model how to read by pointing to and saying each word and then having students practice. Before reading each page, I get students' attention by saying, "My turn." As I read, I hold up the book so students can watch me point to and read the words. Then I say, "Your turn" and make sure each student is ready to successfully practice voice-print match by putting his or her index finger under the first word in their books. I listen to and watch students carefully as they all simultaneously try to mimic me, assisting those who are unable to make their voice match the words or who do not do it to my expectations. As the time for this group to leave the Teacher Center draws near, I gather their books and explain that they will read the books again tomorrow and then take them home to read to their family.

DAY 2

Distribute Books: When students are seated at the teacher table, I distribute the books according to the name written on the front cover.

Echo Read the Book: I tell students to get their reading fingers ready to point to the first word in the title. "My turn," I say, and read the title with discernible voice-print match and finger tapping. Then I cue students with, "Your turn" and observe them reading the title. We echo read the entire book. Since this is the second read-through, it goes quickly.

Instruct Individuals: I use the remaining time with this group to work individually with each student. In order to do this, I assign an easy activity, such as having students read and color the pages in their book on their own. This frees me to listen to and observe individual students as they read their books. The student reads a couple pages or the entire book, depending on the number of students in the group. Based on my observations, I provide individualized, explicit instruction to help develop each student's skill in voice-print match.

Sometimes, as I am listening to someone read, nearby students will stop and observe us. This is a learning opportunity for the neighboring student, so I allow it to happen. When it comes time for this student to read, I may ask him or her to read a different page lest the student only mimic what was overheard. Another solution is to have students choose their favorite page before starting the individual reading so they won't all end up reading the same portion of text.

If you chose a book, or created one, with the proper level of difficulty, students will be quite successful reading it on their own at this point (someone may have to read the title to them), so the book should be sent home or exchanged for a new one the following day. If you retain the same book for a third day of instruction, you may not be able to discover teaching points because students will be too familiar with the text. Of course, even the simplest books contain many teaching points, but most are not appropriate for the first few days or weeks of school when students are focusing so much on the skill and concept of voice-print match.

Sending Books Home

Before sending a book home, write this short note on the cover: *Remember to point to the words when you read this to your family.* This will let parents know what the expectation is and how to initially work with their child. A complete letter about beginning reading skills and how parents can support their young readers is on page 183. This could be sent home at this time, but I prefer to send it later when students start bringing home professionally published books.

Partner Read: Later in the school year, after students begin reading more on their own, I encourage and facilitate partner reading. In order to make this work, I must teach students how to read with a partner during the first few weeks of school when they are all reading the same book with me at the Teacher Center. I usually do this on the second day of reading a particular book, if time allows, because students are familiar with the text by then. Here is how I model what partner reading looks like:

- I ask a student to sit next to me. We each have the same book, and we ensure that the books are closed and we're looking at and pointing to the title on the cover.

- Then I look at my partner and ask, "Are you ready?"

- I place my finger on the first word and check to see that my partner's finger is pointing to the first word, too. When both of us are ready, we begin to read the page together.

- At each page turn, I check to see if my partner is ready—page turned correctly, finger pointing to first word—before starting to read.

I teach students to take turns saying, "Are you ready?" This prevents one partner from reading too quickly or becoming too dominant in the partnership.

Fixing Mistakes

An effective way to instill in children that reading needs to make sense is to recognize and commend their attempts at rereading or fixing their mistakes. When students are reading beginning books and make a mistake that results in loss of meaning, the words not matching the picture, or the text not sounding grammatically correct, most will recognize the error and try to correct it on their own by either rereading the entire sentence or pointing again to the misread word and saying it correctly. Mistakes are easy to fix at this point because students are not yet actually decoding text. They are repeating a pattern of language and changing one or two words to match the picture. This is the time, however, to recognize and commend children for their attempts at correcting mistakes and trying to ensure that their reading sounds right. I call these self-corrections "fix-ups" and make a big deal about students' attempts to fix up their reading. Students quickly learn that making a mistake is not a problem. In fact, it is an opportunity to do a fix-up, and fix-ups seem to result in a lot of positive attention. Students become risk-takers, demonstrating bolder and more fearless reading behavior, knowing that if they make a mistake, they have a chance to self-correct and receive acknowledgement for doing so.

During these first six weeks, I like to introduce several sight words and incorporate them into the paper books I make for students to take home. Recognizing a few sight words helps students master voice-print match because they—and I—can check to see if their reading finger is touching a sight word they recognize as their mouth says it. It is very effective to say something along the lines of, "Wait! Didn't you just say *I*? I heard your mouth say *I*, but your finger wasn't pointing to the word *I* when you said it. You could try that again and do a fix-up!" Known words are precious anchors during the process of mastering voice-print match. Introducing and teaching sight words is covered in depth in Chapter 7.

Assessing Beginning Reading Concepts and Skills

Initially, it will seem like everything you are saying and doing is going right over their cute, little kindergarten heads. But I know from experience that it is not. I know they are soaking up more information than you can possibly imagine. I know that every time I introduce a new book:

- students will begin to write their names more quickly and more legibly.

- students will understand the instructional turn-taking.

- concepts of print and reading jargon become more solidified.

- more and more students will be proficient with voice-print match.

- students will be extremely engaged with the print, noticing letters and words, spaces, and punctuation.

- students already understand that reading should be meaningful.

- students know that if something doesn't sound right, they should fix it up.

All of this is most definitely sinking in, and—wow!—most students will be at an instructional Level 2/B, or beyond, after only six weeks of kindergarten.

Sometimes, when a minute or two remains during whole-class shared reading or at the teacher table, I give students a test. They love this challenge. The test is actually an assessment of their awareness of concepts of print. Sample questions include the following:

- Can you show me the word *a*?

- Can you point to a space between the words?

- How many letters are in this word?

- Can you point to the period?

- How many words are on this page?

- Can you touch the second word?

- Can you read the last word?

- Which word says *dog*?

Though students may not know what a test is, they quickly realize that the goal is to answer the questions correctly. And you can bet that if they were not looking closely at the print prior to the announcement of a test, they most surely will during the test because they want to do well. I tailor the questions for each individual student so that everyone will be slightly challenged yet still experience success in the end.

The Color Book

by

_____

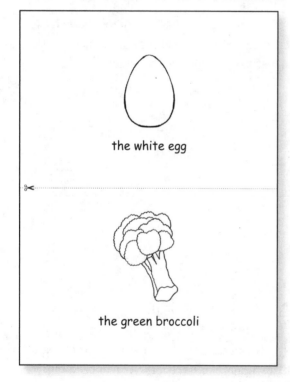

the red firetruck

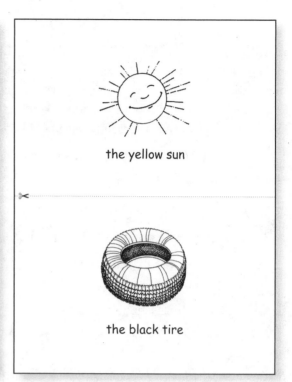

the yellow sun

the black tire

the white egg

the green broccoli

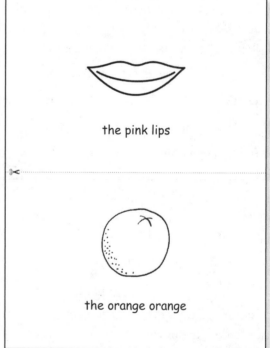

the pink lips

the orange orange

The Color Book *has three words per page—one that is known* (the)*, one that is represented by the picture* (sun, egg, lips)*, and the third that must be inferred (the color of the object).*

Download templates for The Color Book *and* Red Stuff *at* **http://teacherexpress.scholastic.com/teachingreadingK**.

Red Stuff

_____

a red banana

a red apple

a red flower

a red snowman

a red cat

a red stop sign

Students like the book Red Stuff *because they get to, as part of the voice-print match, point to the little laughing figure and make a "ha, ha, ha" noise on the pages that have an object that is not really red.*

Acquiring and Organizing Leveled Texts for Small-Group Instruction

The purpose of six weeks of homogeneous small-group instruction at the Teacher Center is to lay a strong foundation—in all children, despite their skill level and experience with books upon entering kindergarten—in the notion of reading, beginning concepts of print, and the execution of voice-print match. In order to maximize student learning during this time, you will need Level 1/A and 2/B books that enhance and allow students to practice what you introduce and model during shared-reading time. These books should be very similar in nature to the medium size or big books that you are using for shared reading during the first six weeks of school; in other words, they will have three to five words per page, repeating language patterns, supportive illustrations, and some of the sight words that you have taught to the class.

TEACHER-MADE BOOKS FOR SMALL-GROUP INSTRUCTION

While well-written Level 1/A and 2/B student-size books are readily available, I prefer to write and prepare the books that I use for small-group instruction. Here is my reasoning:

- I can ensure that the books will be an extension of what was read during shared-reading time—a similar topic, about the same level of difficulty, and inclusion of sight words that were introduced.

- The books are consumable, so students can write their names, they can color in them, and I can write notes on them as needed.

- The books belong to individual students, who get to take them home after we use them in class.

- It is possible to include photos of students, the Busy Bee, or other highly motivating, community-building features.

- If I used real books, I would have to have ten copies of about 12 different titles. Students' skills will be beyond these levels within a short time and these books would serve no further purpose.

Here are some guidelines for creating books to use during small-group instruction.

- Create two books for each week during the first six weeks of school.

- Each book should be slightly more challenging than the last. If the first book has two words per page, then the next one could have three words per page.

- The topic could accompany the weekly theme, build upon what was recently read during shared-reading time, or coincide with other things going on in the classroom.

- Create and save the books on the computer. A good size for students to hold is 8½ by 5½ inches. Keep the books in a file, modify as needed, and use year after year.

- The title should be short, easy to remember, and have a picture that makes it more predictable.

- Type just one sentence per page (two to five words), with just one word changing per page. Use natural sounding language. For subsequent books, use slightly longer sentences and perhaps two word changes per page. The goal is to create books students can feel successful with but also to make each book slightly more challenging so students' reading skills continue to progress. All of these books will be used within the first six weeks of school, so even though they'll get progressively more challenging, none of them will be above a Level 2/B.

- Include previously introduced sight words and/or the sight word(s) being taught that week during shared reading so students can practice reading them in context.

- Limit the book length to five to six pages.

- Place text in the same position on each page (top or bottom), with the last page possibly having text in both places.

- Include an illustration on each page. Make sure that the art coincides with changes in words and adequately supports students in their attempts to read the book. If you cannot find a complementary picture or clip art for a certain set of words, then rewrite that page. (When I make the books I use clip art with contour drawings so the pictures are easier to color.)

- If possible, incorporate a unique feature or twist at the end. Students love to reread books that will make them smile.

- For ease in assembling books, create the cover on the *top* half of the page in your word processing program and then copy and paste it onto the *bottom* half of the page. Do the same for each page in the book. When you print this out, you'll have a set that will make two books. Make half as many copies as students you have, then cut the copies in half horizontally.

- Staple each book once in the top left corner. Stapling more than that is not necessary and actually makes the books harder for the students to handle.

The first teacher-created book I use at the Teacher Center is a Level 1/A book with the title *I*. Each page has two words—one known and one novel—and the novel word is clearly represented by an illustration. With this text, students can practice reading the word *I* in context: *I jump. I sleep. I cook. I swing. I read.*

I

_____

I __jump__ .

I __swing__ .

I __read__ .

The I book

Download a template for this book at **http://teacherexpress.scholastic.com/ teachingreadingK**.

Conclusion

A well-defined set of routines will result in easy-to-implement, successful centers. It will free both you and your students from distractions related to management and allow students to sustain productive behavior by putting their energy into their learning rather than trying to figure out what your expectations are. As center routines become solidified, you can focus nearly all of your attention on the vital guided practice you need to do with students at the Teacher Center. This first six-week period of daily small-group instruction will lay a strong enough foundation for students to start reading books independently so you can start working with students individually.

CHAPTER 4

Developing Phonemic Awareness and Teaching Phonics

P honemic awareness is the understanding that speech is composed of a sequence of sounds combined to form words (Ellery, 2005) and the ability to notice, think about, and work with the individual sounds in spoken words. Phonemes are the smallest parts, or individual sounds, in our language. Phonemic awareness ranges from the ability to hear individual sounds in language to the more advanced skills of manipulating the phonemes to build, break apart, and change words. Phonemic awareness is different than phonics in that it has nothing to do with knowing letters (graphemes) or associating sounds with letters. The best way to explain the difference is that phonemic awareness can be acquired in the dark; phonics requires light because students must look at and consider letters in relation to sounds.

It is critical that kindergarten students become familiar with the individual sounds in our language and learn to manipulate them in different ways. Students should first learn to hear and isolate sounds. When you hear children or teachers saying things such as, "/P/, /p/, pizza," they are practicing this skill and developing phonemic awareness. Students need to be capable of and comfortable with isolating and saying individual sounds before we ask them to do this during the reading process. We also frequently instruct them in more sophisticated phonemic awareness activities, for example, isolating the ending sound in a word. This, in its purest form, sounds like, "Tell me the last sound in *tub*." Other tasks involve identifying which one of three words starts with a different sound, blending two or three phonemes together to make a word (this is different than reading because they do not look at letters to do this), or segmenting or separating a word into its individual phonemes.

Phonemic awareness is a vital link to a child's reading (and writing) success, yet it remains relatively unknown and/or misunderstood by many parents and educators. While most parents realize that learning the names of letters will help their child learn to read, they are unfamiliar with the notion that he or she needs to learn how to hear the tiny sound components of our language. And listening for individual sounds in speech is not something that children, or even adults, do naturally. As the *Report of the National Reading Panel* (2000) explained:

> *Speech is seamless and has no breaks signaling where one phoneme ends and the next begins. Also, phonemes overlap and are coarticulated, which further obscures their separate identities. Another barrier to developing phonemic awareness is that speakers focus their attention on the meanings of utterances, not on sounds. Unless they are trying to learn an alphabetic code, there is no reason to notice and ponder the phonemic level of language. These facts explain why beginners have difficulty acquiring phonemic awareness and why they benefit from explicit instruction in phonemic awareness* (pp. 2–3).

The teaching of phonemic awareness occurs primarily in kindergarten classrooms, but some teachers at this grade level are not consciously developing phonemic awareness, either because they do not know about it or they do not understand that it is different than phonics. However, phonemic awareness can be developed simultaneously with phonics knowledge through phonics instruction, and it makes sense—time-wise for you and conceptually for students—to accomplish both at the same time.

Phonics is the relationship between the letters (graphemes) of written language and the individual sounds (phonemes) of spoken language. It is also referred to as sound-letter correspondence. In its simplest form, phonics is knowing the sounds that each letter makes. More sophisticated phonics skills include knowing and spelling common letter chunks, such as *th, -ay,* and *-ing,* and, of course, being able to apply this knowledge to the processes of reading and writing. Well-developed phonemic awareness is possible without any knowledge of phonics, but the opposite is not true; the ability to decode words and do early spelling is dependent upon both phonemic awareness and phonics.

A Full Immersion Approach to Teaching Phonics

When I first started teaching kindergarten (after many years of teaching special education and all the other grade levels), I built the framework of my yearlong plan around the letter I wanted to introduce each week. That was how I had seen kindergarten taught and, during a summer of independent research, I planned several activities and ideas centered around the letter of the week. By the end of the first month of the school year, I was frustrated with the pace of my instruction and sensed that my students were, too. Furthermore, I was bewildered by the number of students who were not learning the names and sounds of the letters on which we had just spent an entire week, and I was questioning—ridiculously—whether I was permitted to mention letters that hadn't been officially introduced. Since this approach was not working, I did away with my original yearlong plan and began talking about and making reference to any letters and sounds that arose during the day. I also decided to start providing explicit and structured teaching in real reading and writing immediately. I had a hunch that this would actually accelerate students' acquisition of phonics.

This second approach of immersing children in the entire alphabet and explicitly showing them how letters and sounds are used to read and communicate with written language was not entirely new, but it went against traditional kindergarten teaching. It was considered risky and reckless to not teach letters one at a time in a prescribed sequence. Several literacy experts at the time, however, were advocating this immersion approach in which phonics skills were acquired via reading and writing instruction rather than prior to reading and writing instruction (Marie Clay, 1991; Fountas and Pinnell, 1996; Dorn, French, and Jones, 1998; Lucy Calkins, 2001; Richard Gentry, 2006).

The assessment chart shown on page 76 documents the progression of letter and sound acquisition of the kindergarten students in my half-day program in 2011. This data indicates that immediate and full immersion in the alphabet, together with daily opportunities for students to practice the application of phonics to reading and writing, is highly effective. Almost every single student in several classes learned the names of the majority of the letters and sounds. The inherent upper limit of the number of letters and sounds one can learn precludes data such as this from illustrating real and continuing growth in students' phonics knowledge and application. The number of sight words students learn, their reading level, and their ability to spell and write are all better indicators of what exactly has been learned and

Tracking Students' Progress

I recommend creating a chart, similar to the one on the next page, that tracks student growth in letter name and sound knowledge, as well as other areas such as sight-word vocabulary, and approximate reading level. Data entry is quick and simple with a chart like this, and having all your data on a single page results in efficient tracking and reporting of student progress. I assess kindergartners' knowledge of letter names and sounds as they enter kindergarten and then again at the end of each quarter because I am required to do so for report cards. Data charts like this are also handy for evaluating your teaching and programming, especially when you retain them for several years and look for trends.

2011 End-of-the-Year Assessment Data – Ms. Bergen's Class

Students	LETTER NAMES 54 possible (target is 54)					LETTER SOUNDS 33 possible (target is 33)					SIGHT WORDS from a list of 111 (target is 12)					READING LEVEL see reading level info below (target is level 3/C)				KPA Score (literacy) 216 possible (target 181)		KMA Score (math) 200 possible (target 168)	
	Aug	Oct	Dec	Mar	May	Aug	Oct	Dec	Mar	May	Aug	Oct	Dec	Mar	May	Oct	Dec	Mar	May	Aug	May	Aug	May
1	12	22	39	52	54	2	4	16	26	33	0	2	15	27	30	2/B	2/B	3/C	3/C	17	208	73	181
2	2	24	47	53	54	0	9	23	28	33	0	5	19	37	67	2/B	2/B	4/D	4/D	4	216	102	194
3	54	54	53	54	54	24	30	32	32	33	12+	18	73	110	110	3/C	6/E	14H	28M	188	216	177	198
4	10	45	51	54	54	0	8	19	29	33	0	3	21	36	74	2/B	3/C	4/D	6/E	14	212	117	200
5	8	19	30	43	47	0	0	14	22	31	1	4	20	31	NA	2/B	3/C	3/C	3/C	34	201	95	169
6	NA	NA	NA	46	54	NA	NA	NA	23	33	NA	NA	NA	1	34	NA	NA	2/B	4/D	NA	216	NA	200
7	46	46	53	54	54	16	16	28	29	33	0	4	31	76	103	2/B	4/D	6/E	14H	99	216	111	196
8	42	49	46	54	54	0	16	26	28	33	2	25	65	100	109	3/C	6/E	8/F	16/I	50	214	173	200
9	2	21	48	53	54	0	7	26	32	33	0	5	27	40	64	2/B	3/C	4/D	4/D	4	204	41	191
10	3	10	33	41	49	0	1	6	20	22	0	2	11	20	15	2/B	2/B	3/C	2/B	4	168	50	167
11	53	54	54	54	54	22	25	31	31	33	12+	99	100	111	110	14H	14H	20K	24L	180	216	186	198
12	0	4	28	51	54	0	0	2	20	31	0	5	18	37	36	1/A	2/B	3/C	3/C	1	198	40	189
13	10	28	50	52	54	0	8	17	30	32	0	4	22	34	47	2/B	4/D	4/D	4/D	13	211	122	200
14	40	49	49	53	54	0	19	17	27	33	0	6	17	38	56	2/B	4/D	4/D	4/D	58	210	116	198
15	19	25	38	50	53	0	0	16	23	30	0	2	12	25	29	2/B	2/B	3/C	3/C	23	209	106	187
16	35	47	53	54	54	5	11	23	30	33	0	5	23	60	109	2/B	4/D	4/D	8/F	84	216	110	200
17	5	17	41	53	54	0	7	21	26	32	0	2	22	39	65	2/B	2/B	4/D	6/E	20	209	66	198
18	8	45	52	48	54	0	22	29	31	33	0	5	44	94	105	2/B	4/D	8/F	10/F	10	216	81	194
19	7	32	53	48	54	4	17	25	28	32	0	5	21	39	73	2/B	3/C	4/D	4/D	13	213	94	197
20	20	40	52	54	54	20	17	26	30	31	0	5	25	48	71	2/B	3/C	4/D	4/D	57	214	90	198
21	0	4	27	50	52	0	0	5	29	31	0	1	12	22	28	2/B	2/B	3/C	2/B	0	195	6	163
22	0	6	48	51	54	0	0	21	28	33	0	2	17	35	41	1/A	2/B	2/B	3/C	4	200	100	188
23	NA	NA	49	NA	NA	NA	NA	25	NA	NA	NA	NA	23	NA	NA	NA	2/B	NA	NA	NA	NA	NA	NA

According to district expectations, kindergartners should know most of the letter names (54) and sounds (33) by the end of the year. They should recognize at least 12 sight words and be able to read a Level 3/C book independently by May. We're looking for a KPA (Kindergarten Proficiency Score for literacy) of at least 181 points and a KMA (Kindergarten Math Assessment) score of at least 168.

Reading Levels:

3/C	→ end of kindergarten	8/F	→ December 1st grade
4/D	→ beginning of 1st grade	12/G	→ March 1st grade
6/E	→ October 1st grade	14/H	→ April 1st grade
		16/I	→ end of 1st grade
		18/J	→ beginning 2nd grade
		20/K	→ October 2nd grade
24/L	→ mid 2nd grade		
34/N	→ beginning/mid 3rd grade		
34/N	→ beginning/mid 3rd grade		

how phonics knowledge and skills continue to develop in the course of a year. Nonetheless, the letter and sound assessment data shows that students are capable of learning letters and sounds when they are taught in this manner.

INTRODUCING THE ALPHABET

Singing the alphabet song (to the tune of "Twinkle, Twinkle, Little Star") should be a daily activity for the first several weeks of school. Start by singing it without pointing to or making reference to the alphabet. We want the 26 letter names to become a part of each child's spoken vocabulary. When these 26 names are a part of students' vocabulary, it will be easier for them to assign the names to the corresponding letters. Also, the sequencing of the alphabet and the rhythm and melody of the song will act as a scaffold for naming letters that students do not yet know.

After the first several weeks, begin to point to each letter as you and your students sing the song more slowly. Explicitly state that what you are pointing to are called *letters* and that when these letters are arranged in this order they are called the *alphabet*. At this point, refer to the song as "The Alphabet Song." Emphasize that only one name should be said for each letter. Students will start to associate the letter names with the symbols. Provide opportunities for them to point to the letters as the class sings, guiding their pointer or pointing along with them until they get the feel of the one-to-one match. It is helpful to work on portions of the alphabet rather than the entire set of letters. For instance, initially have students point to the letters *a* through *g*, since, when we sing the alphabet song, there is a natural pause after the letter *g*. There are five distinct portions of the alphabet song: *a, b, c, d, e, f, g/h, i, j, k, l, m, n, o, p/q, r, s/t, u, v/w, x, y, z.*

If your class has access to a computer lab, get students started on using the keyboard for tasks instead of solely using the mouse. Kindergarten students can and should learn how to locate letters on the keyboard. Beginning typing activities, such as typing their first name and then the alphabet, will get them started on learning where the letters are on the keyboard. They should also realize that although the keys show capital letters, a lowercase letter will appear on the screen when they press a key. The keyboard is an amazing tool for helping students make connections between upper- and lowercase letters.

TEACHING THE LETTERS IN STUDENTS' NAMES

As stated, a good goal to set within the first six weeks is for all students to recognize their own first names. Naming the letters in their names will give students a base of known letters upon which they can then build. Though not a word, per se, a name is similar to a word in that the letters work together and its spelling remains constant. As students learn to recognize their name in print, write their name by printing a series of letters in an unvarying sequence, and talk about what constitutes their name and how it stands out from other students' names, they eventually start to learn the letters that make up their own name.

As students practice writing their names daily, circulate amongst them so you can indirectly teach the letters in their names: "Look, the *T* at the beginning of your name is a tall letter." Periodically, quiz students on the names of the letters in their first names to assess their knowledge, and then explicitly teach one or two letters. If students know the name of a letter, put a dot under the letters on their name card. This will serve as a permanent record of which letter names they have mastered and which may require some explicit instruction. Challenge students to learn the remaining letters.

Tips for Introducing and Teaching Letters and Sounds

Though I recommend a full immersion into the alphabet, there are times that are more conducive to introducing certain letters or sounds or at least giving special attention to them. I'm sure you have many ideas that work successfully in your classroom or phonics program. It's always helpful to integrate the tips we come across and develop an eclectic approach for helping students learn letter names and sounds.

USING SIGHT WORDS

Continually introducing and working with sight words is an indirect means for teaching letters, sounds, and even phonemic awareness. Words can be introduced to students as early as the first week of school. The first sight word to introduce, according to my yearlong plan, is *me* because it is a short, two-letter word with two distinct phonemes. The poem on the next page introduces the word *me* and also the concept of what a word is. It also illustrates how learning a sight word can result in learning letter names. Students can easily memorize the first verse of the poem, and you can choose whether to teach the second verse. A fun addition is to do the sign language spelling for the letters as you say them at the end of the poem, but in most instances, it will be important to write the letters so students can associate them with the letter names.

This poem can be used to teach the following:

- the concept of a word
- the word *me*
- the concept of a letter
- the letters *m* and *e*

Download ideas for teaching letter names and sounds at **http://teacherexpress.scholastic. com/teachingreadingK**.

- the individual sounds of the letters *m* and *e*

- the segmentation and counting of the phonemes in the word *me*

- what our mouths do when we make the *m* sound (our lips are together) and the *e* sound (our mouth says the name of the letter)

- what it means to spell a word

- spelling with our fingers

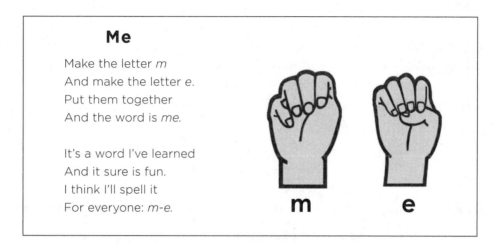

Me

Make the letter *m*
And make the letter *e*.
Put them together
And the word is *me*.

It's a word I've learned
And it sure is fun.
I think I'll spell it
For everyone: *m-e*.

m   **e**

Analyze and discuss each new sight word you introduce like this (whether there is an accompanying poem or not) to address as many concepts and skills as possible within that word and to help students begin to recognize it automatically and memorize its spelling. Students must be expected to learn to recognize, read, and spell sight words. When this expectation, and the necessary supports, are in place, they will learn many letter names while they are learning words. Additional ideas for teaching sight words appear in Chapter 7.

Teaching Phonics Through Structured Writing Instruction

If becoming a better reading teacher to your kindergarten students is your goal, then it is imperative that you also become a better teacher of writing. In *Breaking the Code: The New Science of Beginning Reading and Writing* (2006), Richard Gentry talks about the reciprocity of early reading and writing: "Many teachers still do not realize that beginning reading and writing are almost the same thing, identical processes unfolding . . ." (p. xiii). He believes it is easier to nudge children forward in literacy development by teaching into their writing than focusing only on reading instruction. In fact, he comes right out and says that writing in kindergarten "is as important for learning to read as reading instruction itself" (p. xv).

Like me, Gentry has figured out that consistent, daily writing instruction in kindergarten is a means for ensuring reading success: "Early writers use knowledge about sounds, letters, syllables, words, word parts like onsets and rimes, and phonics patterns, so early writing *advances* reading" (p. xiii). And, in *Reading Essentials*, Regie Routman concurs, stating that stretching out sounds while writing and using invented spelling is one of the easiest and most efficient ways to develop phonemic awareness and phonics. I stated in *Teaching Writing in Kindergarten*:

> *In addition to yielding highly developed written language skills, daily writing instruction as described in this book results in more rapid and advanced reading development than we've previously assumed possible at the kindergarten level. This method immediately introduces and encourages the use of phonemic awareness, phonics, and the learning and application of common letter chunks. The built-in daily practice and individualized support provided during writing time will result in students learning quickly to encode written English. And, once they grasp the sophisticated process of encoding, most will easily pick up the less cognitively demanding skill of decoding required for reading* (2003, p. 7).

Applying Phonics Knowledge Eases the Acquisition of Phonics Knowledge

Letter names and sounds are a big part of any kindergarten curriculum, but the expectation that students apply this knowledge to reading and writing is limited. I have found, however, that expecting more in the application of phonics actually makes the acquisition of phonics easier for most students. It seems that when students realize this information is useful, it sticks with them more easily. The information is meaningful, not to mention empowering. I provide explicit instruction and daily opportunities for writing not only so my students will have an easier time learning and remembering letter names and sounds but also because almost every kindergartner is ready to learn to write—learning to write results in learning to read.

TEACHING PHONICS DURING SHARED-READING INSTRUCTION

A common shared-reading activity in kindergarten classrooms is to use a picture alphabet—on the wall, in an oversized book, on a poster, or that matches the one students refer to during writing time—to chant letter names and sounds. Initially, the teacher chants each letter/associated sound/picture ("capital *R*, lowercase *r*, /r/, /r/, rope") while pointing to the corresponding letter, and then students mimic the language, rhythm, and action. Eventually, however, the teacher and students can chant the entire alphabet together or individual students can point and lead the chanting. Dorn, French, and Jones, authors of *Apprenticeship in Literacy: Transitions Across Reading and Writing* (1998), suggest modifying or shortening this activity on some days by chanting just certain letters—for example, all the capitals, all the tall letters, or all letters with animal pictures.

Modeling Letter Sounds

Students and educators alike often attach a vowel sound to consonants when modeling and teaching letter sounds. For example, a teacher may say, /*bŭh*/ for /*b*/ or /*zŭh*/ for /*zzz*/. Be cognizant of this and try to model a clear, crisp consonant without attaching a vowel. This will help students with blending sounds during reading and not including extra sounds in words they are trying to write.

This activity helps students develop phonemic awareness and letter-sound correspondence, along with the knowledge that the sequencing of the alphabet remains constant. But, since there is no real reading and writing involved with the alphabet chant, it is one of the first activities I cut from my half-day program. Our ultimate goal is to help students apply their phonics knowledge to actual reading. You can use most books to model and discuss phonics knowledge during shared reading and then during students' one-on-one reading time with you. This is discussed at length in Chapter 5.

DEVELOPING PHONEMIC AWARENESS AND PHONICS DURING THE NAME GAME

The Name Game is a meaningful, fun, and easy-to-implement way of teaching almost all letters, all sounds, phonemic awareness, decoding and word analysis, basic spelling skills, and the understanding of common letter chunks. Therefore, the implementation of this activity, or something similar, can serve as the main means for developing phonemic awareness and phonics in your kindergarten classroom.

The game's activities trigger daily discussions about the analysis of the letters and phonemes in students' names. As discussed in Chapter 2, the first half of the school year is devoted to working on first names, and from January to May, last names are studied.

Although many of the letter sounds, chunks, and spelling rules represented in students' names will represent phonics concepts or instruction that are traditionally considered beyond the kindergarten level, students become so enthralled with analyzing their names that it is impossible to not end up discussing these concepts. Students' observations that arise during Name Game conversations become your instructional content. Some students will be incapable of perceiving all the fine distinctions, but the conversations will help them master the basic letter names and sounds that are the standard requirement for kindergarten. For example, the bossy-*r* might be too difficult a concept for a student, but she may remember the letter *r* now that you have drawn her attention to it and referred to it as "bossy." On the other hand, many students will be able to understand these concepts and will, in fact, become fascinated with them. These students will begin to notice the same phonics applied to words they find in books and to environmental print. They will also try to use the applications in their writing. Soon, this knowledge will help students read and write beyond what is traditionally expected of them.

Once students become more competent at guessing letters and the Name Game moves along at a faster pace, you can begin to make a comment or two about every letter that is guessed. These comments can work as 1) positive feedback to increase student participation and confidence, 2) helpful hints for remembering letter names and sounds, and 3) tidbits to promote further thinking. Some ideas include the following:

- **Building confidence:**

   "No. This name doesn't have a p, but I know what you're thinking. You thought it might be the person in our class whose name has six letters and starts with the letter P."

   "Yes, this name does have an h. Good job figuring out that h sometimes goes with t."

   "No, there is not a *five*. *Five* is a number, and we need letters. Letters are in the alphabet. Look at all these letters" (point to the alphabet) "and pick one you like. If you don't know what it's called, come up and touch it, and I'll help you with its name."

- **Teaching/reinforcing letter names:**

   "No, the letter e is not in this name. But it's a good letter to guess. Lots of names have the letter e."

   "Someone already guessed w." (point to it) "Would you like to guess another letter?"

   "No, there is no b in this name. I think you really like the letter b. I think you really started liking it when we were learning about the b-b-bus."

   "I thought you might guess l because your name starts with an L and you know that letter."

- **Introducing/reinforcing two forms for each letter:**

   "Yes, this name has an m. It's the first letter in the name, so I'm going to make it a capital M."

   "No. There isn't a capital G" (write a capital G in the space below) "or a lowercase g" (write a lowercase g in the space below) "in this name."

- **Teaching letter formation:**

   "Yes, there is an h; h looks like n except it has a taller stick."

   "No, there is no y; y is a hang down letter. Watch me make y so you can see how I make it hang down."

   "Yes, there is an s. How do we make an s? Say it with me: forward c, backward c."

Analyzing and Discussing a Name

In addition to teaching letter names, you can use this activity to work on sound segmentation, letter sounds, and chunking of letters. After the special helper (Busy Bee) of the day has been identified through the Name Game, that student can stand before the class and help lead a variety of extension activities.

Sound Segmentation: One of the first activities to do is to help the student learn to segment the sounds in his or her name. Begin by modeling how to pull apart the sounds you hear. Do not refer to the name on the board or chart paper or any other visual clues initially; this is strictly a listening task to develop phonemic awareness. Here's a sample for the name *Shayna*.

- Isolate the first sound /sh/ and raise your index finger.

- Say the /ā/ sound and raise your middle finger.

- Say /n/ and raise your ring finger.

- Say /ŭ/ and raise your pinky.

- Point out that the name has six letters but only four sounds.

Invite the class to separate and count the sounds with you as you did. Then give the student helper the opportunity to try it by herself. It will be difficult for students at first, but each time they get a turn, they will be markedly better at segmenting the sounds in their names.

Letter Sounds: Following the segmentation practice, work on letter sounds by drawing students' attention to the board where the student helper's name is written. Tell them to watch carefully so they will be able to tell you what they notice. Segment the sounds in the name again, circling the letters that are making each sound as you go. Do this quickly and fluidly, with no discussion, so students can hear and see how the letters are working. Here is a sample using *Shayna*.

- Draw a circle around the letters *S* and *h*.
- Draw a circle around the letters *a* and *y*.
- Draw a circle around the letter *n*.
- Draw a circle around the letter *a*.

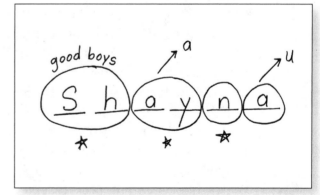

After circling the four distinct sounds in this name, talk about how the letters are functioning. At the beginning of the year, you will do most of the talking, but as time goes on and these names reappear several times, students will begin to tell you what is happening with the letters.

- The *s* and the *h* are working together to make one sound. Introduce The Good Boys or remind students about them if they've already been introduced. Since the *s* and the *h* are making their usual sound, put a star under the chunk to show that they are "behaving."

- The *a* and the *y* are working together to make the *ā* sound. Call this the *a-y chunk.* This chunk will get a star since it is doing what it typically does.

- The letter *n* is making its regular sound, and since it is "behaving," draw a star under it.

- Point out that the last *a* is saying /ŭ/ and remind students that that is the letter *u*'s sound. Show this with an arrow and a *u* and do not give it a star since it is "misbehaving."

Chunking Letters: When a common letter chunk appears in a student's name, take the time to introduce the "friends" associated with that chunk. For example, after analyzing *Shayna*, you may want to introduce The Good Boys—*s* and *h*—and explain that, when they work together and make the /sh/ sound, they make us be quiet and good. Show The Good Boys card, read the names of the friends on the card, Shawn and Shane, and display the card in a place where students can access it. (Students are always excited to learn the names and try to hear the chunks in each one.) The cards will become a resource for students during the Name Game, and reading and writing time. Soon, you will hear students saying, "I see the Good Boys" or "I hear the Good Boys."

It is important to treat *th, sh,* and *ch* with the same priority as letters in the alphabet. These digraphs appear often in beginning books and in student names. Students need to be aware of them to work with the calendar, analyze names and words, and work more independently during writing time. Include these digraphs in your alphabet immersion plan, incorporate their introduction into your yearlong plan, explicitly teach their sounds, and provide scaffolding to assist students in remembering and applying them to reading and writing.

It is important to note that The Icky Twins, The Ouch Brothers, and The Sorry Sisters have been around for many years, but I was unable to determine and give credit to their original source. I changed The Icky Twins (*ew* and *ue*) to The Icky Triplets (*oo, ew, ue*), because, although the double *o* makes a slightly different sound, it is the most often used of the three and the easiest for kindergarten students to remember. They love double letters. I included The Ouch Brothers (*ou, ow*) and The Sorry Sisters (*au, aw*), but do not encourage an over-emphasis of the latter as students will begin to overuse them in their writing and stick in one of The Sorry Sisters every time they hear a short-*o* sound. In addition, I came up with and have had great success using The Bad Boys (*th*; referred to as "the bad boys" because they make you stick your tongue out), The Good Boys (*sh*; called "the good boys" because they make you be quiet), The Chilly Boys (*ch*), The Funny Boys (*ph*), The Oi Boys (*oi, oy*), The Silent Boys (*gh*), and The Whisper Boys (*wh*) (Bergen, 2008). You can also download these cards at **http://teacherexpress.scholastic.com/teachingreadingK**.

Introduce these "friends" slowly, as they appear in student names or other words that arise during instruction. (There are some years when one or more obscure "friend" doesn't appear in a name.) By introducing some of these more common letter chunks, keeping the cards handy as resources, and talking about them throughout the year, students will begin recognizing them while reading and including them in their daily writing.

Adding a Challenge to the Name Game

When most students are skilled at deducing the letters in classmates' first names, challenge them to precede their guesses with the term *capital* or *lowercase*. For example, if a student believes the special helper is Jacob, he might raise his hand and ask, "Is there a capital *J*?" Adding this element to the game draws students' attention to the fact that all names begin with a capital letter and rarely include another capital letter. Another variation to add is having students indicate which blank they are guessing: "Is the third letter a lowercase *c*?" And, once students have learned some of the common chunks, permit them to guess groups of letters rather than individual letters: "Does this name have the *er* chunk at the end?"

Similar Sounds: Another valuable extension activity that covers both phonemic awareness and phonics is to have students brainstorm words that contain sounds similar to one of the sounds in the helper's name. Here's a sample using *Shayna*:

- Start with beginning sounds, since they are the easiest to hear: "Okay, let's try to think of some other names or words that start with the /sh/ sound in *Shayna*." Soon you can make it more challenging by beginning with other sounds: "Can you think of any other words that have a short-*o* sound like we hear in *Monica*?" Or, "What other words can you think of that have the same *sp* blend at the beginning, like Spencer's name?"

- Write students' responses on the board or chart paper and underline the sound or chunk that students are listening for. Doing this moves the activity from phonemic awareness into phonics and adds the elements of spelling and reading for more advanced students.

- You can also think of names that rhyme with the helper's name and teach the class how to change the first letter or two. Write out any rhyming names they come up with, such as *Bayna, Mayna, Tayna*. After watching you do this a few times, students will be able to change the beginning letter and spell the rhyming names aloud as you write them.

Encouraging Participation

Get into the habit of saying, "What do you notice about this name?" This question allows everyone to participate at his or her level. Another trick is to let the special helper call on students who raise their hands. When the class notices that a peer is choosing students, and not the teacher, more hands will shoot up automatically. You can raise your hand, too, if there is something that really needs to be pointed out. Students love calling on the teacher.

■ THE NAME GAME IN ACTION

We're three weeks into the school year. Cedric is our Busy Bee.

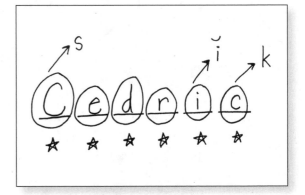

- I remind students to watch carefully as I circle the sounds in Cedric's name so they will be able to tell me what they notice. It is important to connect the auditory with the visual, so I am sure to say each sound carefully as I circle the letter that makes it:

  "/s/ - /ĕ/ - /d/ - /r/ - /ĭ/ - /k/"

- I wonder if students will notice the two different sounds for the letter *c*. They do: "I noticed the *c* sounds like *s*." "I noticed the other *c* sounds like *k*."

- Following both comments, I put a star under each *c* to point out that *c* has two sounds and both are considered "behaving." See the example above.

- Another student can hear that the letter *i* is not saying /ī/, the sound he is most familiar with; we have learned and worked with capital *I* quite a bit in class. I realize that it is very early in the school year to be talking about long and short vowel sounds, but I explain that, like the letter *c*, the letter *i* has two sounds: one is called short-*i* and one is called long-*i*. Most students cannot understand and process this information yet. Many will think that lowercase *i* is "short-*i*." I know, though, that if I introduce this concept, then I can talk about it and make reference to it when it pops up in our discussions and that several months from now, students will begin to understand long and short vowels.

In late September, Krystauna is the helper. I wonder what students will notice about her unique name.

- I have circled the sounds in *Krystauna*. Students raise their hands to tell me what they notice.

One student is not sure how to say what he can hear, but he gives it a try: "For some reason, I can hear */kr/*."

I reply, "You're right! The *k* and the *r* are blending together and making */kr/*." This is the first mention of a blend during the Name Game this year. Instead of talking more about the concept, I put a circle around these letters to show that they are working together. A circle will always indicate any group of letters that students see working together, whether it's a digraph, a blend, a common chunk, or a small word within a name.

It may seem that this is visually overwhelming for kindergarten students, but keep in mind that all the marks and notes added to a name are done one at a time and stem from students' observations. I also use three different colored markers; for example, dashes may be in red, letters in blue, and everything else in green. Here's the breakdown for Krystauna's name:

- I drew nine dashes. (red)

- Then I added the letters, one by one as students guessed them. (blue)

- As the sounds in the name were segmented, I drew circles. (green)

- Stars, arrows, and boxes were applied next, one at a time, with conversation about each one. (green)

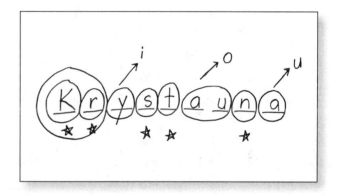

At the end of such an activity, you, and your students, will be amazed that there is so much to talk about in regard to a student's name. You'll also find that, for the most part, the majority of your students participated in and understood, at their individual level, everything that was discussed.

Ashley is selected as the Busy Bee for this fall day.

The Good Boys (*sh*) were introduced to the class when Shayna was the Busy Bee. Today Ashley is the Busy Bee.

- After students guess the letters in the name, and Ashley comes forward to stand by the easel, we go through the process of segmenting the sounds in her name and putting up one finger for each sound.

- Before we even move to the next step, where I will circle the letter(s) making each separate sound so students will get a visual representation of what they are hearing, some faces light up:

"I can hear The Good Boys!"

"Me, too! There's something in her name that sounds like Shayna's name!"

"And it also sounds like Cheyenne! Shawn, Cheyenne, and Ashley. They're all the same."

I can tell that they cannot quite put their finger (or, shall I say, their ear) on why the /sh/ sound in Ashley's name is a little different than it is in Shawn's and Cheyenne's, but some of them will get it once we circle the sounds in her name and they see that The Good Boys are in the middle and not at the beginning.

In November, Solomon is the helper.

- Solomon comes up and tries to separate and count the sounds in his name: "/s/ - /o/ - /l/ - /ŭ/ - /mĭn/"

- I tell Solomon that he's very close, and then all the students and I pull the sounds apart together: "/s/ - /ŏ/ - /l/ - /ŭ/ - /m/ - /ĭ/ - /n/"

- I then begin to circle the sounds in the name: "Now, watch carefully, while I circle the sounds and see if you notice anything." I repeat the segmentation of sounds, circling the corresponding letters as I go. Hands go up immediately. Bodies lean toward me, pleading to be called upon. Here are the responses I get:

    "I noticed the last o, the one by the n, is making i's sound, like /ĭ/-/ĭ/-iguana."

    "I noticed the o by the m is making a's sound." (I take this opportunity to remind the class that /ŭ/ is really u's sound: "/s/ - /ŏ/ - /l/ - /ŭ/, /ŭ/, /ŭ/: Sometimes a says /ŭ/, but whose sound is that really? It sounds like /ŭ/- /ŭ/-umbrella, so really it's u's sound.")

    "I noticed that the l is behaving. Sol-l-l-l . . . sounds like l-l-l-ion."

    "If you turned the o and the n around on the end, it would say Solono." (I don't correct the student and tell him it would say Solomno. Rather, I say, "Oh yeah, what if his name were Solono? That would be weird."

    "S is making the right sound."

    "M is making the /m/ sound so it's behaving."

    "Hey! If you changed the n to an m, his name would be Solomom!"

    "Yeah, only you need to go 'stick, bump, bump' on the last letter instead of 'stick, bump.'"

- I make notes of their observations, using a star to indicate a letter making its true sound and an arrow to show a letter making a sound other than its regular sound, as shown below.

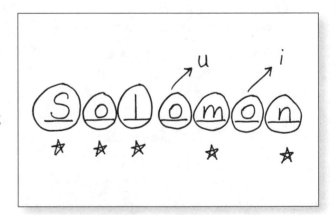

In the spring, we are working with last names. Sanchez is the last name of today's helper.

- After analyzing letters and sounds, we move on to chunks and small words. Students know this is the routine. One student mentions that this name has the -*an* chunk.

- When we have completed the activities associated with the Name Game, a few minutes remain (which is often the case in the springtime because students have become very good at analyzing and conversing about letters, sounds, and chunks), so I ask them to think of words in which they can hear the -*an* chunk, like the one in *Sanchez*. The class has worked with the -*an* word family, so many of the words they brainstorm actually rhyme with *an*. Anyone who suggests a word is encouraged to try to spell the word for me as I write it.

Students love the Name Game and the associated learning activities from day one and will not tire of it as long as the essence of your conversations grow in complexity as students' concepts of phonemic awareness and phonics rapidly increase.

Teaching Phonological Awareness

Phonemic awareness is a subcategory of the much broader concept of phonological awareness. While phonemic awareness focuses on noticing and working with individual sounds, phonological awareness includes the identification and manipulation of larger parts of spoken language, such as words, syllables, onsets and rimes, alliteration, and intonation (*Put Reading First*, NIH, 2003). There is plenty of evidence that shows that well-developed phonemic awareness and, thus, phonemic awareness activities in the kindergarten classroom, contribute to a child's ability to read and to spell at the kindergarten level. While phonological-awareness activities are appropriate and beneficial for more advanced kindergarten students, and definitely for older primary students, I have found, and firmly believe, that structured and explicit instruction in phonological awareness, such as rhyming and syllabication, may initially hinder a kindergartner's process of learning to read and spell.

RHYMING

It is often thought that children who hear many rhyming books and songs during their preschool and/or kindergarten years will grasp the concept of rhyme more easily. I have not found this to be entirely true. Yes, reading to children and singing songs with rhyming lyrics builds the phonological awareness of the concept of rhyme, but it doesn't always result in their being able to hear rhyme. I have had many kindergarten students who could read at a first-grade level and who totally understood and could write word families (e.g., *king, sing, wing*), but were unable to tell me if two words rhymed or to generate words that rhymed.

More important, I have seen no evidence that kindergarten students need an awareness of rhyming to better learn how to read and write. Hearing and supplying rhymes is fun, and rhyming is a vital feature of some types of literature, but it is by no means a prerequisite for learning to read or write during kindergarten. What all this tells me is that children will learn to hear rhymes in their own due time and that we should not waste a lot of instructional time trying to rush the process. Yes, continue to read books with rhyme, sing to your students, and talk about how rhyming words sound and look. But do not fret over whether kindergarten students hear and understand the concept of rhyme by the end of the year.

In fact, overemphasizing rhyming can hinder students' progress in being able to hear and manipulate phonemes in other ways. In *Phonics They Use*, Patricia Cunningham states, "Many children confuse the concept of words beginning or starting with the same sound with the concept of rhyme, so many teachers like to wait until the concept of rhyme is firmly established for most children before focusing on whether or not words begin with the same sound" (p. 36). I would say that, since the concept of beginning sounds is far more important in learning to read and write than the concept of rhyme, teachers should hold off on rhyming and focus on other phonemic-awareness activities instead.

Though the ability to hear rhymes and generate rhyming words is not essential to learning to read and write, it is beneficial, in the latter part of the kindergarten year, to work with the visual aspects of rhyming words. Word families can be brainstormed and listed during the Name Game (in association with a chunk of letters in the name of the day). Students can also work with word families in the computer lab. Once they have learned the keyboard and a certain letter chunk, such as *-and*, you can model how to think of and type a list of *-and* words. The main purpose of such activities is not to understand and hear rhymes; however, word family work at the kindergarten level can help students grasp rhyming by showing them, visually, what it is.

SYLLABICATION

Many different resources and professionals advocate that kindergarten students should be taught how to break words into, and count the number of, syllables. And I have witnessed many kindergarten teachers doing this. I admit that it's fun to teach syllabication: When we model how to hear, separate, and clap the syllables in names and words, students pick up on it almost immediately. We even ask students to identify and label words by the number of claps ("three-clap word"). But breaking words into syllables interferes with what we are trying to do. If students need to break a word into phonemes in order to write it (/h/ /ō/ /t/ / ĕ/ /l/) but have also practiced breaking words into syllables (hō - tĕl), then they might confuse the two skills and when to use them, making it much harder for them to segment words into individual sounds to write words. For example, a student who has heard many words broken into syllables, might say, "*Ho . . ., ho . . .* , I don't know the letter for *ho*" while trying to write *hotel*.

Assessing Phonemic Awareness and Phonics

Traditional phonemic awareness assessments tend to be lengthy and involve several tasks. The easiest and most common phonemic awareness assessment asks students to hear and separate the beginning sound of orally presented words or pictures of those words. For example, when a student is shown a picture of a lamp, the correct response is /ll/. Students do not need to know what letter *lamp* starts with or that *lamp* is even a word that can be represented with letters. In fact, if a student responds with *l*—the letter name—that would be considered incorrect, and the teacher would try to get the student to say the isolated phoneme. Also, students may know the letter names and sounds, but this does not necessarily mean that they have phonemic awareness and will be able to isolate a sound within a word. Students only need to be tested on five to ten words with different beginning phonemes to assess their understanding of this concept.

Traditional phonemic awareness assessments may also include blending together three sounds presented with short pauses between them and identifying the word that the three sounds make: (/b/ - /a/ - /t/ = *bat*), and segmenting a three-phoneme word into its separate sounds: (*mop* = /m/ - /o/ - /p/).

You should not spend time having every student do all of these different tasks. Assessments of the different phonemic awareness tasks can be administered to struggling students to determine specific areas of difficulty if the weaknesses do not surface and become apparent during regular reading and writing activities.

Generally, the most practical way to assess phonemic awareness is to observe students while they are reading or to look at their developmental spelling. A student who spells phonetically is skilled in both phonemic awareness and phonics. A student who is not yet using letter-sound correspondence may be lacking both phonemic awareness and phonics skills or may have developed phonemic awareness but have not yet mastered sound-letter correspondence. Working closely with the student during writing time will help you see where the breakdown occurs.

Kindergarten students have traditionally been assessed on their knowledge of letter names and letter sounds, but they are not always assessed to any real degree on their ability to *apply* this knowledge to actual reading and writing. Teachers need to track student growth in both areas.

How many letters should kindergarten students be expected to know by the middle of the year and the end of the year? My goal is for every student to know all letter names and all letter sounds by the end of the year, but I try to get students to master the majority of them by mid-year. Then my assistant and I focus more on the unknown letters and sounds for each student before year's end. Many teachers, schools, or districts feel that knowing about 50 of the 54 letters is a reasonable goal. Students will most likely forget some letter names over the summer, however, and if they only know 50 at the end of the year, then they may know only 45 at the beginning of first grade. The same is true for letter sounds. My personal, end-of-year goal is for every student to know all 33 letter sounds, plus the sounds for *th*, *sh*, and *ch*.

ASSESSING LETTER-SOUND KNOWLEDGE

Naming each letter—capital and lowercase, and even the "fancy" *a* and the "fancy" *g*, is a traditional and customary assessment in kindergarten, as is assessing the sound (or two sounds) that each letter makes. The development of letter-sound knowledge should be monitored throughout the year. I assess students on every letter name and its sound(s) at the end of each quarter because I want to immediately start intervention if some students are not acquiring them at the typical rate.

To assess knowledge of letter names and sounds, present a student with a sheet that has all the capital letters laid out randomly in rows. Point to the first letter in the top row and ask, "What is the name of this letter?" If a student seems confused about what you are asking, you may rephrase: "What do we call this letter?" If it appears that the student does not know the letter, try a few more letters that you believe he or she knows, such as the more common letters *O, X, A, E,* and *S* or the letters in the child's first name. The assessment continues with a sheet of lowercase letters. In all, students will have 54 letters to name—26 capital letters and 28 lowercase letters because of the "fancy" *a* and "fancy" *g*.

If students do know the names of the first few letters you point to, you can ask them to do the pointing while they name the letters. Teachers usually circle the letters that students are able to name on a separate recording sheet. I have, at times, circled the letters on the student's sheet because I know that the immediate feedback may motivate him or her to come up with the correct letter names. You can decide how quickly students must say the names of the letters to indicate that their knowledge is solid and their ability to name the letters automatic. In my opinion, students should tell the name of a letter within two seconds of focusing their eyes on it. Some students process visual information more slowly and/ or express their thoughts more slowly, so I am flexible with the amount of time I give to different students.

Then assess letter sounds. I present the sheet of lowercase letters for this since, as time goes on, students will be seeing many more lowercase letters in books, in their writing, and during instruction than capital letters. Start with the first letter on the top row and ask, "What sound does this letter make?" or rephrase, if necessary, to "What is this letter's sound?" or "What does this letter say?" If students do not appear to know very many letter sounds, point to letters you think the student knows the sounds for, such as *a, b, m, s,* and *z,* or the letters in his or her first name.

The five vowels and *c* and *g* have two sounds. In some districts, kindergarten students are expected to know and be able to tell both sounds for these letters by the end of the year. In other places, kindergarten students do not yet need to know vowel sounds. I prefer to treat vowels just like any other letter: I introduce them along with consonants, show students how they behave in different words and names, and include them in my assessment of letter sounds. I expect students to be able to tell me two different sounds for each vowel but not necessarily to answer the questions, "What is the short sound?" and "What is the long sound?" Instead, I phrase this as, "What does this letter say?" and follow up with, "What else does it say?" or "What is its other sound?"

In all, 33 sounds for individual letters can be assessed—19 consonants with one sound each, *c* and *g* with two sounds each, and five vowels with two sounds. Kindergartners should also be assessed on their ability to tell the sounds for *th, sh,* and *ch.* These digraphs are essential for beginning reading and writing and should be taught and assessed, though they rarely make an appearance on most kindergarten assessments.

It is common for kindergarten-age students to have articulation problems so they may not be able to produce the correct sound for a letter even though they know it. You will have to use your best judgment in assessing these students. This is the trickiest during pre-testing when you do not yet know your students and are unfamiliar with their speech patterns, but as you become accustomed to the way students speak and recognize their articulation errors, it will be easier to determine if they really do know the sounds for certain letters.

N	T	X	B	W	A	I
P	H	E	Q	L	V	R
Z	C	O	G	Y	K	S
J	U	M	D	F	f	d
m	u	j	s	k	y	g
o	c	z	r	v	l	q
e	b	p	i	a	w	g
x	t	n	a	h		

Assessment Sheet

Quarterly Assessments

After giving the pre-test, it is not necessary, in my opinion, for you to conduct the remaining quarterly assessments in this area unless, of course, there is no other qualified person available to do it. Assessing every single student is time consuming and, as Lucy Calkins (2001, p. 138) says, can cause instruction "to come to a grinding halt." A competent instructional aide collects this information for me. If I had to interrupt regular instructional activities to do this, then I might not assess students as frequently or assess every student each time.

I try not to be overly concerned about students' lack of letter and sound knowledge at the start of the school year. In most cases, this is a result of limited or no exposure to this material, and time will tell if something else is preventing certain children from learning. I hope to see some growth by October, but I realize that during the first quarter students are still becoming accustomed to the whole notion of letters and sounds and are just beginning to see how this information is applied to reading and writing. Still, I want to take a close look at the progress made by all students so far.

Supporting Struggling Students

As soon as I have assessment data, I categorize my students into three groups:

- *Green-zone students* (having sufficient knowledge and making sufficient progress)

- *Yellow-zone students* (having somewhat limited knowledge and/or not making steady or adequate progress)

- *Red-zone students* (having limited knowledge and/or not progressing, sometimes despite receiving extra support and attention during instructional activities)

After each assessment period, I re-categorize students and list the skills they need to work on. This information is provided to my instructional assistant. She pulls yellow-zone and red-zone students to the back of the room for brief (5–10 minute) one-on-one focused work sessions based on my notes. Then we discuss different tactics and approaches for these students, based on their learning styles and personalities. Using the Response to Intervention model, I think of this as Tier 2 support, Tier 1 being regular classroom instruction.

A second way to provide extra support to students is in the form of before-school tutoring. When I taught a full-day kindergarten class, I was able to find time to do this extra tutoring during class, usually right after lunch when students had some down time and I was not involved in direct instruction. This more intense intervention is reserved for red-zone students, the ones who do not know any, or just a few, letter names or sounds or who show very minimal growth between assessments. Their assessment data indicates that they are not picking up on crucial information during regular instructional activities and that they will need intervention to help them attain and retain information.

Before-school tutoring (or any intervention outside of regular class time and conducted by me instead of the instructional aide) is Tier 3 intervention.

Two or three students attend before-school tutoring two mornings a week, 15 minutes prior to the start of school. If I had more students who needed it, I would run different groups on different weekday mornings. For these students, tutoring consists of simple work with picture alphabet flashcards.

I choose five letters to start with and begin by pointing to each component on a card while saying, "Capital *D*, lowercase *d*, /d/, /d/, *dog*. Then I have students mimic what I say while I point to each component on the card. Initially they might not know what *capital* or *lowercase* means (and I have had students with articulation issues and non-English speaking students who could barely repeat these words), and they might not be making the association between the letter and the sound and the picture at all; it will start making sense and coming together for them as the sessions go on. Students will also connect this activity to the whole-class alphabet song described on page 77 and the way I do this with letters on our picture alphabet during the Name Game.

After a few days of teaching and quizzing students individually on these five letters, I introduce another element, which makes the sessions more fun and the learning soar—competition. I present a flashcard and say, "The first student to say the letter gets to keep the card by him or her." All of a sudden, the competition is on. Students try harder than they would in a one-on-one situation. I remind them to look at the picture and actually verbalize: "/z/, /z/, *zipper* sounds like /z/, /z/ . . ." I tell them to be brave and just let that letter name fall out of their mouth: "/z/, /z/, *zipper* sounds like /z/, /z/, z!" Whoever says the letter name first gets to have that card on the table in front of him or her. They don't hold the card, they don't get to keep it, there is no prize; but having the card in front of them motivates students to try for more cards by coming up with the letter names.

You may be concerned that this competition may cause undue stress for struggling kindergarten students. If need be, you can slow the pace by having students take turns when cards are presented and/or choosing easier letters for some students. I have not known one kindergarten student who did not enjoy, let alone thrive on, participating in activities like this. They get much faster at processing the input of visual information and then outputting spoken responses. They can sense this process happening, and it is thrilling for them.

As the sessions go on, students get faster at saying the letters, I teach more letters via the flashcards, and their repertoire of known letter names and sounds steadily grows. I am able to add trickier letters, and we start working on sounds as well. I also may start quizzing them on the sight words that have been introduced in class: to study these words, students must look at and talk about the letters and sounds that comprise them. We also constantly talk about what our mouths are doing ("lips together," "corners back," "top teeth on bottom lip") because some students really cue into this to recall a letter name or its sound.

Most of my students are green-zone students because of the immediate and total immersion into the alphabet, but they will still have some letter names and/or sounds to master. It helps to be very explicit with these students when filling in gaps in their knowledge so they will remember the information; for example, you might say, "We noticed that you could tell us all the letter names except for these three. So I'm going to teach you these three right now, and I want you to try your hardest to remember them. Then, the next time we ask you to name the letters, you'll get all of them." Or, "When I show you this letter and ask you the sound, you need to say, 'This letter has two sounds: /ă/ and /ā/.' That is how you answer the question to tell me the sounds."

Conclusion

In *Guided Reading: Good First Teaching for All Children*, Fountas and Pinnell remind us that "once a small repertoire of information is acquired, it is easier to learn a great deal more" (1996, p. 13). Diving into the entire alphabet on the first day of school supports this notion. In research terms, letter-name knowledge is the most potent correlate of later reading achievement, meaning that the more letters kindergartners know at the start of school, the more likely they become readers down the road (McGill-Franzen, 2006). Knowing a lot of letters, of course, is an indication that a student has had opportunities at home and/or preschool to listen to and talk about books, work with letters, and better understand the purposes and functions of literacy in general. Though many of our students will not start school with a knowledge of letter names, a commitment to immersing students in the entire alphabet and having sophisticated conversations about letters, sounds, and chunks (via the Name Game and daily reading and writing practice) will ensure that *all* children, not just a privileged few, know a lot of letters toward the beginning of their kindergarten year and thus have the equal opportunity to learn to apply their phonics knowledge to real reading.

CHAPTER 5

The Next Six Weeks and Beyond: Moving Students to Independence

After approximately six weeks of school, it is time to start differentiating reading instruction for students. Initially, every student benefits from the same instruction that creates a solid reading foundation; soon, however, you'll find that some students need to continue to work on the same skills within the same level of text, while others are ready to learn and practice more advanced strategies with more sophisticated text. This is why, at the beginning of October, I transition into teaching students on an individual basis. Teaching students one-on-one provides the opportunity to share good books, have intimate conversations, and customize my instruction according to each child's individual needs. To me, working one-on-one with young readers is evocative of snuggling up with my own child at home to read, share, and delight in a good book and appreciate the power and joy of becoming literate.

Preparing for the Transition

A few weeks before I start teaching on an individualized basis, I make sure I have a good sense of how each student is doing with voice-print match and "fixing up" their mistakes.

I also start keeping track of which students are beginning to attend to letters and use them as a source of information while reading. Finally, I note whether students are recognizing the sight words introduced in class. I know most of this off the top of my head—and you will, also—because I have been watching students read every day for six weeks. It remains fairly consistent year to year, with the population I serve, that after the initial six weeks of small-group instruction with Level 1/A, 2/B, and some 3/C texts, most students—about two-thirds of the class—will be ready to start individualized, guided-reading instruction at a 3/C level. The remaining one-third usually consists of one or two students who I feel could start off at a Level 4/D, and the rest of the students showing evidence that they could benefit from reading at Level 2/B a bit longer.

CREATE INDIVIDUAL BOOK BAGS

To prepare for this individualized approach to teaching, I write each student's name on a gallon-size plastic bag that zips. Into each bag, I put the last two books we read at my teacher table when we were working in small groups. I know that students will be able to read these books fairly well, independently, while I begin working with individuals. After the transition, I will always put "real" books into their book bags. I got the idea for individual book bags from *On Solid Ground* by Sharon Taberski (2000) many years ago and continue to use it today. Two books are just right for kindergarten students. I want to make sure students really do know how to read both books in their bag so they know that reading correctly and for meaning is the expectation. Every two or three days, I meet individually with a student and replace one of the books in his or her book bag with a new one.

ACQUIRING AND ORGANIZING LEVELED BOOKS FOR SMALL-GROUP OR INDIVIDUAL INSTRUCTION

In order for young children to learn to read, they must have the opportunity to read many different texts at their instructional reading level. These texts must offer a combination of support and challenge. To choose texts efficiently and effectively, you need to be keenly aware of each student's command of different reading processes and strategies as well as his or her overall approximate reading level. You must then match individual readers with books that are leveled—classified according to their general level of difficulty and according to "a continuum based on the combination of variables that support and confirm readers' strategic actions and offer the problem-solving opportunities that build the reading process" (Fountas and Pinnell, 1996, p. 113). Unlike read-aloud and shared-reading books, which are most effective when utilized at carefully planned points in the yearlong instructional scope and sequence, leveled books are used throughout the school year, at a variety of different times, in accordance with individual students' instructional needs. In other words, a student would read a book with a Valentine's Day theme in November, not February, if that is when that text best matches his or her reading development.

The Characteristics of Each Level of Text

Before you put too much energy into gathering, creating, and organizing leveled books for your classroom, it would behoove you to develop a basic understanding of the gradient of text levels. Understanding what makes a book easier or more difficult will help you identify where to place different texts on the leveled-text continuum. A central tenet of the Reading Recovery program, started by Marie Clay and her colleagues in New Zealand (1993), has always been to move children through a sequence of increasingly difficult short books. Fountas and Pinnell extended this line of thought and, in *Guided Reading: Good First Teaching for All Children*, established their own leveled-text continuum (and included a list of leveled books by title).

I do not recommend, however, that you rely solely on someone else's leveling in order to establish your own leveled-book collection. First, it could be very time-consuming and costly to seek out and buy specific titles. And, many of the titles on the Fountas and Pinnell list are outdated and not as suitable as some of the more recently published books intended for guided-reading instruction. Although many newer books come with a level printed on them, these levels can be unreliable. Some publishers use their own leveling systems that do not correspond with the Fountas and Pinnell system at all. Or, publishers may try to coordinate with the Fountas and Pinnell system but they may be off by a level or two because they don't have a true understanding of how particular text features relate to certain reading levels. Familiarizing yourself with the characteristics of each level of text, learning to level books, and double-checking any pre-assigned levels assigned to books before using them for reading instruction will lessen any confusion.

> Refer to the Reading Level Correlation Chart on pages 5–6 to see the standard book levels and their corresponding grade-level equivalency.

Going through this process will result in a kindergarten classroom in which all the books are leveled, organized, and ready to use for instruction. More important, it will help you acquire a basic understanding as to which concepts of print and strategic-reading processes readers will need to understand and control in order to read at each level.

It is important to know that the process of leveling texts is not an exact science. One teacher may find evidence to label a title as Level 6/E, while another teacher feels that the same book more closely resembles a Level 4/D (one level lower) text. You do not need to be "right on" with your first attempt at leveling a book. Often, a teacher may end up changing the level he or she assigned to a book after using it with readers. And lastly, there is a wide range of texts within any level; for example, a set of Level 4/D books will contain easy 4/Ds (but not so easy that most teachers would consider them 3/Cs) and more challenging 4/Ds (but not so difficult as to be leveled at 6/E). Therefore, it is quite possible that a student reading on a Level 4/D is ready to access some Level 4/D books but not others. There are some titles that most teachers agree represent a certain reading level and some titles that could be placed in at least two different levels on the continuum.

Working with other teachers to level books can be beneficial. As Allington explains, leveling is more reliable when several sets of eyes make the leveling judgment (2006). Also, your expertise in estimating a book's difficulty will develop more quickly and accurately when there is dialogue with colleagues. Because most teachers do share books, students, or student information, it makes sense to approximate Fountas and Pinnell's leveling system as best as you can.

Fountas and Pinnell's original descriptions of the different levels of text were used as a foundation for the information on the Characteristics of Specific Text Levels and Exemplar Books for Each Text Level chart that appears on pages 188–192. I've added thoughts from my teaching experience with diverse students and texts. Reading through and understanding the information in this chart will not only familiarize you with the gradient of reading levels, but it will also highlight which skills and concepts students will need to control in order to progress through more difficult text.

Leveling the Books in Your Classroom

Perusing some well-known titles that typify each level is the easiest way to get a feeling for each level and to start assigning levels to your own books. If you don't already have these titles in your classroom, you should be able to find them in the school or public library, the book room, another teacher's classroom, or possibly through teacher supply stores or catalogs. If there is a book room in your school that houses leveled books, you could also choose a few titles from each level to use as examples. Or, ask a fellow kindergarten teacher or first-grade teacher whose classroom has leveled books if you can look at books that represent each level.

Then—whether you were successful in obtaining leveled book samples or not—use the Characteristics of Specific Text Levels and Exemplar Books for Each Text Level chart to assign a reading level to a small handful of books in your classroom. Do not choose books that have been categorized as read-aloud or shared-reading

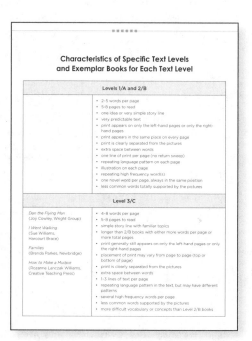

Go With the Higher Level

When you are undecided about the level for a book, always go with the higher level. Experience has taught me that the same book will get more use as an easy 6/E than as a harder 4/D. When I am working with students who are reading instructionally at a Level 4/D, the conditions have to be nearly perfect (quiet classroom atmosphere, ample time, no interruptions) for me to grab a hard 4/D book rather than a medium 4/D book, and since perfect conditions are unusual, the harder book rarely sees any use.

books. Do choose books that belong to you or books belonging to the school, that were purchased specifically for, and will therefore remain, in your classroom. Remember that, as you start to assign a level to each book, it will be perfectly acceptable to change that level later on as you begin to use the book for more structured reading instruction and become more attuned to the characteristics of each level. Therefore, go with your gut feeling, based on what you know at this moment about the different reading levels. Make a quick, informed decision and then move on to the next book.

I write the level of the book directly on the back cover. Stickers fall off or are peeled off by students, intentionally or absent-mindedly. I use letters (the Fountas and Pinnell system) rather than numbers (Reading Recovery), so, for example, I would write a letter in the upper left-hand corner of a book's back cover and circle it.

As you assess the characteristics of each book to determine its reading level, you will simultaneously be evaluating its quality and its worth as part of your structured individualized reading instruction. Only your highest quality books should be used for this purpose. If there are not a lot of books in your classroom, even some lower-quality books will have to be used for individualized reading instruction until you can obtain better books. Also, if you have two half-day classes—and possibly upward of 50 students—then you may need many more leveled books than you have on hand and will have to make do with the texts you have for the time being.

Upon close inspection, some books that appear to be written at a kindergarten or first grade level because they have five to ten words per page are actually quite difficult to read. This can be true if they do not possess the crucial elements of emergent text such as predictable, repeating language; an illustration that supports each sentence; and, a balance of easy sight words and other words, the latter of which can usually be determined from the illustrations. Low-quality books like these were most likely not written for structured-reading instruction and will not be very effective in helping students learn to read. The fact that they don't fall into any category or level is an indication that the text will present too many challenges with too little support for young readers. Books like these should be put away or given away; students will probably not experience success with them.

Organizing the Leveled Books in Your Classroom

Organizing leveled books depends on many factors, including the number of books you have and how you plan to use them. Be wary of creating a complex system that demands a lot of time to maintain. For example, organizing books by topic (sports, animals, and so on) may work with older children who can read titles and labels and help categorize and organize the books, but this system would demand too much of a kindergarten teacher's time and attention. Most teachers like to group books of the same level on shelves or in plastic tubs. The use of tubs makes it easier to move the books around. Since providing books at the right level is an important part of individualized reading instruction, create a system that allows you to quickly and easily locate certain levels of text and/or titles. I keep tubs of books close to my table while I teach small-group or individualized reading because I am constantly in and out of the tubs.

Leveled books are kept near the teacher table. Multiple copies of leveled books are crisscrossed in the tubs to keep them organized.

You can alphabetize the titles within a leveled book tub or on a particular section of a book shelf or order them from easiest to most difficult within a level.

It's also important to consider whether you are going to allow students to use the leveled books outside of their guided practice time with you . Personally, I do not want my students looking at or reading, beforehand, the books that I will use with them for individualized reading instruction. Since I am the only one who is accessing the tubs of leveled books, managing them requires minimal time.

Acquiring Additional Leveled Books for Your Classroom

It's important to always be evaluating the effectiveness of the books you're using for reading instruction and to be proactive in securing new books as needed. When books are ordered across-the-board in an arbitrary fashion, which unfortunately they often are, classrooms often have too few books of decent quality or too many books at some levels—usually the lowest— and not enough at others—usually levels above 3/C, since kindergartners have not traditionally been expected or encouraged to read beyond this level. You may start to recognize that certain titles are not as effective as others and need to be replaced. The size of your class may have increased or perhaps you just have a lot of students who need access to the same-level books at the same time.

Assess and be aware of your needs; communicate these needs to your administrator, PTA, families, or any other source from which you can obtain funds; and maintain a policy of previewing books, whenever possible, to determine their quality prior to expending funds for them.

When you are ready to acquire additional leveled books, consider the following suggestions:

Pay attention to publishers and series. If you already have a variety of leveled books in your classroom, which ones do you like the best? Base your assessment on the books' effectiveness with students, their quality and cost, and how they enhance the variety in your leveled-book collection.

Check out the publishers of the books you like for additional titles you may want to purchase. Be wary, however, of getting too many books that are similar in appearance or content. While the concepts in books should be within the realm of most kindergarten students' experiences, it is important to search for high-quality books on different topics to help them develop new schema.

Books that have worked well for me include the Handprints series from Educators Publishing Service (these books have many high-frequency words); emergent-level science and social studies books from Newbridge Educational Publishing; the Learn to Read series and the Reading for Fluency series from Creative Teaching Press; Pair-It books from Steck Vaughn; Sunshine books from Wright Group McGraw Hill; and some of the Brand New Readers titles from Candlewick Press, which are available in book stores. Larkins Little Readers from Wilbooks are inexpensive but of relatively decent quality for reading instruction. The Little Leveled Readers from Scholastic book clubs contain black-and-white illustrations, but are well-written and quite affordable.

Use resources around you. Talk with other kindergarten and first-grade teachers about the books they like to use. If you find yourself frequently using a title from your school book room, you might want to buy it for your classroom. Perhaps your school has, or once had, a reading program and there are several leveled books in your classroom that came with the program. Double-check the leveling on these books as well as read through each title to ensure their quality.

Print books from the Internet. If you are in desperate need of additional books but have limited resources, think about printing and copying books from a wide variety of Web sites, such as Reading a-z.com, that have hundreds of books and other resources that teachers can print, use for instruction, and then send home with students.

There is a fee to access most of these sites and then, of course, there is the expense, in terms of money and time, of printing, copying, and assembling the books. Another drawback is that these books all tend to look very similar to one another: they are approximately 8½ by 5½ inches and have black-and-white illustrations. These books can be a godsend to some teachers and, if that is the case with you, can be used as part of your instructional program; however, also try to secure funding for books from publishers, too.

Making the Transition to Individualized Reading Instruction

It is simple to transition from the beginning-of-the-year reading instruction where every child is reading the same book and practicing the same skills to a model based on individualized instruction, especially if you had this in mind as you were establishing your classroom set-up and routines.

The overall setup and flow of the three centers remain basically the same. I begin by assigning one-third of the class to a center. I still do not group students by ability or need because a heterogeneous group can better learn from and support each other as they move through the centers. Groups continue to rotate through the centers in the same way.

TEACHER CENTER

During the first six weeks, small groups sat with me at the teacher's table and received the same instruction. For the remainder of the school year, a group sits near my table in the independent reading area and reads on a fairly independent basis while I work with one student at a time from the group. It is an easy transition for students. First, the Teacher Center is in the same place, so students know where to go. Also, though I will now be working with one student at a time, I keep myself available to the rest of the group, especially at the beginning while students are getting accustomed to reading independently.

Introducing Independent Reading at the Teacher Center

One of the first steps to take when initiating independent reading at the Teacher Center is to explicitly tell students what independent reading is and why they will be doing it. You can explain this to the whole class before sending students to their centers. If your students are not familiar with the term *independent*, then be sure to explain it at their level. For example:

"Today you're going to try something called independent reading. You know how you work all by yourselves at the Independent Center without a grown-up? Well, today you are going to try *reading* all by yourself without a grown-up. Don't worry; you are already such good readers. The first thing you will read independently—by yourself—are the books in your book bag. You will find the bag with your name on it, then sit down on a beanbag or on the rug or at a table and read both books in the bag. If you want, you can do partner reading. We already know how to read with a partner because we've practiced it at the teacher table. If you get stuck and you can't figure out a word . . . listen because this is really important . . . I want you to sneak over to my table, and I will help you. Don't just sit there and do nothing. Come over and get some help."

As I talk, I model finding the right book bag, sitting down, reading, and walking over to the teacher table for some assistance. Then, in the same explicit manner, I show students how to read charts and/or shared-reading books once they have finished the books in their book bag. I don't expect them to remember everything, but enough students will recall most of what I say and do so they can provide sufficient modeling for their classmates. And they will be reading near the teacher table so I can provide further guidance.

ASSISTANT CENTER

The classroom assistant (or parent volunteers) will continue to work on various activities with groups at this center. After about six weeks of school, when most students have mastered basic voice-print match, I start an activity at this center that happens on the same day each week called Take-Home Books. Students are provided with two books that are at their approximate reading level. I do not send home the high-quality leveled books that are reserved for individualized instruction at the teacher table. Instead, the books that go home come from a collection of slightly lower-quality books that are more loosely leveled and that, in addition to being used as Take-Home Books, also serve as a library for independent reading.

Take-Home Books

Once a week at the Assistant Center, students are given two books at their approximate reading level from the tubs of independent reading books. I provide a list to my assistant as to which level of books each student should get. Students put the two books into their take-home book bags along with a note about how parents should read with their children (see page 184). A week later, students are expected to bring the books back to school and must read a bit from each book to the assistant while at the Assistant Center. The assistant informally determines whether they did enough reading at home. If a student can read the books fairly well, then he or she is given two new books to take home; if not, the same books are sent home with them for the upcoming week. It is not necessary to write down titles that students check out. Students know they are responsible for the two books; if one goes missing, then it will either have to be found or paid for. Reading just-right books at home ensures that parents are involved in their child's reading development, understand their child's current reading level, and learn to recognize the books representing that level. Also, the fact that students will "know" several books from these tubs will serve as a scaffold when it comes time—usually in January—for them to choose and read books on their own as an activity at the Independent Center.

INDEPENDENT CENTER

Students continue to work independently on different activities—listening to recorded stories, doing structured work with math manipulatives, completing Word Wall work or other paper/pencil activities, or doing art activities that do not require adult supervision. This center will serve much as it did during the first six weeks of school, but, of course, students will be able to do more and more on an independent basis. What used to happen at the Assistant Center may now be a possible activity for the Independent Center. As the year goes on and students gain the strategies, confidence, and decision-making skills needed to read on a truly independent basis, this center can morph into the Independent Reading Center.

Establish a Library for Independent Reading

The highest-quality texts in my classroom are reserved for reading instruction at the teacher table, and these are the books that make it into students' plastic book bags. Books that do not quite meet my standard for personalized reading instruction but that are written well enough to truly represent a specific level, and have the necessary built-in supports, go into independent reading book tubs. These are also the same books that I send home with students to read with their parents. These books get a lot more haphazard handling than the books I reserve for individualized-reading instruction at the teacher table—and sometimes get lost or destroyed—so they need to be replenished more frequently than my highest quality books.

In my classroom, the independent reading book tubs are used at the Independent Center two or three times a week beginning mid-year. I want students to participate in the Take-Home Books activity for approximately six weeks before trying this type of independent reading, where they get to choose books on their own. Since the books they take home come from this center's stash of books, they should be able to find some of the same titles that they have already read at home. They'll know these books well, making it possible for them to get started and feel confident.

The texts in the independent reading book tubs are loosely leveled and color coded. Students are assigned a color that represents books that will be "easy" for them; since this is the Independent Center, there will be no adult to offer support. If students are between the levels represented by the color coding, then they may be assigned two colors. Students know that I expect to see them using books coded with their color during independent reading time. Since quite a range of reading levels is associated with each color, students still need to think about and determine on their own whether a book is working for them. And because of the variety of texts, they also know that they are sure to find something that interests them.

Color Coding Books

In my classroom, the books that students use for independent reading and as take-home books are color coded with a sticker in the upper left corner of the front cover and loosely arranged in bins or tubs in the following categories:

- "Blue" books have text representative of levels 1/A, 2/B, and 3/C.

- "Red" books represent reading levels 4/D, 6/E, and 8/F.

- "Yellow" books are at written at Levels 12/G and 14/H.

- "Green" books are levels above 14/H.

Having less discrete divisions allows students to make important decisions on their own about whether a book is just-right and gives them room to read easier books or more challenging books. Most years, I do not set out the green book bin until spring, and then only a few students have the option of choosing books from this bin.

■ SET EXPECTATIONS FOR INDEPENDENT READING

As students transition from independent activities at the Independent Center to independent reading at this center, I explicitly explain how independent reading works and what it looks like. There is independent reading at the Teacher Center, where students read the books in their books bags, and now there is another kind of independent reading—independent reading at the Independent Center where students choose books on their own. I show the students how the books are arranged—blue dots, red dots, and yellow dots—and explain that they may only have two books out at a time. I model the thinking the students should do:

A colored dot sticker in the upper left corner of each book supports students in finding just-right books as well as in keeping the book tubs organized.

"Okay, my two colors are blue and red. I remember Ms. Bergen said to get two books at a time. So, I'll start with one blue book and one red book. Oh, cool! I took this book home once so I'm going to read it again. And over here in the blue tub, there's a book about a dog. This looks good."

I sit down and carefully read the easier blue book first, pointing to the words and reading just as I have taught them to do. Then I try the red book and act as if I can't figure out the title:

"This title is hard. Ms. Bergen said we don't have to read the title, so I'll just start reading inside." (I feign trouble with the first page.) "Hmm . . . maybe this book is too hard for me. I'm going to choose something different."

I model this again, or variations of it, from time to time.

When independent reading is one of the centers for the day, I ask students a series of questions to remind them of my expectations:

"How many books should you have?"

"When I peek at you, should I see you mostly reading or mostly standing by the tubs looking through the books?"

"Is it okay to read with a partner?"

"What should you do if someone is bothering you?"

"Can you put a book with a blue dot in this tub that has books with yellow dots?"

"If a book is too hard, should you interrupt and ask me what every single word says or should you put the book back and choose a new one?"

Again, students are not usually ready for this second type of independent reading until January and it works well if they've had opportunities to read some of the books in the independent reading books tubs, as my students do with the Take-Home Book activity.

Supervising Independent Reading

Independent reading should always be supervised. I know it's supposed to be done independently without the oversight of an adult—and it will be—and the teacher should be working with students individually at this time—and you will be—but students need guidance in how to be actively engaged during independent reading time. To ensure that students are actually reading, that they are trying to use the techniques and strategies they have learned, and that they are behaving in a way that demonstrates an understanding of the purpose of reading and the shared community goal of everyone learning to read, it is imperative that independent reading time be used appropriately. We want students to understand the importance and pleasure of daily independent reading time.

Carrying Out Individualized Reading Instruction

In this section, I will provide the structure and routines for working with students individually at the teacher table during center time. In the next chapter, I will advise you on how exactly to help students develop a network of strategies necessary for reading increasingly challenging levels of text.

SELECTING A STUDENT TO WORK WITH

Students love coming to the teacher table to work with me on their reading. Sometimes they stand and stare at me, hoping I will choose them, or they frequently ask, "Is it my turn today?" I always remind students that I will choose someone who is doing the right thing—sitting down and reading a book—to ensure that they do not waste precious reading time trying to get chosen for individual instruction. Not only do I tailor instruction during this one-on-one time, but I fulfill that need that all students have to be recognized and get attention, to be known.

I do need to ensure that I am meeting with all students approximately the same number of times per week. To do this, I list students according to their approximate instructional reading level. As I work one-on-one with students, I cross off their

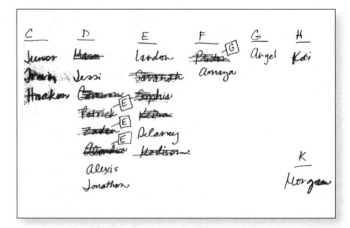

Tracking students' turns at the teacher table

name. The list thereby reflects who still needs a turn reading with me at the teacher table. If I want to move a student up to the next text level, I make a notation next to that name. When almost all the names are crossed off, indicating that it is about time to start another round of one-on-one teaching, I relist students according to the reading levels, being sure to move those who are ready to a new level. This is basically all I do to maintain a steady pace of meeting with students and to keep track of which level of book each should get.

Sometimes I work with two students simultaneously. I do this for a variety of reasons, always with intention:

- I can see more students within a given time period.

- Students can experience the fun and excitement of reading with a partner.

- I know that one particular student may motivate another.

- I use the partnership to introduce the idea and skill of reading silently (about level 12/G).

Teaching How to Read Silently

I work with two students simultaneously. The two students need to be at the same level—usually around Level 12/G—and be provided with the same title. Sometimes students read the book together. (I teach them how to check to see if the other student has turned the page and is ready, and I expect them to track the words at about the same pace.) Sometimes one student reads a page first and then the other student reads it, then they reverse the order on the next page; sometimes one student reads a page out loud while the other points to the words and reads in his or her head. I make comments such as, "Even though it's not your turn and you're not saying any words, I can tell you're reading the page in your head." This is how I transition students into reading silently when they're ready.

RECORD KEEPING

I truly feel that since I know my students as readers, and their instructional reading level, that I do not need to record our daily interactions, such as which title they read, which strategies we discussed, or students' success in implementing them. When it comes time to choose a new book for a student at my teacher table, I'll look through the appropriate tub and ask, "Have you read this book yet?" "How about this one?" Most of the time, I can recall which books each student has read and how he or she did with it. This is because I know my books well. You might want to document some information, especially when you are first starting to teach reading; however, I believe that much of the record keeping teachers do, or are led to believe they must do, is unnecessary and actually takes away from the amount of teaching we can accomplish.

Running Records

Running records are highly informative tools, not only for getting a detailed picture about how a student goes about the task of reading, but also for sharpening a teacher's observational powers and understanding of the reading process. Taking a running record involves sitting next to a child and making a record of every word he or she reads. Words read accurately are recorded with a checkmark, and self-corrections are noted. Errors or "miscues" are coded by writing the word the child says above the word that appears in the text. Teachers can analyze the running record later for the three types of errors students might make while reading: 1) *semantic*: it didn't sound right, 2) *syntactic*: it didn't make sense, or 3) *graphic*: the student didn't attend to the visual cues.

A running record yields the percentage of words a student read correctly in the selected text and range of the text.

Independent	Instructional	Frustrational
98%–100%	94%–97%	93% or below
An easy book: A student can read text at this level on his or her own.	**A just-right book:** A student can read text at this level but should be receiving some instruction or assistance with it.	**Frustrating:** A student may not be able to sustain meaning.
An easy book does not present challenges, and a teacher will be hard pressed to find any teaching points, making the instructional time nearly worthless.	This is the level at which a teacher is most likely to find appropriate teaching points and will be able to teach in the zone of proximal development.	A too-challenging text will present teaching points that the student is not developmentally ready for and will therefore not be conducive to furthering his or her strategic thinking.

It is generally not necessary to calculate the percentage of words read correctly to know the level or range of a book. If the child is not making any errors and there are no teaching points to offer, then the text is easy, and you have missed a teaching opportunity with that student. If you must stop and assist with several words in the first few pages and the child is already frustrated (and so are you), then the text is obviously too difficult. Again, the perfect text is one that offers plenty of support with just a few challenges and that presents opportunities for teaching into a child's zone of proximal development. This is a text that allows the student to strategically think through most of the reading but that requires you to intervene and offer guidance in a few places.

Teach in the Zone of Proximal Development (ZPD)

The "zone of proximal development" (Vygotsky, 1978) represents the small window of student development between what can be done with a little bit of adult support and what can be done independently. This is the ideal teaching zone—addressing what students are on the verge of doing on their own and what they will do tomorrow (or sometime in the near future) without assistance. This philosophy entails knowing each student, which skills an individual demonstrates on a regular basis, which skills he or she is beginning to understand and use, and which skills are not yet developmentally appropriate for a specific child. The way to know your students this thoroughly is to work with them in small groups, and then individually, as frequently as possible. We want to instruct at this "point of almost" so students will have the support they need to try strategies on their own while reading independently. I call this "being aware of the point of almost" or "teaching in the zone."

I do caution against making decisions about a text based on accuracy percentages alone; one error on a short, emergent book can result in a frustrational level (below 94 percent accuracy), but it's likely that the student wouldn't really be frustrated with the book. And, if that text is abandoned for something less challenging, then the new text may not offer any teaching opportunities. If you don't recognize this, then you may keep students in texts that are too easy and thus present no opportunity for growth.

Furthermore, I believe that what a teacher can learn from a running record can also be learned from simply observing a student reading and getting to know that child as a reader. And if you are working with your students one-on-one a few times each week, you *will* know them as readers. It is important to observe and be aware of the types of mistakes students are making and to adjust your instruction accordingly. During one-on-one reading instruction, when you observe that a student is making a certain type of mistake, you can address it right away; while conducting a running record, you cannot—theoretically—instruct the child because anything you say might affect his or her reading later in the passage, which would make the record less valid. The role of the teacher during a running record is as a neutral observer. Well, kindergarten students aren't used to that; they are used to their teacher teaching and supporting them along the way. They do not understand why, one day, we are suddenly not talking to them about the text. It cannot be good for a young reader's understanding of what reading is to let them make mistakes that go uncorrected. In fact, as the example below shows, it must be downright confusing to a student why, during a running record, the teacher is not insisting that his reading make sense.

I once watched a teacher conduct a running record. The student read, "The farmer gets up early . . ." (with a long-*e* sound in *early*), and the teacher made a written note of it.

Since the teacher was involved with assessment and not teaching, she could not intervene on an instructional basis. The student looked perplexed. The sentence did not make sense to him, and I believe he thought he should try and correct it. However, the teacher was acting as if what he had said made perfect sense. She wasn't reacting, and the student may have thought that the dissonance he perceived was, perhaps, not there at all. Watching the student struggle was hard enough, but I also wondered what would become of the teacher's written note. Was she just going through the motions or would she use her note to get back to the student and/or guide future instruction? It was such a teachable moment. Think how much more valuable it is for the learner to learn, at that moment, that his hesitation was warranted and that something should, indeed, have been done to ensure that the sentence made sense.

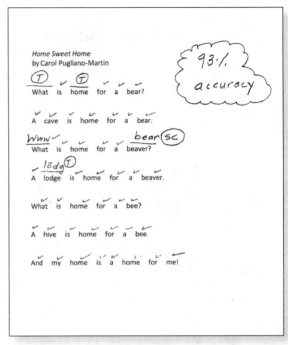

A sample running record of a kindergartner's reading

I do, however, recommend doing a few running records with your students just so you become familiar with the process and understand how to analyze errors. The sample above shows the simplest way to take and analyze a running record. And, being familiar with the three types of errors—semantic, syntactic, and graphic—will sharpen your observation skills and make you a more effective teacher. If you feel the need to take running records on a regular basis, I suggest that you instruct during this time as well. Again, students, especially kindergarten students, benefit from instruction right at the point of error, not a few days or even a few moments later, when the running record is complete and you have had time to analyze it and talk to the student about the errors he or she made.

CHOOSE TEXTS THAT OFFER ADEQUATE SUPPORT AND CHALLENGE

It is crucial to understand that students need to be reading just-right texts during one-on-one instruction. A text is just right for a student when that student is able to read most of the words and when he or she can put to use some strategies to read the few remaining unfamiliar words.

I select books for students at their instructional level, not their independent level. First, I need to ensure that some teaching points arise as the child reads alongside me. If, after reading aloud the title and the first page or two, a student is able to read the rest of the book without making errors, or immediately corrects mistakes, then the only teaching action I can do on that day is some reinforcement. My one-on-one time with this child is invaluable, and I need the opportunity to model, scaffold, and prompt for the different strategies I eventually want him or her to try independently with new books.

Second, because students have any given book in their book bag for four or five days, the text should be slightly challenging for the first day or two and then seem just right after they've had a chance to practice using the strategies that the text demands. If a book is initially just right, it will become too easy with repeated readings, so students won't have the opportunity to try new strategies or push themselves. It is okay to put an easy book inside a student's book bag sometimes. Reading an easy book gives the child, and you, a little breather and will build his or her fluency and confidence.

Providing slightly challenging books to students when they come to the teacher table also allows you to move them out of the early emergent level texts (2/B) that are typically written with repeating language patterns as soon as it's appropriate. These books require students to use voice-print match to repeat the same language and then to look at the picture to "read" the one or two words that change per page. This is no longer challenging for most students after they've been doing it daily for six or more weeks. Moving students to level 3/C and 4/D books provides them with the opportunity to try the very strategies they need to be practicing—namely, cross-checking with all three sources of information: semantic, syntactic, and graphic—in order to progress with their reading development. I do not want students to think that reading is just about parroting back words and looking at pictures. We need to start the real work of reading that will build their network of strategies and a solid reading foundation.

Sometimes, says Taberski (2000), we run the risk of not giving children enough room to grow. We need to make sure the support is there, but we can't overdo or prolong it, or

Approximating Reading Levels

It's okay to say that a child is reading at *about* a certain level based on the books you are using with him or her in your classroom. Variability can occur when leveling books. And there are different levels of support you can give a student during the reading of a book. For example, you might want a student to read a text at his or her *instructional* level, which will require some assistance, or read a text on his or her *independent* level on his or her own. Also, students will need more help with texts on the first read than they will on subsequent reads. Therefore, be sure to think of students as being at an *approximate* reading level. When it comes time to formally assess a student and be more precise about a concrete and final reading level, then you will most likely be using a pre-leveled, standardized formal assessment that will yield a fairly accurate reading level.

where's the challenge? Pat Johnson (2006) agrees, explaining that early-emergent level books made by publishers tend to hold fast to patterning all the way through the text. While these patterns are great for getting voice-print match awareness underway and for giving children a sense that the pictures and the words of text must match, the rigid patterns don't allow for enough self-monitoring/cross-checking on the part of the child. Johnson supports moving children out of early patterned texts at levels 1/A and 2/B and into more challenging texts at levels 3/C and 4/D, which are not as easy to memorize and have more opportunities for building up a network of strategies.

STARTING THE READING INSTRUCTION

Here are the steps I take when a child comes to the teacher table.

- I ask the student for the "oldest" book in his or her book bag. This is a hard concept for kindergartners at first, but they catch on soon that they need to give me the book that has been in their bag for the longest period of time. I put this book away.

- I choose another book at the same level, or at the next level up if I have made a note that the student is ready to advance to a new level. The new book should have something different to offer or be slightly more challenging.

- I read aloud the title of the book selected for the student. (The title is usually much more challenging than the text itself; there is no reason to have students read the title on their own until they are at about Level 8/F.)

- The child reads the title back to me. I have the child read the title again on the title page, if there is one.

- I then read the first page or two so the student can get a sense of the text structure and repetitive language used throughout the book.

- Then I let my instruction unfold, depending on what the student shows that he or she can do and what the book offers in terms of strategy instruction. I may need to read another page to the student, but if the text I have chosen is appropriate, he or she should be able to start taking over the responsibility for reading.

Usually, no matter what level of text a student is reading, I don't begin strategy instruction in earnest until the second or third page when the child understands the text structure and can try to make sense of it and make it sound right. Lucy Calkins (2001) does this with emergent readers, too; she points out that one-on-one reading actually starts with a bit of shared reading as the teacher reads the title and the first few pages. I, too, start my session with the child as shared reading and ease into guided reading as he or she takes over the responsibility for most of the reading.

PICTURE WALKS AND BOOK INTRODUCTIONS

Doing a picture walk and/or book introduction is a distinct component of traditional guided reading, as outlined by Fountas and Pinnell in 1996. This involves having students look at the pictures on each page and get a sense of the story and its vocabulary and concepts, through conversation, before actually starting to read. I have found, however, that picture walks are time-consuming and disrupt the strategic thinking and problem solving a young reader might do if he or she did not first look through the book. Since I only have about 5 minutes with each child and want to scaffold and prompt according to what a particular learner needs, I want to see how he or she reads the book without knowing the outcome. I want to observe the ways in which the child makes meaning. I want to see him or her struggle, somewhat, with new words and concepts. Finally, I want to watch the reader's face as he or she learns how the story ends, *during reading*, rather than prior to reading the book, to get a sense of his or her understanding. To me, picture walks and book introductions provide too much support for the child and lessen the strategic thinking I can facilitate during this short, precious instructional time.

ADVANCING STUDENTS

Fountas and Pinnell (2006) recommend being especially careful about moving quickly—advancing readers up to higher levels. It is important, just as before, that students actually be able to understand what they are reading: "The point of reading instruction is to ensure both growth and breadth as well as steady vertical movement. When readers move to levels too far above their current grade level, the content often becomes developmentally inappropriate" (p. 153). Fountas and Pinnell believe that once students are reading about one year above grade level, they might not understand as much of the content as they should. Taberski (2000) explains further that semantic and syntactic cues cannot be accessed when books are too hard, and that readers are forced to rely solely on visual information when they should be using all three sources of information.

When I have a student reading at an end-of-first-grade level or higher, I select books that are a level or two below that level. I do this to enhance the breadth of the reading experience and knowledge and practice. I am careful not to put readers in a position where they cannot depend on all three sources of information for support. I have found that there are some higher-level texts (first- to third-grade reading levels) that kindergarten students can deal with, relate to, and continue learning from. These are typically shorter books (not chapter books) in the genres of realistic fiction students can relate to or nonfiction about a topic they are interested in (e.g., animals or insects) that does not introduce too much advanced vocabulary.

TEACH THE READER, NOT THE BOOK

Once we start teaching students individually, we no longer have to worry about addressing several strategies and concepts with every student in some magical way that is timely and appropriate for all. Instead, we select two or three teaching points to use with a book that matches each student's zone of proximal learning.

Because instruction is individualized, it is important to note that not every teaching point presented by a text has to be taught. We must know what is appropriate for a particular student, that this reader can construct knowledge from the text, that he or she can connect with it, and that it coincides with his or her zone of proximal development. At times, it will make sense to tell the reader a word or abandon a book before putting it into a book bag if it does not seem to be a good match for the reader at that point. Our goal is to teach the reader, not the book.

Teaching the reader and not the book also means that a book does not have to be mastered before a student exchanges it for a new one. When a student comes to the reading table, and I ask for the oldest book in the book bag, I usually know if he or she has been struggling with this text. Again, I keep an eye on the group of independent readers at my center and listen in on their reading while I work with an individual at my table. And, since students are allowed and encouraged to ask for assistance, a student may have come over several times to ask me about the title, the repetitive language, or a certain word or two in a book. This is usually a sign that the text is a mismatch and that the student is not having much opportunity to practice strategy use with it. It makes sense, then, to replace the book with a new one rather than insisting that the student keep practicing with the same text. Of course, if this becomes a pattern, then I know that this reader is probably not working up to his or her potential while reading independently and will need additional monitoring and encouragement.

SET EXPECTATIONS FOR TEACHER CENTER READING

In order for you to focus your attention on the student reading alongside you at the teacher table, and for students to make as much progress as possible during their kindergarten year, it is necessary to establish high expectations for students to read on their own, and to the best of their ability, during independent reading time. You can promote this by continually monitoring students as they read independently and supporting them so they are successful. I frequently remind my kindergarten students of the following independent reading area expectations:

- When you arrive at the Teacher Center, find your book bag and start reading right away.

- You may sit on the floor, at a table, on a beanbag, or near a friend, but you have to be reading.

- Don't do pretend reading. I can tell if you are really reading and I am always peeking at you.

- You may read with a partner, but both of you have to be looking at the words.

- Read both of the books in your book bag. When you finish, you may read other books in this area or you may use pointers and read charts that are hanging on the wall.

- Don't leave this center. Stay on the rug.

PARTNER READING

At this point, students know how to partner read the same book. During independent reading, however, there are times when students will have different books in their book bags, so it is necessary to model what partner reading looks like in this case. I let students know that it is okay to have one student pointing and reading, but only if the listener is sitting up, sitting closely, and looking at the words as the reader says them. This is not the time to just be hearing a story. If that were acceptable, many students would listen the entire time instead of doing some of the reading work themselves.

I encourage students to partner read because it ensures that they can be engaged during independent reading in at least one way, but primarily because they learn so much from each other. For the most part, they watch each other closely, more closely than if I were the one reading to them. They expect the reader to self-correct upon making a mistake and hold him or her accountable for doing so. Sometimes they are paired with, and hear, a more fluent reader. They get exposure to other books with new vocabulary and concepts. And, they experience the joy of sharing a good book with a friend.

HANDLING INTERRUPTIONS

I permit students to interrupt me at the Teacher Center when they really need assistance in order to carry out a task, or when they are excited and want to share something. I want to know what they are thinking, what they are struggling with, and what connections they're making. I want them to always construct meaning while reading and often times they need my help to do so. I want them to feel successful. Often, students need to share their excitement or a discovery with me. They may come over and say, "I found the -*ar* chunk that we were just talking about!" Of course, I teach students how to approach the teacher table and politely interrupt. Here is my procedure:

- The student(s) reading with me take precedence.

- The student who is interrupting stands back slightly and waits quietly until I look at him or her. Then the student speaks quickly and quietly.

- I say the minimum number of words to acknowledge or assist the student.

- Then I return to my teaching, and the student goes back to his or her reading spot.

Because I work with students one-on-one for short periods of time, rather than small groups of students, it is easy to attend to both individuals. The student at my table rarely gets distracted and will often just keep reading while I am briefly speaking to another student.

Conclusion

Working individually with students on a regular basis is not only good for each and every student's reading development, but it is also easy to manage and requires no preplanning or materials preparation. Once you start working one-on-one with students and are aware of the different teaching points in the books you have at your disposal, you will know how to approach the instruction for each child. Strategies should not be taught in a predetermined sequence, nor should they be introduced to every child at the same time or in the same manner. The whole purpose of teaching kindergarten students one-on-one is to better adapt your instruction to the different learning level, rate, and style of each child.

CHAPTER 6

The Network of Strategies

Learning to read is not an innate process; unlike learning to walk or to speak, children are not going to learn to do it just by listening to and watching adults do it. Still, I rarely feel as if I am *teaching* students how to read; rather, it's as if I am *facilitating* the development of reading by creating the space, sharing the joy, "bringing to conscious attention"—as Frank Serafini (2001) says—a variety of strategies that students can use to make sense of written language, and offering fitting books at the right time. Though reading does need to be taught, many kindergarten students seem to acquire this skill almost effortlessly when they are in an environment where the development of the skill is properly nurtured.

Serafini also talks of facilitated reading instruction. He describes it as an approach where the teacher works alongside the reader as he or she engages with a text and tries to make sense of it. This is the context in which the teacher "brings to conscious attention" the strategies that successful readers employ to make meaning from written language. According to Serafini, facilitated reading instruction happens in two main ways:

- Teachers rely on preplanned curricular engagements, in which they plan and facilitate specific classroom experiences, to help develop reading strategies. This teaching situation is described as teaching "in front of" a child's experiences. It would occur, for example, during shared reading, wherein a teacher carefully selects a shared-reading text ahead of time and then decides what to introduce or model through the reading of this text.

- Teachers make time for individualized response-centered engagements with students, which is called teaching "into" a child's experiences. This would occur while a teacher works alongside an individual student, supporting and responding accordingly, at the point of need and in the midst of the child's real reading moments.

The Missing Link

Traditionally, reading instruction in kindergarten has been more about teaching "in front of." The teacher knows how to do the skill or use the strategy and does it; students watch and absorb but get too few experiences to try it out for themselves. And, too often, when students do get to try it, perhaps in an unstructured independent reading situation, the teacher is not alongside them, so that crucial in-between step, the teaching "into," doesn't happen. This is often the missing link in kindergarten reading instruction and what typically holds kids back from learning to read beyond a Level 3/C.

In *One Child at a Time,* Pat Johnson discusses how to teach the various behaviors and strategies that successful readers employ. Semantically speaking, a behavior is something that can be seen, while a strategy or process is a cognitive action that constructs meaning. Usually a student's reading behaviors will hint at what is going on in his or her mind, but not always. Sometimes, students go through the motions but are not engaged cognitively. Johnson explains that when we teach strategies, we are teaching students ways to solve problems that they can apply now, and as well on another day with a different text. Readers need to learn many strategies, come to own a "network" of strategies, so they can use a part or parts of this repertoire as the need arises.

Developing a Network of Strategies

Johnson outlines five teaching actions that describe, to a tee, what I do during shared-reading and individualized-reading instruction with kindergarten students. These actions are used in teaching "in front of" and "into" students' reading experiences. And though I've been teaching kindergartners to read for many years and these actions come quite naturally now, they are still at the forefront of my mind each time I work alongside a child. The five teaching actions to always keep in mind are:

1. **Modeling:** Clearly demonstrate what you want students to do, using explicit language.

2. **Scaffolding:** Present creative and flexible temporary supports during guided instruction that students can attempt and rely upon while reading independently.

3. **Prompting:** Use questions or comments, or nonverbal cues, that remind students to think about a scaffold or try a strategy or behavior.

4. **Backing off:** Dismantle scaffolds and prompt less frequently or overtly, making students more responsible for initiating strategies and behaviors.

5. **Reinforcing:** Bring students' attention to the strategies they use, highlighting the effectiveness of strategies, and intimating their continued use or application in different situations.

Modeling Reading Behaviors and Strategies

Formally introducing a desirable behavior or strategy by giving it a name, showing students what it looks like, and explaining its purpose are important aspects of explicit teaching. Shared reading and read-aloud are the perfect venues in which to present and demonstrate the use of specific strategies and behaviors and to teach "in front of" students' own reading experiences.

While you should have one teaching point as the focus of a shared-reading lesson or read-aloud, realize that you teach many strategies, behaviors, and concepts simultaneously each time you demonstrate reading in front of your class. Likewise, a student uses a network of strategies each time he or she engages in reading. Readers never use just one strategy. Usually with whole-group shared reading, you will have a specific teaching point in mind, but if you let students take the pointer and do the reading, any number of reading situations could arise. The same is true when you and a student are reading during one-on-one instruction. The key is to be flexible; look for opportune teaching moments; and introduce, review, or focus on any relevant strategic reading action.

Keep in mind that as the school year progresses, it is less likely that the entire class will receive the full benefit of whole-group instruction. As students' individual rates of learning, attention, and motivation come into play, some will not be quite ready to comprehend and incorporate what you are demonstrating into their network of strategies; some will already know the strategy and be capable of accessing and applying it while reading independently; and some will be right at the cusp of understanding what you are doing and how it relates to what they already know (the zone of proximal development).

Certain processes and behaviors can be introduced to the entire class, and others—usually those that are more sophisticated and associated with reading higher-level text—should be introduced at the point of need while working with individual students. The Strategic Reading Behaviors and Processes Associated With Each Level of Text chart on page 180 shows a list of somewhat developmentally sequential reading behaviors and strategies that need to be taught and suggestions for text levels to complement the teaching and use of each strategy. It starts with the most basic and gets progressively more sophisticated and advanced; however, it is not intended to be used sequentially. Most of *what* you teach will remain constant from year to year; however, exactly *when* and *how* you teach these behaviors and strategies may vary. Which strategic reading behaviors you teach, and how, will depend on the unique characteristics of your classroom, the texts you have, your distinctive teaching style, and the learning needs of your class as a whole and, most important, as individuals.

Follow this process to introduce and model reading behaviors and strategies:

- **Be explicit about your teaching point.** This will help students focus on it instead of casually observing the many other behaviors they see happening; for example, you might say, "We've already learned how to look at the *picture* to figure out what a word says. Today, we're going to learn how to look at the *letters* to figure out a word. Watch me, and I'll show you how to look at the first letter and say its sound when reading." It will be impossible for students to *not* look at the picture, and to *not* think about what makes sense, and to *not* predict the word based on what would sound right, so stating the strategy right before modeling helps them focus on it as the key strategy.

  It is not important, however, that kindergarten students be able to name every strategy or use explicit instructional jargon. The goal is for them to eventually access and use the strategies automatically. Sometimes, bringing too much attention to the strategies, talking too much about them, or insisting that students explain which strategies they know puts the focus on the strategies instead of on actual reading.

- **Choose a text that complements the strategy.** Or, choose a specific strategy based on the text you will be using. With the strategy mentioned above—looking at the first letter to figure out a word—it would be effective to use a book with illustrations that do not necessarily match the key word or that will create some uncertainty as to what the word might be. For example, if there is a picture of a rabbit, students will absolutely have to focus on the first letter in the word to know if it says *rabbit* or *bunny*. In a few of the books I wrote for instruction during the first six weeks of school, I deliberately alternated the words *the* and *a* so students would be required to look at the letter(s) instead of just repeating a language pattern. The text on one page read *I see a black tire* while on the next it read *I see the red wagon.*

- **Think aloud to model strategic processing.** As mentioned earlier, strategic thinking happens inside the head. Students cannot observe it so you need to explicitly share your thinking: "Okay, I'm going to read this page, and I'm going to try and look at the first letter and use the letter sound to read the words. I see the Good Boys so I'm going to make the *sh* sound. */Sh/, /sh/, she is* . . . I'm going to look at the picture, but I'm also going to try to use the letters. *She is* . . . I see an *r*. *She is* . . . */r/, /r/ reading a* . . . I could just say *book* because I know that's what we read, but today I'm trying to use the letters. The next word has a *b*. *She is reading a /b/, /b/ book.* The word is *book*."

- **Read fluently on some days.** On occasion, the purpose of shared reading or read-aloud should be to demonstrate what reading sounds like when an entire network of strategies is in use. When you read fluently, children can hear what good reading sounds like; hear a story straight through without the usual strategy instruction; and build up their listening skills, background knowledge, and ability to comprehend. One way to model fluent reading is to read a shared-reading or read-aloud story straight through without any discussion and, on subsequent reads, demonstrate additional strategies and behaviors.

- **Mention the strategy whenever it is appropriate to do so.** Like everything in kindergarten, once a strategy, concept, or bit of knowledge has been introduced, it can, and should be brought up from that point on. It is now common knowledge in the learning community. Students have an established schema about it. What you teach during shared reading and read-aloud is what you'll emphasize when appropriate during one-on-one instruction. The same strategies will be demonstrated and talked about again and again and again.

Scaffolding to Support Reading Development

You create scaffolds to support your instruction and student learning naturally, whether you are aware of it or not. The idea of scaffolding was first introduced by Jerome Bruner, a cognitive psychologist, in the 1950s. Scaffolding is the helpful interactions between a teacher and students that allow students to participate in something that they cannot yet do independently.

If a scaffold falls within a student's zone of proximal development, then he or she will probably catch on to the gist of the scaffold. If the student is not yet developmentally ready or, conversely, if his or her abilities surpass the zone, then the scaffold will most likely be disregarded.

Scaffolding also encompasses the supports inherent in any well-written, leveled text. The organization of the book, repeating language pattern, illustrations, number of known words compared to unknown words, and predictability of the language all contribute to textual scaffolding. If the textual scaffolds, in conjunction with the support you provide, do not help a student successfully access the text, the text may be too difficult or leveled incorrectly—or it may be of poor quality.

CREATE SCAFFOLDS TO GO

When a student is at my table, I think about which scaffolds might be helpful in making sure he or she will be able to read the book independently. If a word appears several times in a book and is proving to be a challenge, then I try to come up with something that will assist the student in remembering the word. An example is the word *here*, which can be hard to decode when it appears at the beginning of a sentence. I show the student that the word begins with *he* (*he* is on our Word Wall by mid-fall) and is followed by an /r/ sound and a silent *e*. I have the student practice saying *he-/r/, he-/r/.* For other words ending in silent-*e*, I have the student watch me draw an arrow from the *e* back to the preceding vowel. Sometimes this visual cue is enough to remind the student to make the vowel long, especially if he or she watches me draw the arrow as we talk about it. (Remember that having to strategically deal with a silent *e* won't occur until about Level 6/E or 8/F text when readers are more advanced; this is why the arrow scaffold is appropriate.) I provide support for the word *look* by drawing dots in the two *o*'s so they look like eyes.

A temporary scaffold in a book

When marking in a book to scaffold a child's reading, I explain that it is okay for teachers to make marks in books but not for students to do so. Also, if I come across a temporary scaffold that I created for a previous reader but that is not needed with this reader—either because he or she can be successful without the scaffold or because the skill or concept is not yet in the child's zone of proximal development—I erase the mark so it is not distracting to the student now reading the book.

Prompting Students to Help Them Access Their Network of Strategies

In the setting of individualized instruction, you can customize scaffolds for each student based on previous teaching interactions, shared books, and his or her unique personality and learning style. When working with students one-on-one, you are more at liberty to tailor your use of prompts to remind students to think about scaffolds.

Prompting is the art of using limited comments or questions, or just expressions or actions, to get students to think about a scaffold or to try a strategy you've already introduced. Questions such as, "What can you do to figure out that word?" or "That didn't make sense, so what do you need to do?" remind students that they have learned some strategies for problem solving while reading. But be wary of turning prompting into a long, reflective strategy discussion. Lucy Calkins (2001) reminds us that the goal is to help readers develop unconscious habits; if we always stop students and engage them in prolonged conversations, then we defeat that purpose. The goal is reading, not talking about reading. It is critical, therefore, that intervening as a child is reading be done as lightly as possible so you don't interrupt his or her momentum and meaning making. Tapping an illustration to bring attention to it, twisting your fingers to remind students to be flexible with letter sounds, or scowling a bit to express that something didn't sound right are examples of less invasive prompting.

Teaching "Lightly"

Many teachers have visited my classroom over the years to witness for themselves what kindergartners are truly capable of doing with reading and writing. During centers time, the visitors usually observe and converse with children as they choose books to read at the Independent Center, read the books in their book bags, or read charts or other shared-reading materials. They watch my assistant work with a small group of students. And they always come over to the teacher table where I am reading alongside a student. I know from experience that they will not stay at my table and observe the one-on-one instruction for long, but it wasn't until recently that I realized why they moved on so quickly. I now know that my teaching there is so "light" and unobtrusive to the work that the student is doing—as it should be—that onlookers are not aware that it is happening or cannot, because they do not know the reader well enough, readily make a connection between what I am doing and how it will benefit that student's reading development. Often, it must look as if I am doing nothing other than sitting there and listening to the child read.

MOVING STUDENTS INTO MORE CHALLENGING TEXT

When you model the strategic processing that good readers do and then employ creative and artful scaffolding and prompting to get students to apply the strategies, it becomes possible, and advantageous, to move them into more challenging text. Because of the intentional design of quality leveled books, students cannot practice certain skills and strategies unless they are reading a text that demands the use of such strategies. A more difficult text level will demand that students use new skills and strategies, which will in turn move them along the continuum of learning to read. Of course, you will advance students based on their individual ability. My belief in, and commitment to this approach—intentionally teaching the new and necessary strategies and behaviors associated with the next level of text and then providing students with those texts—is the instructional foundation for moving kindergartners through the levels and getting them beyond a 3/C reading level.

The key structures of each level of text and the strategic thinking needed to successfully read them are shown in the Strategic Reading Behaviors and Processes Associated With Each Level of Text chart on page 180. You can see from the chart that students have to be attending to and using the beginning sounds of words in order to access Level 3/C texts. I must model this strategy in shared reading and emphasize it during individualized instruction with those students who are ready to try it. When a student knows several letter sounds and demonstrates an understanding of the concept of using beginning sounds, it is time to bump that student up to a Level 3/C text. I don't wait until the student has *complete* control of a strategy or knows *all* of the letter sounds, for it is the provision of the next level of text that will make these things happen more quickly.

Unlike a Level 2/B text, Level 3/C text is designed to provide opportunities to practice a particular strategy. This is just the way good, leveled texts are written; they do not ask too much from a reader too soon. Keeping students at a Level 2/B text for too long and thinking they are not ready for Level 3/C, or shouldn't be at a Level 3/C until the end of the year, is one of those ways that teachers may inadvertently hold kindergarten students back. Students are ready to move to the next level of text when they have the strategic processes and behaviors needed for reading their current text level well under control. You will know which strategies students consistently utilize because you'll be teaching them one-on-one on a regular basis.

Backing Off and Releasing Responsibility to Students

The teaching actions of scaffolding and prompting are, inherently, part of releasing responsibility to the students. Different types of scaffolding and prompts provide varying levels of support. When you meet individually with students on a regular basis, you will get to know them quite well as readers and will always have a good grasp of the level of scaffolding and prompting necessary for them to be successful. As a student internalizes scaffolds and you become more subtle in your prompting, his or her network of strategies will expand and become more efficient.

Reinforcing the Use of Strategic Reading Behavior

When students stand before the class and take a turn pointing to and reading the words in a shared-reading text, or when you work with them individually, reinforce their strategic reading behaviors—whether they are doing them naturally or with intention—by mentioning and making them aware of exactly what they did that helped them read accurately or construct meaning. Of course, you are not going to do this every time a student reads a word, sentence, or page, nor should you always mention the strategy they just put to use, but you should offer reinforcement frequently enough to remind students of the power of strategy use and to develop their metacognition. Reinforcement helps students understand that their ability to read is not happening magically but rather because they are cognitively engaged and actively processing information while they read. Keep your comments brief, so your precious time goes to reading and not to too much talking. Examples of quick reinforcement include comments such as the following:

- "You looked at the picture and figured out the word without even slowing down your pointing and reading."

- "I'll bet you were reading along and thought that long word was going to be *elephant* and then you saw the *e* and you knew it was."

- "Did you hear yourself twist the sounds? Because I did! First, you said, '*I wănt . . .*' with an /ă/ sound, then you twisted the *a* a little and turned it into a real word that makes sense. That's exactly what you're supposed to do."

I also reinforce strategic reading behaviors with kindergartners by making them aware of the fact that I am watching and listening as they read in more independent locales. Because I situate myself closely enough to overhear them as they read their books independently and can observe them as they use pointers to read charts, I am able to reinforce their positive reading behaviors even when they are not sitting alongside me. Often, I will stop the entire workshop and make an announcement: "Sorry to interrupt, but I just have to tell you! I was spying on Angel while he read, and I saw him breaking a word into chunks to figure it out, just like we do with our names during the Busy Bee. And he got the word. He figured it out!" Pronouncements such as this help all students to, once again, start thinking metacognitively about the strategies and how they are putting the strategies to use.

The Network of Five Critical Strategies for Kindergarten

When children read continuous text—text that is ongoing, contextualized, and meaningful as opposed to isolated words or phrases—they rely upon three sources of information to help them figure out the words:

- **Meaning:** what makes sense contextually (Readers use the *meaning* of the passage and what would *make sense*, as determined by any illustrations, their background knowledge, and the context of the story.)

- **Syntax:** what sounds right according to the structures and conventions of English (Even young students have a good idea about how phrases and sentences should be structured, and this allows them to predict the words based on *what sounds right*.)

- **Visual clues:** pictures, letters, letter chunks (Students look at the *visual cues*, which, initially, are picture clues, but then are mainly the *letters or chunks of letters* in words.)

The processes, or strategies, that must be developed in children should be based on the effective use of all three of these information sources. Good texts will allow students to use and rely upon each of these information sources. It is impossible to systematically address how to teach all the reading behaviors and strategies that can be taught in kindergarten. Instead, I will cover, with explanation and examples, the five most critical strategies for the kindergarten grade level. The five categories that follow encompass what I consider to be the most crucial processes to nurture in young readers in order to establish a foundation that ensures a future of fluent and meaningful reading. These five critical strategies should be taught to all students, whether they are struggling the entire school year with Level 2/B texts or have advanced into first- or second-grade level books.

- **Learning behaviors**
- **Word analysis**
- **Predicting and cross-checking**
- **Fix-ups (self-corrections)**
- **Relevant comments and questions**

In the next section, I offer whole-class shared-reading (teaching "in front of") ideas as well as an easy-to-manage context for working one-on-one with students as they practice these strategies with your personalized guidance (teaching "into" students' reading). After reading about ways to teach the main strategies, you will have a much broader concept about, and several ideas for, teaching any of the other strategies on the Strategic Reading Behaviors and Processes chart (page 180) as well as others you come up with as you work with young readers.

CRITICAL STRATEGY: LEARNING BEHAVIORS

There are general learning behaviors to address as well as behaviors that are more specific to reading achievement. Many of the behaviors that would fall into the latter category are included on the chart on page 180. The teaching of learning behaviors, like the teaching of reading strategies, should be done during both whole-class instruction and while working with small groups or individual learners. Whole-group discussions about how best to learn are often consistent from year to year, but should also arise from the unique circumstances of your current class. If, for example, during independent reading, you observe that Maya is looking at books and pretending to read, you should review what it looks like when kids are really pointing to the words, searching the page, and trying their hardest to read. You could do this with just Maya or with the entire class, if you feel that others need the scaffolding as well. If some students rarely participate in class discussions, you can plan for some explicit teaching on how and why to join in.

Using Five Teaching Actions

The cultivation of behaviors that support learning should start at the beginning of the school year before there is time for other behaviors to become habit. As with the teaching of content and skills, use these five teaching actions to show students exactly what you expect from them and to help them gradually gain control over the desired, positive learning behaviors:

- **Modeling**
  "This is what my body and my face look like when I am *really* paying attention. My body is facing the teacher. My head is up. I might lean to one side to see better if someone is in front of me. My eyes are sparkly because I'm listening and thinking. I might raise my hand to say something so the teacher knows I am paying attention."

- **Scaffolding**
  If a child is consistently unable to sit still and attend during read-aloud, I may seat him or her on the floor directly in front of me. I gently tap my shoe against the child's, when needed, to remind him or her to think about what his or her body is

doing. The child also has a better and more sustained view of the book and my face, which helps focus his or her attention.

- **Prompting**

  "Should we be looking at our shoes? Does that help us read the words correctly?"

- **Backing Off**

  I open a book and am ready to start reading, but one student is not attending visually. I wait. He notices the silence and that I am not proceeding and changes his behavior accordingly.

- **Reinforcing**

  "Remember when I had to show you each time what independent reading looked like? Now all of you just go to the Independent Reading Center, choose the right books, and read, read, read."

From the outset, request that students look at you or the appropriate visual when instruction is delivered. Usually, kindergartners are so interested in shared-reading materials and the process of learning to read that they will automatically attend to the best of their ability. Do not write off wiggly students or those who have trouble maintaining focus as incapable of sitting quietly and learning and do not think they're not developmentally ready. Expect them to exhibit the behaviors you model. If they can't do it at first, they can steadily improve. If students are sitting quietly but are clearly not engaged, wake them up. Explain that they should be thinking about whatever is going on in front of them, what you are saying, or what is happening in the book. Let them know that you can tell if they're thinking because thinking bodies and faces have a certain look. Show them what active engagement looks like compared to someone who is not thinking. Again, always be explicit.

CRITICAL STRATEGY: WORD ANALYSIS

When kindergarten students read, they must do two things—figure out the words and construct meaning from the words. These two skills need to develop simultaneously in an integrated fashion. Traditionally, reading instruction with kindergartners has focused more on being able to read words, but words are often presented in isolation, or as controlled words (consonant-vowel-consonant pattern or word-family words with the same chunk of letters) or even as nonsense words. The focus has been on decoding.

Now, we understand that kindergarten students, like everyone else, have a much easier time figuring out words when they are contextualized. Children will comprehend better, in the long run, if they understand from the beginning the purpose of reading. Figuring out words and constructing meaning mutually complement one another. This is why there is an emphasis on having young readers read continuous text (stories) and having them start this right away in their formal schooling. When students learn to read with authentic, continuous texts that encompass all three of the sources of information, the meaning they construct as they go along helps them predict upcoming words and be more successful with figuring out what a text says.

Efficient readers generally predict what the text says and then cross-check against the visual information to confirm or refute their predictions. But young readers will not be able to make use of visual clues unless they are receiving instruction and practice in letter recognition, the blending of sounds, and chunking, both "in front of"/prior to real reading experiences and "into"/during the reading of books. Below are several ideas for building up the critical strategy of analyzing words.

Attending to Beginning Sounds to Decode Words While Reading

Initially, students should be free to concentrate on repeating a word pattern on each page and changing it slightly each time by looking at the picture. Soon it will be time to emphasize to readers that they must look at the letters in words.

Introducing Color Words: Around the fifth week of school, I start working with the color words. I begin with *red*, and students learn that *red* can be spelled and that *red* always begins with the letter *r*. We sing songs for all the other colors, too, and I point out salient features of each color word, but I do not expect kindergarten children to memorize these words or features. Next, students do activities that require the "reading" of color words, an example of which is shown in the photo on the next page. Most students do not actually use letter sounds or sounding out to read the colors; rather, they match the word they see to the one on the color chart. Determining if two words match, letter for letter, helps them learn how to look closely at the letters in words. Students begin to notice that *yellow* starts with *y*; *green* has two *e*'s; and, for *blue*, *black*, and *brown*, they must look past the first letter. They are starting to visually analyze words without having to know letter sounds. It is crucial to do activities like this and have conversations about the visual aspects of words throughout the entire school year, so students develop the habit of looking closely at and thinking about the letters and letter chunks in words.

Introducing Beginning Sounds: After a few weeks of school, I ease my students into looking at the letters and actually doing something with them. I model during shared reading and then reinforce it at the teacher table. I read the repeated words on each page in the same voice, and then emphasize the beginning sound of the one word that changes. This is the word that is usually represented by the illustration in 1/A and 2/B leveled books: *I can see a b-b-banana. I can see a w-w-wagon.* The numerous supports—meaning, syntax, repetitive language, the visual cue from the illustration, and the hint provided from the beginning sound—will not only ensure that

R-E-D Red Song, sung to the tune of "Are You Sleeping?"

students are successful, but also will have fun. Modeling the skill, doing it together with students during whole-class shared-reading time, and then following up with small groups at the teacher table helps students understand that the message is in the print and that there are other ways to figure out words besides looking at the picture and thinking about what would make sense.

When I have students practice the skill, I want them to do it just as I did, by isolating and overemphasizing the beginning letter sound. Normally, students will parrot back exactly what I do, but if they do not, I model it again and ask them to copy me. If students have good control and coordination of voice-print match, I may ask them to put the pointer or their finger directly beneath the first letter of that word as they say the sound to further draw their attention to the letter. The modeling and practicing of this not only helps transition students into looking closely at the words for additional information while reading, but also helps develop phonemic awareness and phonics.

A student practices matching color words.

Pronouncing Beginning Sounds

When isolating and saying beginning sounds of words, be careful to *not* attach a vowel sound to the beginning sound. For example, with the word *lamp*, produce the /l/ sound and hang on to it—*l-l-l-lamp*—rather than saying *lu, lu, lu, lamp*. This will remind students to completely isolate the one phoneme and always produce a clear, crisp letter sound anytime they are working with sounds.

Another way I help students learn how to move from looking at the picture to focusing more on the text is teach them, explicitly, how to answer this question: *How do you know that word says _____ ?* Here's an example from a conference with a student:

The student was reading a book in which a character named Mike appeared on each page, and she read the name correctly.

I asked, "How do you know that word says *Mike*?" I continued, "When I ask you how you know what that word says, I want you to say, 'Because, Ms. Bergen, it starts with an *M. M-M-M-Mike.*'"

As the student kept reading, I repeated the question for several pages so the student had to say, "Because, Ms. Bergen, it starts with an *M. M-M-M-Mike*" over and over again.

Students think this is quite humorous—to say the same thing repeatedly, including my name. Soon they begin to search for the beginning letter and are ready to answer my question before I even ask it. After a few pages of practice, they almost always start saying, "Look, there's the *M*!" or they'll just point to the first letter and smile, daring me to ask them my question again.

The point here is to realize that although we can learn a lot from listening to and analyzing how students may answer questions on their own, it is okay to tell them how to answer our questions, especially when we have formulated an answer that will aid their understanding and learning.

Modifying and Extending the Use of Beginning Sounds

As you customize instruction for individual learners, you can modify and/or extend this idea.

Practice with other words: You can have students try to isolate and say the beginning sound of prominent, easy-to-predict words—rather than the one represented by the picture—in the book. Have them practice with the first word on the page and words that are mid-sentence to help them attend to and use visual cues as a source of information for their reading on a consistent basis. Doing this exercise with words in all positions will be more challenging because readers will not be able to predict the words as easily, and the pictures may not provide obvious support.

Rain, Rain, Go Away

Offer prompts: I frequently prompt students by asking, "What do your eyes see, and what does your mouth need to do?" In the beginning, or when the student does not know the letter's sound, I will scaffold by supplying the answer: "Your eyes see an *m* so you need to put your lips together." or "Your eyes can see a *p* so you need to make the pizza sound." (An illustration of a pizza is on our picture alphabet for the letter *p*.) I tend to offer the following types of scaffolds in a sing-song voice: "When our eyes see an *r*, our mouth goes *r-r-r*." or "When our eyes see an *f*, our mouth goes *f-f-f*."

Students catch on to this quickly and start repeating it. Some go through a phase of overdoing this—noticing and separating the beginning sound of several words on every page, so their reading sounds like this: "Th-th-there i-i-is a b-b-bird in the n-n-nest." Emphasize that they should *only* do this if they are stuck on a word and have to use it, strategically, to figure out the word.

Substituting names: Because of the daily work we do with names during the Name Game, any activity that involves the use of student names helps students realize and generalize their ability to scrutinize names and identify someone based on the letters they see. I like to make charts like the ones shown at the right, so students can create different versions of a shared-reading text by inserting different student names. (There are magnetic strips on the charts and on the back of student name cards, which are different than the main set of name cards we use in class.) Students tend to be quite particular about, and place a lot of value in, the names they want to include in the text. They will work hard at looking at and thinking about the letters before sticking a name card onto the chart. I like to observe students as they choose a name card; they are highly motivated to figure out whose name it is, and though their cognitive processing is going on inside their heads, it is also written all over their faces and exhibited in their body language.

Who Took the Cookie?

Model blending sounds: Another way to extend the skills of looking at and doing something with visual cues is to model blending sounds. The opportunity to do this usually arises during the Name Game, where I might say "Pr-Pr-Preston" or "St-St-Stefano" with follow-up prompting during one-on-one reading with students who are ready: "Hey, did you notice? There's one of the blends we've seen before. We saw that in Slade's name. Let me hear you do it!" All students will benefit from "in front of" teaching about blends during whole-group instruction, but applying blending in their own reading will not be in their zone of proximal development until they are reading Level 6/E or 8/F books (see the Strategic Reading Behaviors and Reading Processes Associated With Each Level of Text on page 180).

Chunks

I use the term *chunk* for any consistent and recognizable group of letters that work together in words. It covers digraphs like *th* and *sh*; word endings such as *-ed* and *-ing*; rimes that the class has been introduced to, like *-at, -and*, and any others that are in the names we analyze; and consonant blends—*st, fl, pr*, or others represented in student names. I do sometimes use the term *blends* when I want to emphasize to students that we blend two letter sounds together: *St-St-Stefano*. Otherwise, it is not important that they know the separate terms, like *digraph, rime,* and *ending*. I just want students to know that letters sometime work together and that when the letters are working together, we need to see them as a group or chunk and use them in this way.

Scaffolding From Beginning Sounds to Sounding Out Short Words

Once you've had students practice with visually and orally isolating the first sound of words while they read, scaffold them into sounding out two- or three-letter words. By the time students are ready, developmentally, to do this with continuous text (usually when they have moved into Level 4/D or 6/E texts), you will have modeled it for them in plenty of different whole-group instructional situations. Students should also be quite familiar with the separating and sequencing of sounds from their daily work with the Name Game and writing.

You should try to prevent students from relying on sounding-out as a primary strategy for reading, or as their first strategy when a problem is encountered, because it is not a very efficient strategy. Many words cannot easily be sounded out. Plus, sounding out words is difficult, especially when a young reader is not yet familiar with all the letter sounds, may not be flexible with trying different sounds for the same letter, and/or does not yet recognize letter chunks in words.

Your role is to encourage students to try sounding out words at the appropriate times while reading and support them in their attempts. Readers should only do this if the combination of other sources of information is not helping them decode an unfamiliar word. It's too complicated to explain to five-year-olds *when* they should sound out words; it's better to suggest it as an option when you know they have exhausted other strategies, but only if you know that they have the skill to sound out the word and that the word can actually be sounded out.

Some students tend to "sound out" words internally. If they can do this successfully for the most part, then I don't tell them that they have to do it out loud. If, on the other hand, they are not often successful, I will ask them to do it out loud for me and, if necessary, I will model again for them what it should sound like. I need to know if the breakdown is occurring with the initial saying and separating of the sounds or the blending back together of the sounds. Also, it is easier for students to hear, and thus learn, the process of twisting sounds if they do it out loud.

Teaching Flexibility With Letter Sounds

Students need to learn—and it may not be until first grade for some—that in order to be successful with sounding out words, they need to be flexible with trying different sounds for some letters; for example, a student may initially pronounce *city* with the more common hard *c* rather than a soft *c*.

A scaffold and prompt that I use to help teach this is to "twist" the sounds. Twisting a sound means trying a letter's other sound or just massaging the sound a little to make the word sound like a real word.

To model twisting the sound in *city*, I would do the following:

- Pronounce the word with a hard *c* (*kitty*)

- Stop and think aloud that it didn't make sense ("We went to the *kitty*? That can't be right.")

- Think out loud about which letters in the word have more than one sound ("I know *c* has two sounds and that *i* and *y* can make different sounds. I think I'll try to twist *c* first.")

- Think aloud about which sound I've already tried and then try the other sound for that letter to see if it works better. ("/K/, /k/, *kitty* didn't sound right; how about /s/, /s/, *city?* We went to the city. Yeah, that sounds better!")

After students know how this process works, I use a prompt such as, "You tried a short-*e* sound, but it didn't turn into a real word. Do you want to try long *e*?" Shorter prompts that support the release of responsibility to the student include "You could try *g*'s other sound." or "Is there a letter that has more than one sound?" or "Is there another sound you could try?" or "You can twist some sounds."

I can also prompt them quietly and without interrupting their reading too much by rubbing my thumb on my middle and ring fingers as if I am twisting a piece of yarn or massaging a word until it sounds right.

The flexibility with sounds that I model and we practice daily during the Name Game (e.g., when the *o*'s in Solomon have three different sounds) greatly enhance students' understanding that letters may make more than one sound and their ability to twist sounds as they read. While analyzing names during the game, they learn that vowels and some other letters have more than one sound, that sometimes letters behave—make the sound they're supposed to make—or misbehave—make a sound that belongs to another letter, and that some letters can be silent. Working with names not only demonstrates these concepts but also sends a message to students that it is perfectly okay, and actually necessary, to twist letter sounds and try different things while reading.

It's important to choose the words carefully that you ask students to sound out. A word should have two, three, or four distinct phonemes that will turn into a real word when broken apart and then blended back together. Starting with two-letter words like *am* and *up* is great, but you wouldn't ask students to first try this strategy with *we*—because *e* has two different sounds—or *do*—because the *o* is not behaving. Words with a consonant-short vowel-consonant pattern, called CVC words, work well: *pig, man, jet.* But don't ask students to sound out harder words unless you have done some "in front of" teaching about what they're going to encounter in that particular word. For instance, it's unfair to have students sound out a word with a silent *e* unless you've already talked quite a bit about how *e* can be silent at the end of words, not to mention what it does to the vowel sounds. If *ing* appears in a word, then the student needs to be familiar with it, be able to see it as a chunk in words, or understand what to do when prompted about it. I only have students attempt to sound out more difficult words if I have previously successfully worked with them on sounding out easier words, *and* if we have already talked about the letter or phonics concept that is going to cause some difficulty (through the Name Game or the study of sight words that we put on the Word Wall), or if I am aware that they know most of the letter sounds, including two sounds for some letters, and some common chunks.

Reading at Home

If you provide books for students to read at home, be sure to educate parents about what beginning reading entails and how they can support their child's efforts. Parents tend to know more about sounding out words than any other strategy, so this is typically the only way they know of helping their child. Communicate to parents that students should *not* be expected to sound out words at the beginning of the year when they may not even know letter names and sounds and that asking them to do so will hinder their growth and confidence in reading. The way for parents to help is to have their child listen and watch as the parent points to and reads the words. Then the child can try to emulate the behavior. A sample note to parents to include with books sent home is on page 184.

Scaffolding From Looking at Individual Letters to Looking for Chunks

Students need to learn how to chunk while decoding words. For example, if a student comes across the word *staying* and has no prior knowledge of chunking, he would probably try to sound it out letter by letter, which wouldn't work very well. He might be able to figure out the word if he already knows *stay* as a sight word and can flexibly manipulate the remaining three letters. Or, if he is familiar with some chunks and has been taught about the common word ending *-ing*, he might see the word as *st* plus *ay* plus *ing* and decode it fairly easily.

To help students develop this skill, introduce letter chunks as groups of letters that work together to make a certain sound. Model how to read a chunk as a whole instead of breaking it apart into individual letters. Students will be highly interested in and retain the sounds of most of the chunks you talk about in their names during the Name Game, as well as the more common ones: *th, sh, ch* and *ing*.

It is necessary and acceptable, developmentally, to start talking about chunks early in the school year and to model how to work with them long before students actually need to apply this skill during real reading experiences. For instance, I introduce *th* as a chunk the day we first talk about *Thursday* on the calendar. The chunks that appear in students' first names and last names are discussed during the Name Game. *Ing* is on my yearlong plan for January because of Martin Luther King, Jr. Day, and because several students need to know this chunk at this point in the year. We also start studying and working with word families about that same time.

Play "What Do You Notice?" A great way to teach about chunks and draw students' attention to the visual details in print is to occasionally play "What Do You Notice?" during shared-reading time. This works particularly well with charts because the entire text is visible. Asking this simple question: "What do you notice on this chart?" encourages students to search for anything that they know and can talk about in the print. Students may notice certain letters, see words that are on the Word Wall, mention something that leads you to your teaching point for the day, point out punctuation, or mention chunks that have been previously discussed. As you can imagine, this activity allows all students to participate on their own level and to further their skill in analyzing text. It's a good activity to use any time you have a few minutes to fill.

Chunking words at Level 6/E and 8/F text: Texts at these levels have longer words with more syllables and inflectional endings like -*ed* and -*ing*. Students will have to start seeing words as chunks of letters and using these chunks to decode and cross-check while reading. This will be the time, developmentally, to scaffold and prompt for this reading behavior, as it will be in the students' zone of proximal development.

One way I do this is by alerting a student to any upcoming chunks that I know they will recognize and can do something with. I do this just as the reader is about to come upon the word by saying "I see -*ing* on the end of that word." or "Here comes the *ill* chunk." Although the student probably knows the chunk, he or she does not yet have much practice with discriminating it in continuous text. Even if the student is not going to rely primarily upon the visual cues to read the word, I still want to facilitate his or her ability to see chunks and develop an awareness of them in text so the student will be able to rely upon this skill when it is needed. If I want to be less intrusive, I might underline the chunk with a pencil, without saying anything, as the student is coming upon it. This also puts a little more responsibility on the reader. Another reason I might underline the chunks in a word if it contains two or more prominent chunks (st ar) is if I think it might help the student to chunk on his or her own while reading the book independently later.

As described earlier, I also teach students to answer a question in a way that will help them think about chunking:

"How do you know that says *into*?"

"Because, Ms. Bergen, it has *in* and then it has *to*."

The important thing is to not waste precious learning time by waiting for students to notice chunks on their own before you encourage them to use this skill, which could take months and keep them from moving into Level 6/E text and beyond. Point out the chunks you know students are capable of using.

Recognizing Two Types of Words

In *Teaching Writing in Kindergarten,* I write about teaching kindergartners that there are two categories of words and two ways to write words:

- If the word is a known word, write it from memory or find it on the Word Wall.

- If the word has not been taught yet, then listen to the sounds in the word and record as many as possible.

This also applies to early reading instruction. Beginning readers sometimes don't say the words they recognize and know as they are reading continuous text; they may, especially once you start focusing on visual cues, isolate and repeat the beginning sound or think they have to sound out the word (even if they already know it). Kindergartners do not always know what they know, so they might not think of a word as a word they know even if they have actually reached a point of automaticity with it.

Therefore, I frequently ask students if a word is known or unknown. If it's a word they know, I will prompt them to just say the word with one of the prompts below:

- "I think you know that word."

- "Is that word on the Word Wall?"

- "We've been seeing this word on every page of this book."

- "You wrote that word in your journal earlier today."

- "When we know a word, we say it fast and move right on to the next word."

- "Remember—don't do the sounds on words you know."

The words on our Word Wall are not necessarily the words that students know. About half the students will know all the words on the Word Wall, but some will not be able to steadily learn them as they are added. Some students will know many more words than the ones that have been officially taught. As you work with students on a daily basis in both reading and writing, you will develop a general sense of how many words each student knows. If you can't keep track of who knows what, that's okay; you can ask students as you're working with them: "Is that a word you know?" They need to become aware of what they know and what they don't know; this is a part of their developing metacognition.

Of course, students are not going to know very many words unless the teaching and learning of sight words is an integral part of their reading instruction. Chapter 7 contains more information on introducing and using sight words.

CRITICAL STRATEGY: PREDICTING AND CROSS-CHECKING

Predicting makes reading more efficient: it is faster to guess what the words say and quickly cross-check these guesses than it is to figure out each word, one at a time, as if they are unrelated and unfamiliar. Prediction, explain Fountas and Pinnell (2006), provides a forward motion, which enables the reader to spend much less attention on letters and word parts and more attention on reading.

Encouraging Making Predictions While Reading

Cloze activities: The cloze procedure allows students to practice predicting and also helps them understand that making predictions can make reading a lot easier and a lot faster. It is important for students to realize that they can probably guess, as they read, what the text is going to say because the author has to write words that make sense and sound like real talking.

Cloze activities require students to supply a missing word or words, in order to complete a phrase or sentence. Usually, to practice this particular concept with beginning readers, I cover the last word on each page of a shared-reading book with a blank sticky note. As I read, I draw out my voice as I approach the covered word: "My job is to bake. . . ." Students guess the missing word as a group or when called upon, and then we talk about how they will determine if their guess is correct.

Building confidence: I believe that we have to build up students' confidence to make predictions as they read and encourage them not to be overly concerned about making incorrect predictions. Beginning readers who struggle often do so because they are not very good at, or are uncomfortable with, predicting what will happen in a text. To encourage students to be brave and predict, I always celebrate when a prediction is confirmed. I also celebrate when a prediction turns out to be wrong, perhaps even more so, because it creates an opportunity for using a fix-up. Initially, I try to turn making a prediction into a game, or model some outlandish predictions just to show students that it's okay to guess anything as they're reading—as long as they're predicting the words as they read. This encourages students to voice their ideas and realize that, although not all their predictions will be correct, they can still be brave and have some fun trying it. Soon, I emphasize that readers should only guess words that make sense, and then that they should only guess words that make sense and have the right letter sounds. Here's how I might work with a student who is uncomfortable making predictions because she doesn't want to make a mistake:

We're reading a book about adding ingredients to vegetable soup.

Ms. Bergen: What do you think the word is? *I could get some . . .* I could get some cookies? I could get some popcorn? I could get some popsicles?

The child starts shaking her head and smiling, and though she still hasn't taken a risk with predicting a word, I at least know she understands what we're doing.

Ms. Bergen: I could get some /p/, /p/, . . .

Student: Potatoes.

If the student still cannot guess or doesn't want to risk getting the prediction wrong, I'll prompt further.

Ms. Bergen: Could she get some potatoes for the soup? Yes? You should read it and guess the word *potato*. See how the word sounds and then tell me if you think you're right!

The act of predicting applies not only to single words but also to phrases and entire sentences. Of course, early emergent books, with their repetitive language patterns, totally support the development of making predictions while reading. Students—even those who do not have a good command of English—can repeat a sentence from the first page and predict that it will be the same on every page. When you're reading this type of book, point out to students that they are predicting or guessing what the words are saying and that they are getting them right (the teaching act of reinforcement). As students read more challenging texts, their ability and confidence with predicting will have grown right along with their other strategic thinking.

Is a child predicting the text? Pat Johnson (2006) explains an easy and reliable way to determine if students are predicting the text as they read: a child substitutes a known word for an unknown word rather than stopping or waiting for someone to give him the word. If, for example, a student says, "The dog crossed the street," when the text says "The dog crossed the road," then he or she is predicting based on meaning, syntax, and perhaps a picture clue. This is what we want readers to do. To be effective, however, the ability to use prediction while reading must be accompanied with the strategic process of cross-checking.

Cross-Checking

Cross-checking is basically self-monitoring one's reading by first using one or more sources of information to predict a word and then confirming the prediction with another source. For example, if a page of text says "The duck swims in the lake," a student might guess that the last word is going to be *river* but then look at the first letter *l* and decide it is *lake* instead. Or, the opposite can occur. A student might start reading "'Wake up,' said my mother" by looking at the letters in the first word and saying *walk* and then, using the meaningful information that follows the first word, realize that *wake* would work better. Pat Johnson says that self-monitoring via cross-checking means that "a child is checking and confirming that what he is reading makes sense, sounds right, and looks right. Therefore, any time you see an indication of the child stopping to attempt to work something out, you could infer that the student is monitoring his reading. He may not always be able to fix the error, but he is still monitoring that something is not quite right" (2006, p. 160).

If students are encouraged and expected to attend to all three sources of information—meaning, syntax, and visual—from the beginning of their reading instruction, then their ability to cross-check and self-monitor while reading will develop somewhat naturally as they move through the levels of text. In fact, my encouragement and expectation are probably why I have seen so many kindergarten students progress with their reading well beyond a Level 3/C.

Though many students will cross-check naturally, we must nurture the use of this strategy and make students aware of what they are doing, thereby sharpening their metacognition. Because we start children off with texts that have highly supportive illustrations and repetitive language patterns, predicting will happen automatically. Then, we want to start encouraging them to cross-check their predictions by looking at the letters in words. The sequence of instruction is important: encouraging beginning readers to concentrate first on the letters and then use that source of information to predict what the text will say usually results in stilted, labored reading. This is brought on by too much sounding out and not enough focus on what would make sense and sound right.

Well-written emergent reading texts, especially those at Level 3/C and up, will demand that readers use some sort of cross-checking or self-monitoring, as shown in this example with a student named Cedric.

The text had somewhat of a repeating pattern:

> *"Bird sees a little leaf.*
>
> *Bird sees a big leaf.*
>
> *Bird sees a little bird.*
>
> *Bird sees a big bird."*

Toward the end of the book, the text changed:

> *"Bird does NOT see a big hole."*

It was obvious when Cedric saw the word *does* and said, "That's not *see!*" that he had made a prediction based on the repeating language and then changed his mind after cross-checking his prediction with the visual information.

Structuring teacher/student interactions to start developing the strategy of cross-checking is necessary for building a solid reading foundation and moving students beyond Level 3/C texts.

I also encourage students to cross-check by asking questions or making minimal comments when they are getting ready to transition from Level 3/C books into Level 4/D:

Ms. Bergen:	How do you know that says *ducks*?
Student:	I saw ducks in the picture.
Ms. Bergen:	How else do you know it says *ducks*?
Student:	I know this word says *ducks* because this book is about ducks and there are ducks in the picture and I can see a *d* so it's /d/, /d/, *ducks.*

This lets students know that they should have at least two reasons for how they know the word says *ducks*, one of which must be based on the letters in the word.

Students who already know how to cross-check usually just need occasional reminders rather than direct instruction. Using *The dog crossed the street/road* example again, when the student substituted *street* for *road,* I might say, "Hmm, it seems to me that *street* would start with an *s.*" This puts the responsibility on the student to problem solve using the different sources of information.

Initially, students are taught to cross-check by looking at the first letter(s) in words. And, often, just noticing and thinking about the beginning of a word will be enough to determine whether a prediction is correct. There will be instances, however, in more advanced texts, when students must look beyond the beginning sound and read all the way through a word before deciding whether their prediction can stand. To develop the ability to consider visual information beyond the first letter(s), look for teaching moments to encourage students to look at the end of words. If a text says "I want to go sledding" and the student reads, "I want to go sled," he or she might be using visual information to cross-check but is not checking far enough into the word. Prompting with, "Do you see a chunk on the end of that word that you know?" or "Did you look all the way across the word?" will remind the student to do more than just look at the first letter or few letters, even when the first letter(s) seems to confirm the prediction. A prompt that demands more from the reader is, "Hmm, it seems like *sled*" (said with an emphasis on the /d/ sound) "would have a *d* on the end and I don't see that."

Once students are skilled at considering the beginning of words and the end of words to cross-check, they move into searching the middle sounds and, finally, to reading through the entire word to see if all parts of it support their prediction. Efficient readers do this on the fly, with hardly a hesitation. It might look as if they are not cross-checking, but they are. All good readers constantly cross-check the three sources of information against each other.

CRITICAL STRATEGY: FIX-UPS (SELF-CORRECTIONS)

When young readers are encouraged to cross-check while reading, most will automatically correct their mistakes on their own, without even having been taught to do so, when they sense the "dissonance created by a mismatch" (Fountas and Pinnell, 2006, p. 47). Self-correcting is the natural result of predicting and attending to all three sources of information while reading. Though it may come quite naturally for most readers, it is probably the most strategic reading behavior so it also needs to be explicitly taught and reinforced.

We see young readers self-correcting initially either when what they say does not match what they see in a picture or when it does not match the repetitive language pattern they've been using so far in a book. In these instances, they are self-correcting because they spoke too quickly or carelessly or let their attention wander. Soon, students also start self-correcting based on the visual information presented by the letters, along with what makes sense and sounds right. When less-experienced readers sense that they have made a mistake, they typically prefer to go back to the beginning of the sentence and reread it correctly. They like, and need, to hear the sound of the sentence read correctly in its entirety. As readers gain experience, they will self-correct at the point of the error and will not necessarily have the need to repeat the whole sentence.

Explicitly Teaching and Reinforcing the Fix-Up Strategy During Shared Reading and Read-Aloud

The fix-up is critical because it emphasizes to children that reading must make sense at all times, so it should be introduced and modeled to the entire class as early as possible. Stressing fix-ups from the beginning will result in far fewer issues with comprehension when students move into more difficult text. I let students know that fixing up our reading as we go along is one of the most important things that readers do. Teaching the fix-up strategy as a positive, meaning-making reading behavior, rather than an action that must occur because of a reading mistake, can also boost students' confidence and risk-taking. If most errors can be nullified with a fix-up, then students tend not to view mistakes as wrong or embarrassing. And, when kindergartners start taking risks as readers and gaining confidence, they do a much better job of predicting text and maintaining a forward motion with it.

Since it is difficult to feign errors while demonstrating reading with a read-aloud or shared-reading text, it is best to introduce and revisit the fix-up strategy when real errors actually occur. When I make a mistake while reading aloud or sense that I need to reread a sentence to adjust my pacing or intonation to make the text sound more like the author intended, I point this out to students: "Oops! I need to do a fix-up!" Occasionally, during read aloud, I will make a correction without realizing it, and a student or two (or several!) will point out that I did a fix-up.

As described in Chapter 3, I have students pointing to and reading words as soon as the first day of school in the shared-reading setting and at my teacher table in small groups. As soon as they make an error, I say something along the lines of, "Whoops! That didn't sound quite right. You get to do a fix-up. Any time we are reading and we make a mistake or it doesn't sound right, we try it again and we fix it up." Later, I can shorten this to, "Yea! You get to do a fix-up!" It only takes a few instances of me saying, "You get to do a fix-up!" or other students saying, "I heard her do a fix-up!" for students to realize that making a mistake, and then correcting it, is a good thing.

When almost all students are doing fix-ups fairly automatically, cease to point out that a fix-up is necessary. It is important to provide the time for students to sense for themselves the dissonance in the sources of information. When students fix mistakes on their own, I reinforce this by pointing it out; for instance, I might say, "Did you see that? She just did a fix-up. We like fix-ups, don't we?"

Explicitly Teaching and Reinforcing the Fix-Up Strategy With Small Groups and One-on-One

While working individually with students, it is critical not to do too much prompting or correcting. Students should not become dependent on external monitoring from the teacher rather than internally monitoring their own reading. They shouldn't anticipate being interrupted—whether for encouragement or correction—because that tends to make them hesitant and/or more apt to read word-for-word and pause between words.

Often, students who are accustomed to receiving lots of external feedback, or who are seeking it, will look at the teacher's face while reading. To deter this habit, tell students to keep their eyes on the words in the book, and avoid making eye contact with students by keeping your own eyes on the book as well. Also be conscious of nodding your head. Students will pick up on this slight movement and use it as external confirmation.

When we pay attention to children's attempts to self-correct, we can learn a lot about their reading development and the processes that are going on inside their head. If they do not try to correct mistakes, then they are either not listening to or thinking about their reading, they do not yet understand that reading must at all times make sense and sound like talking, or they do not yet have the language skills to know if what they are saying makes sense, which is sometimes the case with English language learners. For students with limited English and/ or limited oral language skills, it is better to model how the phrase or sentence should sound rather than question them about it or have them try to determine on their own if it made sense.

When a student's attempts do not match the visual information, then you can probe to find out if the child is not attending to the visual information or just doesn't know what to do with it. For example, a child might see an *f* but might not remember the sound for *f*, or a student may be using the visual information at the beginning of the word but not at the end of the word.

CRITICAL STRATEGY: RELEVANT COMMENTS AND QUESTIONS

For the most part, students can understand the meaning of the words in levels 2/B and 3/C texts, and if they cannot, they can derive meaning from the accompanying illustrations. Still, at this very emergent stage of reading development, students must be guided to think and talk about the books they are reading to develop their understanding. If students are encouraged to think, and wonder, and talk about books, then doing so will become a natural part of their reading behavior.

The observable reading behaviors of making comments or asking questions about a book soon grow into an internal ability and the habit of critical thinking. What we initially model and students practice out loud becomes strategic processing that helps young readers think about and understand what they are reading on a deeper level.

Modeling and Whole-Group Practice of Thinking While Reading

Read-aloud and shared-reading time are excellent settings in which to model what a reader thinks about while reading. When we stop reading and make a comment to ourselves about the book, or wonder aloud about something ambiguous, we are "thinking aloud" and sharing our thought processes with students. Modeling should always be done deliberately and always when you truly are noticing or wondering about something in the text.

Students, especially those in kindergarten, need explicit instruction and structured guidance in how to convey their thoughts. Most students will think about a book as it is being read to them, but they might not be aware of their thinking. Modeling how to think, and then following up with opportunities for practice, will create an awareness in students about their own thought processes. Ideas for implementing discussion about books and improving the level of talk, and thus understanding, are discussed in Chapter 8.

Encouraging Thinking, Commenting, and Asking Questions During One-on-One Teaching

Each time I work with a student, no matter what his or her reading level is, I model the following:

- Sharing my thoughts about something in the text

- Making a relevant comment about the words or the illustrations

- Asking a question about something I am wondering about in the text

Then, often, all I have to do is listen as students offer comments and ask questions of their own. Basically, I just want to ensure that students are thinking and are aware of doing so; I want them to be thinking about their own thinking. As time goes on, students begin to independently raise questions in their mind. This is observable, even when nothing is said: a student may turn the page to re-examine a picture, look confused, reread to clarify, or hurry ahead to learn if a question he or she has is going to be answered.

I welcome this time to talk with students one-on-one about the books they are reading. Not only does it develop their understanding that reading should be meaningful, but it also provides an opportunity to have a conversation with a child about a book and how it might relate to his or her prior knowledge or experiences. All children, especially those with less developed oral language skills, need the opportunity to engage often in productive talk. Working on this strategy a little bit each time I read with a child gives me the chance to develop these thinking and discussion skills two or three times each week.

Conclusion

Most kindergarten students can easily learn to read Level 3/C text and beyond. This is facilitated by expecting them to demonstrate certain learning behaviors and by explicitly teaching them to analyze words, predict and cross-check while reading, self-correct, and employ relevant commenting and questioning while talking about books. By working with students individually and providing them with just-right books at their instructional level, you will have many opportunities to develop these key strategies and reading behaviors.

CHAPTER 7

Building Sight Word Knowledge

Students need to have a repertoire of words that they instantly recognize and are able to read. Many of the most frequent words that they come across—*the, of, are*—are not pronounced or spelled logically, making these words nearly impossible to decode. It is, therefore, imperative to start teaching such words at the beginning of reading instruction and to steadily increase the number of words that students can recognize and instantly read. If this important component of reading instruction is ignored, students will not even be able to read a Level 3/C book by the end of the school year.

Instantly recognizing and reading high-frequency words frees the reader's mind to attend to less common words while reading. Stopping to figure out words while reading requires not only time, which slows the reading process, but also mental energy. Even more consequential, it takes attention away from the making of meaning that is usually happening prior to encountering an unknown word. Patricia Cunningham (2009) provides a thorough explanation as to how encountering unknown words affects the reading process:

> *Decoding . . . a new word takes all our short-term memory space. In fact, when this decoding process begins, all words already read . . . and stored in short-term memory are dumped out. . . . This dumping explains why, once the new word is decoded . . . we must quickly reread any prior words in that sentence so that we may put them in short-term memory again. It also explains why children who have to decode many words often don't know what they have read after they*

read it! . . . they never get enough words in short-term memory from which to make meaning to put in long-term memory. All their attention is required for figuring out words, and there is no capacity for putting together meaning. (p. 87)

The acquisition of sight words positively impacts children's first attempts at reading real books with continuous text. As you recall, one of the first skills kindergarten students have to learn is voice-print match. At first, when they try to accurately point to two, then three, then four or more words on a page, they use the kinesthetic movement and auditory tapping of their finger as it hops beneath the words, in conjunction with the spacing between words and the sound and feeling of one word at a time coming out of their mouth, to assess whether they are succeeding with this task. But, as soon as students recognize and are able to really read even one of the words on a page, that word then serves as an anchor for their voice-print match. Most students realize, proudly, when they point to a known word and their mouth says *that* word instead of just *a* word. They can sense that they are doing something more important than what they do with the unknown words; they understand that they know the word and that they are saying the word *correctly*.

KINDERGARTNERS CAN ACQUIRE MANY WORDS

Earlier, I discussed how the Level 3/C standard actually limits our expectations for kindergarten students. The same applies for the learning of sight words. If a standard is set— say, of ten words—then many teachers will strive to teach their students ten words. Most likely the sequencing and instruction will be orchestrated so students learn those ten words slowly and steadily over the course of the year, or perhaps just the second half of the year, ensuring

Number of Sight Words Learned by Kindergarten Students

School Year	Range of Number of Words Learned	Average Number of Words Learned
2008	6–96	69
2009	25–99	62
2010	1–98	64*
2011	15–100	63
2012	0–100	69*

* *One student, who had an identified learning disability, was not included in the average.*

that the tenth word is taught and mastered by most students just prior to the end of the school year. Teachers may also think that no other words should be taught.

I know that the majority of kindergarten students—even if they have underdeveloped language skills, a slight learning disability, no knowledge of letters or sounds upon entering kindergarten, and/or limited experience with books and literacy before entering school—are capable of learning far more than ten sight words. And since they are capable of this, it is our responsibility to give them the opportunity to do it. The assessment data shown on page 147 suggests just how many words kindergarten students can learn to recognize and read, both in context and in isolation.

This data was collected by having students read words from the list of 100 High-Frequency Words on pages 186–187. Though typically thought of as a list of words that students should be able to read by the end of first grade and spell by the end of second grade, I like to use this list as an assessment tool because it lets students show me what they have really learned. To test them on just the district-required words without determining what else they know is synonymous with testing students up to a Level 3/C text but not beyond. We need to know what our students are capable of doing in order to adjust our instruction and best meet their needs academically.

INTRODUCING HIGH-FREQUENCY WORDS

I recommend introducing and teaching words as early as the first week of kindergarten. First of all, kindergarten students are enthralled with learning, and they will be excited to know they are learning words, especially if you really play it up. More important, however, is that once students accomplish the sometimes difficult task of learning their first few words, they will be in position to learn additional words much more readily. As Cunningham so aptly put it, once students pick up a few sight words, "they have learned how to learn words" (2009, p. 223).

Why High-Frequency Words Are So Difficult to Learn

The first words we introduce to kindergarten students (after their first name) are among some of the hardest words they will encounter in their first few years of school. Students will need to know these words to be successful with their efforts in reading and writing. And, reading and writing will naturally give students practice with these words. Because of their abstractness and unusual pronunciations and spellings, it will take several years for students to learn the first 100 high-frequency words; therefore, the sooner we introduce them to students, the better.

Cunningham explains that the first problem students have with the high-frequency words is that most of them have no meaning. Unlike words that represent concrete, observable things, such as *dog, apple,* or *running*, "words such as *are, is,* and *have* are functional, connecting, abstract words children cannot connect any meaning to" (2009, p. 88). In addition, many of the frequently occurring words share the same letters, such as *of, for, from* and *went, want, what.*

The result is that trying to remember these words is like trying to remember the pronunciation and spelling of words in a foreign language.

Spelling patterns can be helpful in pronouncing words while reading; however, the most frequently used words are often not pronounced or spelled like other words with the same spelling pattern. As Cunningham explains, *to* and *do* should rhyme with *go, so,* and *no*; *what* should rhyme with *at, cat,* and *bat*; *said* should be spelled like *red* and *bed.*

LEARNING BY ASSOCIATION

Since many of the high-frequency words have no meaning in and of themselves, it is best to help students associate them with something meaningful. Cunningham reminds us that associative learning is always more permanent than rote learning.

I teach words through association in three basic steps:

- **Introduce new words with associative learning:** First, I use a memorable story, chant, or activity to introduce a sight word. In this way, students associate the word with the situation in which it was introduced and have a better chance of recalling it.

- **Refer to words as "words we know":** Next, any word that is formally introduced and taught is added to the classroom Word Wall and referred to as "a word we know." I incorporate activities that center on practicing and reviewing these words so students have a better idea of which words are "words we know," and they gradually commit more and more of them to memory.

- **Get creative with associations:** Last, any time we work with a specific word and a student shows signs of not remembering it, I either reiterate the initial association tied to the word or try something entirely new and different since the first attempt at association did not have the desired effect.

Introducing New Words With Associative Learning

When teaching a word to kindergarten students, it is best to present it in the context of shared-reading material, shared writing, a fun chant or song, or an activity that focuses around the word. Students will then associate this word with the memorable way in which it was presented. For example, I introduce *up* as a Word Wall word during the apples-themed week via the book *Ten Apples Up on Top!* by Theo. LeSieg; *can* is introduced with *Dan, the Flying Man* by Joy Cowley and then solidified during the canned food drive in December with many "can" activities. As the photo on the next page shows, I wrote *can* on a label and put it on a can of food as a scaffold during reading instruction.

I point out the word *little* and add it to the Word Wall when we learn about the Little Red Hen, as well as *not* (and sometimes *will*) because the characters are always saying, "Not I" or "I will." Since these stories and related activities become near and dear to students, they tend to recall the sight words associated with them.

Introducing words by association is much more effective than introducing and teaching words randomly or in a specific sequence that is not tied in with anything else going on instructionally. The sample yearlong plan on Teacher Express demonstrates several ways in which words can be introduced in association with the weekly theme, a class activity, or a piece of literature.

Referring to Words as "Words We Know"

As words are introduced and placed on the Word Wall, I refer to them as "words we know." This means that I have introduced

A scaffold for the word can

the words and they are accessible to students, so I can begin to make references to them and hold students responsible for knowing them. As part of the process of learning to recognize words instantly, it is crucial to constantly remind students about the words they know. I review these words and, when we encounter one in various texts, point it out as "a word we know."

In the previous chapter, I talked about explicitly teaching students that there are two types of words: words that are known and can be written (either from memory or by copying them off the Word Wall) and unknown words that students must listen to and write down the sounds for. This concept carries over to reading. When working with students I can prompt them with, "You know this word," "That's on the Word Wall," or "That's a Little Red Hen word." Or, on the other hand, "This is a new word. What can you try?" Encountering both types of words—known and unknown—on a regular and frequent basis requires students to use meaning, syntax, and visual cues to figure out the text. High-quality texts have the right balance between the two types of words and thus tend to support students in using all the sources of information equally as they learn to read.

Emphasizing Known Words

Whenever I bring out a new chart, I, at some point while reading it, say, "Hey, there's *the*. We know that word!" I do this to model my exaggerated observation and thinking as I come to the realization that I see a word from our Word Wall, which can easily and quickly be read. I do this just a few times, with each of the words we "know," before students start searching for words they know and exclaiming, "Hey, there's a word we know! *Is!*" This sometimes happens with read-alouds and shared-reading books, too, as I present the book and students take their first look at the cover and title.

Getting Creative With Associations

Though I teach sight words right from the beginning of the school year, there will be a few students in my classroom who are not developmentally ready to commit words to memory. This means I will need to reteach words, on an individual basis, at different points throughout the year. I can use the association or scaffold with which I originally taught the word to the class or I may try a new trick; it all depends on the student, the situation we are in when I am reteaching the word, and, often, what I come up with at that moment. I've found myself telling kindergartners things like, "I see double *e*'s," (for the word *see)* or "I *do* know this word" *(*for *do*) and then teaching them how to utter the scaffold when they come across the word so it serves as a reminder on how to read it. When you come up with something that works well, make a note of it and be sure to use it again in the future with other students.

USING WORD WALLS TO SUPPORT THE ACQUISITION OF KNOWN WORDS

Cunningham is well known for her work with Word Walls and how they can support students in learning to read and spell high-frequency words. She explains that one way to associate meaning to abstract, connecting words is to display them in an accessible place so students can find the words as necessary when they read and write. Many teachers display these words on the wall or a bulletin board and call it the Word Wall. But, as Cunningham cautions, though teachers often *have* a Word Wall they don't necessarily *do* the Word Wall. *Doing* a Word Wall, according to Cunningham, means:

- being selective and limiting the words to those really common words that children see a lot and use a lot in their writing.

- adding words gradually.

- making words accessible by putting them where everyone can see them, and writing them in big black letters on a variety of background colors to help students more easily distinguish between them.

- practicing the words to help students remember them.

- making sure students spell Word Wall words correctly in their writing.

Choosing Words

You can introduce and teach sight words in any order that makes sense to you and your circumstances. It is important to start with words students will be seeing and reading—*the, a, is*—as well as a more concrete words, such as *I, red,* and *see.* After thinking about which words to teach and their sequence, make a long-range plan (such as the yearlong plan on Teacher Express), gather supporting books and resources, develop activities that will allow students to practice using the new sight words, and be willing to constantly change and update your sequencing and methods for the teaching of sight words.

I know my students are capable of learning between 20 and 100 sight words during their kindergarten year. In my planning, I consider the powerful effect of knowing how to read and spell the most frequently used words in our language and incorporate these into my teaching. According to Cunningham, the ten most frequently occurring words in the English language account for almost one-quarter of all the words that we read and write. These words are *the, of, and, a, to, in, is, you, that,* and *it.*

Some of the other words I select are words that students will use in their writing and that demonstrate the relation between rhyming and spelling: *I, can, my, said, on, like, we, he, she,* and *at.* Since kindergartners tend to write personal narratives, those words frequently appear in their writing: "On Saturday I . . . ," "My mom said . . . ," "I like . . ." "You can . . ." As students learn to spell these words, they gain confidence and are able to start writing—and keep writing. And, their writing becomes more readable because correctly spelled words anchor the text, making it easier to predict the incorrectly spelled words.

These high-frequency words also appear in shared-reading books and books used for guided reading, allowing for additional analysis and discussion. *She* has the *sh* chunk, just as *the* provides an opportunity to teach *th.* Some of the words are phonetic and lend themselves to segmenting and blending; others are not and, therefore, help students to understand the importance of the wholeness of words.

The 20 most important words for kindergartners to read and write are:

the	*I*	*of*	*can*	*and*
my	*a*	*said*	*to*	*on*
in	*like*	*is*	*we*	*you*
he	*that*	*she*	*it*	*at*

Adding Words Gradually

Introduce words slowly and steadily at the beginning of the school year. I recommend

Words to Include on Your Main Word Wall

Words such as *Mom, Dad, cat, dog,* and *love* do not appear on any standard list of high-frequency words but are some of the most regularly used words in kindergartners' writing—and are encountered often in reading—and thus could and should be posted on the Word Wall. Post student names and color words in the classroom, as well as other words you and/or students deem important, but don't display them on the main Word Wall. Adding words that are not high-frequency words will clutter it and make it difficult for students to use as a resource. If too many words appear on the Word Wall, then it isn't realistic to expect students to learn all of them, and it would not make sense to refer to the words as "words we know." Both Cunningham (2009) and Gentry (2006) agree that though names are valuable in teaching phonics, they do not belong on the main Word Wall of high-frequency words.

one, maybe two, per week to begin with. Each word will need to be introduced with intention; that is, you should know in your mind that it is the most important word of the week and you should have a plan as to how to introduce it and what type of follow-up activities will help students to learn it. The word should be added to the Word Wall and then referred to often.

Soon students will come to understand the concept of a word and learn several words. Then you can start introducing words more quickly; for example, students might be able to learn two new words per week rather than one, or they might be able to learn three closely related words, such as *he, she,* and *we.* Gentry (2006) concurs, stating that, generally, two words per week is appropriate for kindergarten. Be wary of adding too many words at the same time or teaching new words before students have had adequate time to work with previously added words, or they will not be able to absorb the words into their repertoire of known words.

Colors for Words

The words on my Word Wall are written on different colored paper. This is helpful, especially when students try to find and copy a certain word. During writing time, I might say something like, "You're trying to write *my.* Don't forget that's on the Word Wall." I then watch the student search for the word *my.* If he is not looking in the *Mm* area, I will remind him that our lips go together on that word and that means the word starts with the letter *m* or that *my* sounds like *mouse* so he can search for the mouse picture. Once the student finds the general area (or I point it out), I can then say, "Okay, now which of these words says *my*? Is it the green one or the pink one or the yellow one?" This will guide the student to find the word on his or her own and then, when trying to copy it, not confuse it with other *Mm* words—*me, Mom*—that are on different colors.

Orchestrating the Practice of Word Wall Words

In addition to creating a memorable association for a new word, you will need to give students many opportunities to use it in writing and to read it within the context of phrases or sentences that appear on charts, books, or in their own writing. Isolated, skill-specific practice is appropriate and highly effective with sight words. When you introduce a word, arrange many learning situations, especially immediately following the introduction, in which students can practice reading the word in real contexts and applying it in their writing in meaningful ways. Without these follow-up opportunities, students will not be able to start the process of committing the word to memory. Again, they will need constant exposure to the high-frequency words in order for those words to become permanently known.

PROVIDING PLENTY OF INDEPENDENT READING TIME

Lots of easy reading, says Cunningham (2009), in which most words are immediately recognized, is essential for the development of sight word vocabulary. Independent reading time, where students choose from books that are at their independent reading level, is the venue for making this happen. Remember that at the beginning of the school year, students will use the texts that you introduce during shared reading and the books you provide during small-group instruction for independent reading material; however, as the year goes on, and they gain more skills and come to know more sight words, kindergartners can choose from all sorts of books at their level, whether the books have been taught by the teacher or not. Reading easy books, in great volume, is crucial to the solidification of sight words.

Creating Texts That Intentionally Include Sight Words

As previously discussed, you can easily create books that showcase a particular word. If you are introducing the word *can,* for example, you could create a book that features the word *can* on each page. It is easy, too, to bring in recently taught sight words to help review and solidify those words as well. The repeating language on each page might be *I can pet the* . . . and each illustration would show a different animal. Students would get practice in recognizing the new word *can* as you emphasize, "Hey, there's our new word *can,*" while at the same time continuing to work on the previously introduced words *I* and *the* as you declare, "Oh my gosh, I see some other words we know, too."

Asking "What do you notice?"

Continuing to ask, "What do you notice?" during shared-reading time will elicit opportunities to discuss and reinforce the sight words that have been taught. For example, when students respond with something like, "I see the word *and,*" you can say, "Yes! That's a word we know. It's on our Word Wall by the letter *Aa.*" This activity reiterates the importance of these words and that students should be learning them.

INCORPORATING SIGHT WORDS INTO DAILY WRITING

You can facilitate the use of sight words in your students' daily writing. For instance, if you have recently taught *the*, it is easy to get students to try writing it by giving them a topic and then suggesting a few ways in which they might write about it. If you read a book about a fox, you could have them write about the fox and facilitate their writing by saying, "Today you're going to write about the fox. You might want to write about how the fox was sad, or you might want to write 'The fox was cute,' or you could talk about how the fox tried to save the leaf." Seemingly random suggestions like these will lead students to start their writing with "The fox . . ."

While circulating about the room and assisting students during writing time, it is easy to get them to use certain Word Wall words by suggesting that they write a little bit more and then giving them some ideas that would require the use of a certain word. For example, you could

Using Sight Words Makes Them Less Abstract

Having opportunities to practice applying letter-sound knowledge to the process of writing definitely increases the rate at which students acquire letter-sound correspondence. And the same is true for words. When a high-frequency word is introduced and then students read that same word in a book or try using it in their writing, the word becomes less abstract and more meaningful, and thus easier to remember. Calkins agrees, ". . . if I was to teach high-frequency words and then post them on the Word Wall, I'd still expect the real learning would come not from the five or ten minutes I had spent teaching the word but from the children encountering that word repeatedly in the midst of their ongoing reading and writing, and using the Word Wall as a tool to help them recall and use conventional spellings" (2001, p. 213).

get a child to write *like* no matter what the topic by saying, "Do you like _____? Because if you do, you could say that in your writing."

It is important to hold students accountable for writing Word Wall words correctly. Once a word is placed on the wall, it is a known word and should be spelled correctly. I usually circle any misspelled Word Wall words during writing time and remind students that the circle means they should try to find the word on the Word Wall, erase what they have, and spell it correctly.

Typing Sight Words

If you are fortunate enough to have a lab that allows all your students to work simultaneously at computers, then you can have them practice letters and words in this setting. I have found it quite effective to have students practice the words on the Word Wall by typing them while we are in the lab. By removing the physical act of writing, students are better able to focus on a word and its characteristics. Of course, we do not attempt this until a few months into the school year because there are many prerequisite computer skills for students to learn.

I first have students try to recall which words are on the Word Wall by letting them brainstorm words for me to type on the big screen that is visible to everyone. As they suggest words, I have students try to spell them, and I type them as they spell. After they've suggested five or ten words, I either have students copy the words I typed on their computers or clear the words on my screen and encourage them to type any and all Word Wall words they know. The differing variables are dependent upon how far we are into the school year, how many words are on the Word Wall, and how well students can, at that point, find the letters on the keyboard, spell, and stay on task. No matter the time of year or parameters, students always finish the task by reading back to me the words they have typed.

Using Magnetic Letters

Working with magnetic letters also frees students from the physical act of writing. I do two activities that utilize lowercase magnetic letters.

- The first is a whole-group activity that uses giant or standard-sized magnetic letters and a large magnetic board (or a smaller board that I hold). A student suggests a word, and then either that student or another student comes up and tries to spell it with the letters. I encourage the other students to "do it in their minds" and then check to see if they spelled the word right.

- The second activity can also be done with a small group; for example, at the Assistant Center. Each student has his or her own personal-size magnetic board and a set of letters for the words I've selected. I have students work simultaneously on their board as I start with a simple task and make tasks progressively more difficult. I keep this activity as fast-paced as possible, helping those students who need it so that others do not get off-task and start playing with the magnetic letters. A series of tasks might sound like this:

  » Start with the same letters in the same order across the top of each student's board. "Let's point to and say all the letters on our board: *t, r, h, e, d, s, m, i*."

  » "Pull down the letter *e*." Check each student's action. "Put the letter *e* back." Repeat for all the letters in the set, spending just a few seconds on each one. Students should be permitted and encouraged to watch their peers and "copy" them; this will keep the activity moving at a fun, fast pace.

  » "Pull down the right letters and spell *it*." When all students have the word *it* on their board, say, "Let's point to and read this word." Do this as a group. "Now, let's point to each letter and spell the word *it.*" Again, encourage everyone to do this together. Repeat for the words *red, is, he, she,* and *the.* Of course, only ask students to make words that are on the Word Wall.

  » If appropriate, have students leave the *e* and remove just the beginning letter(s) to then make *me, he,* and *she.* This can lead into and/or support conversations about word families and rhyming.

  » "Make sure all the letters are back up at the top of your board in this order: *t, r, h,* . . . *e, d,* . . . *s, m, i.*" This prepares the boards for the next group during center time.

Practicing Words on Personal Dry-Erase Boards

The primary purpose of this activity is to solidify sight words through the process of writing them. This is also a good time to practice correct letter formation and handwriting. Because I want to observe students closely as they write the words, I have them gather around me on the floor. Supplies—small dry-erase boards, markers, and tissues—are distributed. The expectations for using these supplies are explicitly taught and then quickly reviewed each time we do the activity, and students know they must take a short break from the activity if they do not honor the expectations. We go over everything that I predict might be detrimental to the effectiveness of the activity, such as not taking the lid off the marker until I say it is time; not writing on anything except the top surface of the board (a few students colored the edges of the board, which cannot be wiped off, and that led to this guideline); not smelling the markers; not pressing too hard or smashing the tips of the markers in any way; not writing or drawing anything extra on the board other than the word that is being practiced; erasing the word as soon as I imply that their work is correct ("Perfect! Erase it!"); and, thoroughly wiping the board clean before putting it away.

Then I give students the first word to write. Students are allowed and encouraged to look at the Word Wall if they need to. My glance shifts quickly as I try to catch each student writing at least a portion of the word. I keep a close eye on the way in which they are forming the letters. I try to catch students as they are *about* to make a formation error (e.g., starting a letter at the bottom and going up instead of starting at the top and going down) and supply an appropriate prompt or scaffold: "Remember, we always start at the top and go down" or "Your marker is way down at the bottom; you're not going to go up, are you?" It is usually possible to tell if a letter was formed incorrectly, even if I didn't observe the action, and I will ask the student to try it again as I watch. Making changes is easy since erasing is done with a tissue. When a student has spelled the word correctly and also formed the letters correctly, then I tell him or her to erase the board. They then must sit patiently until everyone else has written the word. This activity is time-consuming with a whole group; with a competent assistant, it can be done effectively during center time.

Playing "What's the Word?"

"What's the Word?" is a quick game I play with my kindergarten students to ensure that they stay in touch with the words accumulating on the Word Wall. I start this about midyear when there are quite a few words on the Word Wall. I often do it at the end of the day as a final fun activity that the Busy Bee can help lead.

- I give clues about one word on the Word Wall to students and ask them to guess what it is.

- I whisper the first clue to the Busy Bee, and she announces it to the class. The act of whispering in someone's ear and then waiting for the whisper to be shared with everyone keeps students listening and engaged. The first clue almost always tells how many letters the word has or what color card the word is on.

- Students search the Word Wall for words that match the clue. I write their ideas on the dry-erase board, ensuring that each word meets the criteria. Students like to spell the word for me as I write it.

- Succeeding clues may be "starts with a tall letter," "has one vowel," (if it is later in the year when we have started talking about vowels), "has a hang-down letter," "rhymes with . . .," "is the opposite of . . .," or "has the _____ chunk in it." For the ensuing clues, students look at the words written on the dry-erase board and choose words, one at a time, that now meet both criteria.

- I circle these words. The choices narrow and the clues become more specific until there is just one word left.

Playing the game is a whole-class effort because the class is working together, not against each other, to determine my word.

Word Sorts

Once introduced, word sorts can be done as a whole group, in small groups (either with or without adult supervision), or on an independent basis. You will need to create a recording sheet with boxes in which students can write words. I usually start with two boxes; an example is shown (right).

Another example is words that have an *i* and words that do not have an *i*. Later I move into three boxes (e.g., words that start with a short letter, words that start with a tall letter, words that start with a hang-down letter) and possibly four boxes. By the time students can handle separating words into four different categories, they also understand that words might fit into more than one group. For example, if the categories are words with an *a*, words with an *e*,

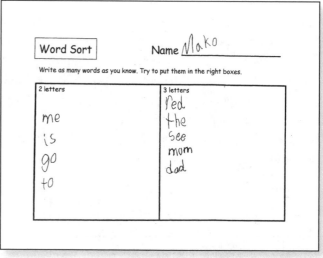

Word sort

words with an *i*, and words with an *o*, some words, such as *like*, could be written in two boxes.

I try to simplify the category heading as much as I can, usually by writing a word that represents the category or a short clue rather than writing out the name of the category. This makes it easier for students to remember the criteria after I first explain it. I use the same format on each sheet I create for this activity, as it will serve as a scaffold to remind students that they are sorting words. If the sheet is made and saved on the computer, as shown on the next page, you can easily change the category clues in each box. This activity is very helpful in getting students to know and remember which words are on the Word Wall and where each one is located.

Word Wall word search completed by a kindergarten student

■ INVOLVING PARENTS IN WORD PRACTICE

Since the teaching of sight words is fairly straightforward, it is the main component of reading development that parents are capable of and willing to help with at home. I truly believe that most parents want to be involved with their child's learning but are unsure of what exactly is being taught and how to go about supporting their child. It is easy to periodically provide parents with a list of words that you introduced in class and some short and simple instructions on how to help their child work with these words at home (see page 185). Notice that this note to parents emphasizes that these are *sight* words and that the best way to practice is to have the child look at the word and repeat what the parent says until the child can look at it and say it by himself or herself. It is okay if parents point out a certain feature of the word, such as double *e*'s, but they shouldn't encourage their child to sound out these words.

I sometimes send home a note saying that in a few weeks I will be testing students on how many sight words they know and that, in the meantime, it is acceptable to practice these words at home. The list of words that should be known (the ones on the Word Wall), along with others that can be practiced if the student already knows the Word Wall words (any of the remaining 100 high-frequency words), is attached to the note. Also, by making available assessment data, such as that shown on page 76, parents can see whether their child is learning words at an appropriate pace, based on the standard or expectation and in relation to how many words the other students in the class have learned. After parent-teacher conferences, when I go over the data I have collected and share the number of sight words that students are learning, or after I send home an updated assessment chart, I notice that parents start working on sight words more at home. Having that data in front of them—how many words their child knows in comparison to the other students—is quite motivating.

■ PROVIDING SUPPORT FOR STRUGGLING STUDENTS

There will always be some students who struggle with recognizing and learning to read sight words and who need extra support. I offer support on two different levels with my students: Students can get extra one-on-one time with the classroom aide (Tier 2 intervention) and/or participate in short, concentrated before-school tutoring sessions with me (Tier 3 intervention).

Working with the classroom aide: There are certain times of the day when my classroom aide is available to pull students aside and work with them one-on-one. These sessions are short—usually 5–7 minutes—so students can return to the class instruction or activity without missing too much. After assessing students on how many words they have learned, I analyze the class data and prepare a list for my aide of the students who could benefit from additional instruction in and practice with sight words. My aide teaches the words in the same manner that I would and in the way in which we encourage parents to, but, since it is one-on-one instruction, he or she also has the opportunity to tailor prompts and scaffolds for each student.

Before-school tutoring sessions: I invite struggling students to before-school sessions during the middle part of the school year. These twice-a-week sessions are short, commencing about 15 minutes prior to the start of the school day. Students come into my room after getting off the school bus, or parents bring them in. I usually work with three students in this setting, having found that a group of three provides motivation and momentum that would not happen were I to work with a child one-on-one.

While there are many ways to work with and practice words, I have found that, with struggling learners, the most effective way is to do good old-fashioned flashcard drills. There are many tricks of the trade that can really escalate the effectiveness of word flashcards.

- The only words in my stack of sight word cards are those that are currently on the Word Wall. From this stack, I choose the three to five easiest and most frequently used words. I display a card, say the word, then make sure all three students look at the word and say it. I quickly repeat this with the other words to keep the pace going. We go through these words until most of the group can recognize and say them. Then I shuffle the word cards, and repeat the process until I am satisfied that all three students know almost all the words.

- I slowly add one or two new words to the stack of initial words. Words are never removed from the stack, just added. Prior words continue to be practiced, so students get better and faster at recognizing them.

- I might point out a salient feature of the word (*the* has the Bad Boys) or give the students a scaffold to use (pull the corners of your mouth back when you see the *i* in *it*) until the word, and the way in which it can be attacked, becomes automatic.

There are very few words that I encourage students to "sound out." With each session, more and more words are added and practiced.

- As students get to know the words, I sometimes have them take turns. This takes some of the pressure off those students who cannot process information as quickly and also allows me to assess who is having difficulty and which types of prompts and scaffolds might work for them.

- Often, spelling a word out loud helps students remember and say it. Or, if I ask a student how he or she knows a certain word and that student is able to verbalize it, then we might use that as a means for helping the other students learn the word.

- Though it is important to let students occasionally take turns reading the words, I tend to keep this activity in "race format" more often than not. (See the description below.) I have done this enough to know that when students say the words together, or try to say them before their peers can, students who process visual information more slowly and/or take longer to spit back information show a marked increase in the speed at which they can do this task. The momentum of the activity and the pressure of saying the word simultaneously with, or even before, the others in the group seem to increase the firing speed of their neurons. Also, with this format, all students look at and process every word, whereas during turn taking, some may tune out when it is not time for them to read a word.

- It is necessary to talk about staying focused, being ready, and watching my hands in order to know exactly when the next word will be shown.

- There are two simple techniques I use to motivate students to say the words as fast as they can.

  » The first is to give the word card to whomever says the word the fastest. I do not hand cards to students to hold because they tend to fiddle with and bend them; rather, I lay the cards on the table in front of them and put subsequent cards in their stack. This, alone, is enough of a reward to get kindergarten students to try their hardest. Once all the cards are read and each student in the group has a stack, we count and find out who got the most. This is competitive, yes; the competition is motivating, and students recognize how much they are learning as they acquire more and more words each time.

  » If no one in the group knows the word I present, I say the word and then stick it back in the stack, reminding students that they will be seeing that word again very soon. As students say the words, the stack of remaining words gets smaller and smaller, meaning that a troublesome word will reappear soon. Each time the troublesome word appears, students are better able to recall it.

- Sometimes one student in the group struggles far more than the others. I want to ensure that this is a positive learning experience for that student and he or she feels confident that he or she, too, is learning words. I can do this by incorporating more turn-taking sessions and making sure that the easiest words, or words that this student is more likely to know and read, are flashed when it is his or her turn. I can also be ready for that split-second when this child is ready and watching and perhaps the other two are not, so he or she has a better chance of saying the word before the others.

PRACTICING WORDS DURING TRANSITION

In my attempts to utilize as many minutes as possible for learning, I have students practice reading sight words as they are moving through the drinking fountain line. I have placed a metal cabinet alongside the line-up area and attached magnetic sight words that students can point to and read while the line is moving along. I also have them read three words written on a small dry-erase board as they move away from the drinking fountain and back to the gathering area. Students can discuss, quietly, the words and assist each other in reading them. Or, I have my assistant supervise the line of children and provide prompts and feedback as they read the words.

A SAMPLE WEEK OF EXPLICIT TEACHING AND INTENTIONAL PRACTICE FOR THE WORD *STOP*

A good example of arranging for the practice of a particular word occurs in Week Four of the yearlong plan on Teacher Express.

Theme and Word: The weekly theme is *bus*, and the word to be learned that week is *stop*. Although *stop* is not one of the top 100 most frequently occurring words in the English language, I like to teach it because it is a word that links environmental print—words and other graphic symbols that children learn to recognize because they are frequently seen in their environment—and print that actually needs to be analyzed and processed in order to be read. It is a good word to use to solidify the concept of a word.

Essential Read-Aloud: *School Bus* by Donald Crews is an essential read-aloud for the week. It contains dozens of pictures of school buses with stop signs.

Activities: Here is a list of the ways in which students learn and practice the word *stop* throughout the week:

- As I read *School Bus* aloud to the class, we find and read every stop sign on every bus.

- We draw a picture of a bus one day during writing time, and students write *stop* on the bus.

- Another day, we draw an intersection with a stop sign. Students write *stop* on the sign, and we then write the phrase *a stop sin* (sign) together.

- We add the word *stop* to our Word Wall, and I also hang a stop sign in the classroom.

- I draw students' attention to the stop sign on the Stop and Drop Box where they put important papers for me.

- During small-group reading time, students get their own copy of a book I wrote called *Stop* (*I see a stop sign. The bus has a stop sign. The lady has a stop sign. The boy has a stop sign. Stop signs are red.*) They learn to read the book and then they take it home and read it to their families.

- Toward the end of the week, when an actual school bus arrives to take students for a quick trip around the neighborhood, the first thing we do is find the stop sign on the outside of the bus and ask the driver if she can extend it and make it light up. I take a photo of students beneath the stop sign and hang it in the classroom.

By the end of the week, nearly all students recognize the word *stop*, and several have learned to spell it as well, meaning that they have probably learned four new letters and a few new sounds to boot.

ASSESSING SIGHT-WORD VOCABULARY

Assessing the number of words that students know by sight is a practical and purposeful activity. A school or district should decide how many and which sight words they expect kindergarten students to learn. (Remember, though, this list should not determine the number of words you teach or limit the number of words students actually learn.) These words should be included on the pre- and post-test and assessed two or three times mid-year as well.

It is a fairly easy process—though time-consuming—to present a list of words to students and see which ones they can read automatically without having to sound them out. "Because sight words should be recognized 'at sight,' children should have only a couple of seconds to identify the word," explains McGill-Franzen (2006, p. 122). If it takes longer than that, a child might be trying to decode the word, which is different than recognizing it on sight. You should observe what a student is doing during the few seconds it takes to say a word. Is the child trying to recall the word? Is the child working through an association he or she has made for this word? Or, is the child visibly or mentally sounding the word out? Perhaps the student hasn't even looked at the word yet. Students, especially those who process visual information slowly, should be given a couple of seconds to retrieve a word from its place of storage in the brain, but if a word is sounded out, then it should not be counted as a word that is known by sight.

I do not painstakingly check every student on every word at the end of every quarter. When the first quarter ends in October, my classroom assistant points to the words that have been introduced and asks the student if he or she can read them. The assistant then points to a few other words she thinks the student may know and finishes by giving the student, especially if we know this student is already reading a little, an opportunity to look over the list to see if there are any other words he or she knows. By the end of the second quarter of school, in December, students are able to focus on the tip of a pencil running down each column of words and, for the most part, read the words they recognize or say "skip" or "don't know" for the other words. If this proves too difficult for a particular student, then we go back to the first quarter method of pointing to the words that we think the student might know. Around the second or third quarter, students start to "sound out" some of the words on the list. This is an indication that they do not know the word and that they are trying to quickly read it. Again, even if they are able to read it, we do not count it as a known sight word. We only count the words that are automatic for the student. At the end of the year, almost all students have the ability to look through the entire list, one word at a time. Additionally, they have a strong sense of which words they know, reading some instantly and saying "no" or "skip" with the others.

An assessment like this is purposeful, meaning that it is worth my time to conduct. It helps me think about the level of books each child should be reading, which students I might want to provide additional support for, and, of course, whether I need to make some adjustments to the way in which I present the words to students and find ways for students to practice using them.

Conclusion

The explicit and ongoing teaching of sight words is a vital component to teaching kindergartners to read. Known words help anchor voice-print match and make it easier to predict the text. And, the more words readers know instantly, the more energy they'll have for decoding unknown words. Most important, a growing sight-word vocabulary means that students can read more and more texts independently, and this increased reading time helps add to and solidify their number of known words.

CHAPTER 8

Teaching Comprehension and Fluency

Comprehension is, ultimately, the goal of all reading experiences. And though it appears here as a separate entity and at the end of the book, it is, of course, embedded in all reading instruction and of utmost importance. Traditionally, kindergarten teachers have not been overly concerned with this aspect of reading instruction, but as kindergarten students become better and better readers, it will be crucial for their teachers to learn how to intentionally teach and foster comprehension, both "in front of" students' reading experiences during whole-group instruction and "into" their experiences while working with them individually.

Comprehension

The ability to process a text is called comprehension and it is, inarguably, the most important part of reading. Thus, comprehension must be at the forefront of our minds as the end goal of literacy instruction and learning. The processing needed for comprehension is embedded within the five critical strategies discussed in Chapter 6. If young readers are encouraged to read quality texts using these processes (reviewed below), it will be nearly impossible for them not to be comprehending at the same time.

- Proper **learning behaviors** will support comprehension.
- A reader's ability to decode by **word analysis** is reciprocated by his or her comprehension.

- A reader cannot **predict and cross-check** unless there is some comprehension going on.

- Comprehension is the basis for **self-corrections**.

- When a reader **makes relevant comments or asks questions** related to the text, he or she is demonstrating and furthering comprehension.

As teachers, we deal with comprehension in a less explicit manner because, from the very first day of instruction, the notion of reading is about making meaning, even though our instruction focuses on the behaviors and strategic thinking necessary to decode. Students practice voice-print match with two- and then three-word phrases that are linguistically correct and match the picture on the page. What comes out of a student's mouth must make sense or it has to be fixed up. It must sound like talking. It must be meaningful. Most of students' attempts at reading are supervised, which means that the majority of mistakes are corrected and nearly all words they read will be meaningful. Not making meaning is not an option.

Many kindergarten teachers tell me that their students can often read the words in a Level 3/C or higher text but that comprehension is an issue. Other than a small percentage of ELL students or students with an underdeveloped language base, comprehension should not be what holds students back from progressing to more challenging levels of text, such as Level 4/D, 6/E, or 8/F. There is, perhaps, some confusion about what "good" comprehension is. It is neither possible nor desirable, say Fountas and Pinnell (2006), for readers to remember every detail of what they read. Instead, we should look for evidence of comprehension while students are reading: Do they accurately predict most of the words? Do they substitute a word with another that makes sense in the sentence? Do they self-correct? And we should engage them in talking about what they are reading and gauge

Literal Understanding

Most lower level texts do not demand a lot in the area of comprehension. This is intentional: young readers must put their energy into their budding reading behaviors and figuring out the words. The literal understanding that is required in order to read one of these books, however, is vital and can be challenging for some students. Fountas and Pinnell (2006) explain that grasping the literal meaning of a text is, in itself, a complex process that requires a reader to decode the words and, even more important, to understand the meaning of the words as they exist within the context of sentences. We should not assume that students understand the literal meaning of a beginning text. Comprehension should not be overlooked or downplayed. Without a strong foundation in literal understanding, higher levels of thinking and processing will never be possible.

the relevancy of their comments and questions. I honestly believe that my kindergarten students do not, in general, struggle with comprehension because I provide ample opportunities for small-group and one-on-one reading experiences; I focus my instruction on the five strategies I believe to be most critical for kindergartners; and, I model how, and allow students plenty of opportunities, to talk about books and learn that appropriate commenting and questioning is a part of reading. The last component—teaching students how to talk about their reading—is discussed in this chapter.

READING ALOUD TO DEVELOP AND DEEPEN COMPREHENSION

As discussed earlier, reading aloud is one of the four important parts of a balanced approach to teaching literacy. It is the component that requires very little reading work on the part of students, which means they are free to put their mental energy into understanding the story and thinking more deeply about its meaning. Most likely, you read aloud to your kindergarten students. But, knowing more about the importance and purpose of read-aloud may alter how often you do it, how you do it, why you do it, the books you choose, and its overall effect on students' reading development.

Fountas and Pinnell (2006) consider reading aloud to be an essential foundation of a good language and literacy program: "Reading aloud supports learning in every other area. It is a way of nourishing the intellect of your students, expanding background, vocabulary, and language, developing an appreciation for inquiry, and creating a literary community in your classroom" (p. 215). All of these things are, of course, what builds understanding, and thus comprehension, in students. Students develop schema about new ideas and will then have some background knowledge when they encounter the subject in another book. Each read-aloud introduces several new vocabulary words or at least shows the different ways in which words can be utilized. The more language our young students hear, the more language becomes accessible to them. And this is especially critical for those students who do not have a lot of life experiences, are not engaged in extended and meaningful conversations on a regular basis outside of school, and are not being read to at home.

Gathering Read-Aloud Books

There are many engaging read-aloud books available today. But, with instructional time being so precious, read-alouds should serve another purpose—or perhaps several purposes—in addition to providing sheer pleasure and getting young children to love literature.

Those absolutely-must-read books you know off the top of your head are a great starting point for listing and organizing read-aloud books. It will be immediately obvious which time of the year you will most likely use some titles, such as *Fall Leaves Fall*. With other titles, I suggest really looking closely at content and concepts, repeated use of one or more sight words, ability to provide practice with specific reading strategies, and/or other ways in which it might complement a weekly theme or instructional unit. Read-alouds can be an important component in helping students make connections throughout a theme, and these connections will deepen their comprehension. Therefore, keep your yearlong plan and weekly thematic units in mind when considering which books to use as read-alouds.

Collecting high-quality, purposeful read-aloud books is an ongoing process. Whether you have plenty of read-aloud books at your disposal or are just starting to gather books, always be on the lookout for new possibilities.

I suggest creating a list of books you want to purchase. It is convenient to own the read-aloud books you will read to your class every year—as opposed to having to request them in advance from the school or public library or borrow them from another teacher—but you may decide that it makes more sense to pledge school dollars not toward read-aloud books that you may use once or a few times with each class, but toward books that will be used repeatedly throughout the entire school year with many students. I prefer to own favorite read-aloud books and let the school district purchase books that students will handle regularly and will thus need to be replaced on an ongoing basis.

While it is best first to borrow a book from the library—and then test its effectiveness with your students—or preview it at your local bookstore before purchasing it, this is not always possible and may, in fact, prevent you from discovering some real gems. I have uncovered many quality read-aloud titles through the following two-step process:

- First, I find titles for different units on the many Web sites devoted to kindergarten thematic unit planning.

- Then, I peruse online bookstores to read summaries and reviews of the books and, perhaps, get a peek inside to see the layouts of the text and illustrations.

With this process, I can usually gather enough information about books before I actually invest in them. Online bookstores are good, too, at suggesting related titles that may interest you.

FIVE WAYS TO INCREASE THE EFFECTIVENESS OF READ-ALOUD

I have discovered five main ways to increase the positive effects of read-aloud in the kindergarten classroom.

1. **Try to increase the number of books or times you read aloud to your students.** Every time you read to your students, you create opportunities for them to hear language, develop vocabulary, and create schema for new concepts. You also establish shared experiences that contribute greatly to the overall community of the classroom. Instituting a balanced approach to teaching literacy will make it more difficult to find time each day to just read aloud to your students. But there are so many good books out there and this is a crucial foundational activity in kindergarten, so do try to commit to reading at least one, and up to four books, to your students each day. When I had a full-day kindergarten, students might hear three or four books per day. I had time for repeated readings of the same book, which I highly suggest doing if you can find the time.

2. **Intentionally and effectively plan the titles to read and the order in which you read them.** By doing so, you can help students develop a schema on a certain topic and then build upon it with related books. You can sequence read-alouds so students can make connections between a current text and a previous one. Knowing the vocabulary, characters, or the message from one story can assist them in activating prior knowledge and better comprehending a subsequent book. This is why I list the read-alouds for each weekly theme in my yearlong plan.

3. **Have students share the same experiences and the same books.** When a group shares the same background knowledge about certain topics or titles, powerful things happen. The amount of follow-up talk amongst students increases. Thus, the shared knowledge of the learning community is yet another way to enhance comprehension.

4. **Assign writing topics based on the books students have shared.** If we read *The Cat in the Hat* and I ask students to write about the cat, there will be no dearth of knowledge or ideas. As students write, their thinking and understanding about the character will expand. As I work with students while they write, I get a good glimpse into their comprehension and can help shape their ideas as they write. If there is time to share, students listen to others' writing and consider whether that thinking matches their own. Sometimes, they want to revise what they wrote based on another student's thoughts. This sharing greatly increases the knowledge and concepts of everyone in the group as well as their ability to comprehend future, related stories.

5. **Make read-alouds interactive.** In an interactive read-aloud, students are expected to participate in thinking about, talking about, and responding to the text. Pause occasionally at strategic, talk-worthy points, and ask students to briefly talk about the book. This is an essential update to the more traditional read-aloud in which students sit quietly and listen politely as the teacher reads.

The following ideas will help you incorporate interactive read-alouds into your classroom. These activities will assist students greatly in learning how to make relevant comments and ask related questions while reading individually with you or on their own during independent reading time. Interactive read-aloud not only deepens comprehension, but it also teaches children how to have intentional conversations with each other about literature.

Say Something to the Group

Kindergarten students need a few weeks at the beginning of the year to learn to sit quietly and listen politely during read-aloud time. Once they understand that they cannot interject whenever they have a thought to share and that they should not be having side conversations while you're reading, then it is time to model exactly how they can participate in an interactive read-aloud.

To get my students involved in meaningful conversation about books, I start with an activity called "Say Something to the Group." I tell the class that as I read, I will periodically put the book down on my lap and that will be their signal to say something about the book. Students must raise their hands, wait to be called on, and then say their idea loud enough for the entire group to hear. In addition to learning how to make relevant comments, I also want them to learn how to listen to their peers' comments. To encourage this, I teach them how to say, "I agree with . . ." when they realize a classmate had the same thought they did and got to share it with the class before they could. This keeps students attending more closely to what others are saying. Keep in mind that it is quite difficult for kindergartners to formulate a thought and keep it in their mind while at the same time listening to others' ideas. When you call on certain students, they might respond with, "I forgot." That is why we want to transition into talking to a partner—because all students get to participate and talk right away while their ideas are fresh.

Say Something to a Partner

When most students are able to hold their remarks until the appropriate time and then say something that is related to the story, I transition them into "Say Something to a Partner." I teach students how to turn to someone near them and start the conversation, facilitating a few groups of three if there is an odd number of students or if there are personality conflicts. Some teachers prefer to assign partners; they feel this alleviates any confusion there might be about who should talk to whom. I also model ways in which students can encourage their partner to talk if he or she is hesitant by asking questions such as "What do you want to say?" "Are you thinking the same thing I'm thinking or something different?" While students are talking to one another for the 1 to 2 minutes I allow, I listen in on as many partnerships or groups of three as I can and offer feedback if it seems necessary. Mostly, I listen for any remarks that suggest students are thinking about and comprehending the read-aloud book.

Ask a Question

Understanding the difference between a statement and a question is a difficult concept for kindergarten students, and it often takes most of the school year for them to get it, but modeling and having students practice will develop their awareness of both. In addition, teaching students how to ask questions while reading or listening to a story will give them yet another way to talk about books, as well as deepen their thinking and, thus, their comprehension.

There are two things that I have found to be especially helpful with aiding kindergartners to recognize a question:

- The first is to point out that a question needs an answer. I tell my students that if someone says something that requires an answer—*yes, no,* or something more specific—then he or she must have been asking a question. I'll sometimes preface my questions with, "I'm going to ask you a question, so get ready to give me an answer." This advance labeling helps students listen more closely to the variety of questions I ask throughout the day. Or, if students respond to me or their peers with an answer, I'll say, "Oh, you just answered, so that means that was a question."

- Asking questions is easier and more worthwhile when students can be spontaneous and natural rather than limited to formulating questions that begin with certain words. I haven't found it that helpful to teach kindergartners to listen for or use specific question words, such as *who, what, when, where,* and *why* because, really, questions begin with a wide variety of words. Instead, I tell students who are struggling with the concept that they can start their question with the words, "I wonder . . ." if they would like to. In the framework of this scaffold, I overhear students saying to one another, "I wonder what's going to happen next." "I wonder if she did that to make the other kid feel better." "I wonder if he'll find his mom." These, of course, are not questions, but they serve the same purpose as actual questions: students must continue to listen to see what the answers to their wonderings will be.

Saying something relevant and asking questions during read-aloud lays the groundwork for expecting students to do this when I work with them one-on-one. Talking about and asking questions about books will, over the course of the next few years, move from an outward, premeditated, or directed behavior to the independent ability and habit of thinking critically.

I Remember

"I Remember" will help students improve their listening comprehension. Tell students to listen and think about the read-aloud as well as they can and try to remember everything that happens. Then periodically stop and ask open-ended questions about the text such as, "What do you remember from this page?" or "Do you remember what the author has talked about so far in this book?" Open-ended questions allow students to respond in a variety of ways, ensuring that almost all their responses will be appropriate. Once students are good at remembering, recalling, and sharing information, you can start asking questions that require more specific answers: "Who remembers the girl's name?" or "Do you remember what he did right after he went to bed?" "I Remember" can be combined with "Say Something to a Partner." Talking about what they remember with a partner will keep all students engaged.

Important Words

This task encourages students to listen for and recall the most important words on a certain page or section of a book. You can help students find the most important words by preparing them to listen more closely as a significant word is about to come up in the story: "I'll bet there's an important word on this page. Let's listen closely while I read." The words to focus on are typically the subject of the story, names of characters, setting, crucial dialogue, new vocabulary, and words that advance or resolve the plot.

Balancing the Flow of the Story With Stopping and Talking

The story must flow. Pausing too often or for too long can easily, and quite abruptly, destroy any sense of the story that you were trying to develop by talking about it. Calkins (2001) cautions against pausing too often during a read-aloud. Just as we do not want to interrupt one-on-one reading instruction so frequently that a student cannot stay engaged in a text, we should not overdo turn-and-talk activities to the extent that they overwhelm the story. After students are familiar with these different activities, one way to ensure that they are more engaged in the story than in focusing on certain strategies or assigned conversations is to encourage them to turn and talk about the read-aloud in any way that lets them communicate and clarify their thinking.

ONE-ON-ONE INSTRUCTION ENHANCES COMPREHENSION

Interestingly, I find, year after year, that most of the instruction I do with individual students at my teacher table has to do more with the decoding aspect of reading than with the comprehension of text. This tends to be true even as students move beyond Level 3/C and into books that demand more in terms of comprehension. I have thought about this at length—especially since many kindergarten teachers tell me that their students struggle with comprehending texts beyond those considered standard for the kindergarten level— and have come to the conclusion that students will better comprehend what they read when comprehension—making meaning—is a nonnegotiable requirement of the process starting with their very first reading experiences. Frequently reading with students one-on-one, and monitoring their reading behaviors during independent reading, creates more opportunities where they are expected and encouraged to reread when meaning is lost.

ENCOURAGING REREADING WHEN COMPREHENSION BREAKS DOWN

Kindergarten students may not always realize when a story has stopped making sense to them. But, when I sit beside an individual at my table, I can hear in his fluency and expression when something in the text is not making sense to him. I encourage the student to reread by saying: "That didn't sound quite right. You better go back and read that again."

Rereading seems to be the easiest and most effective strategy for beginning readers. Regie Routman has found that most readers, including adults, tend to employ rereading for clarification first and foremost when meaning breaks down: ". . . rereading is the strategy that is most useful to readers of all ages. When given opportunities to reread material, readers' comprehension always goes up" (2003, p. 122). Routman, then, is encouraging all teachers— and not just kindergarten teachers—to have students reread as their main strategy to ensure comprehension.

Writing Demands Reading and Rereading

When we write, we must go back and reread what we have written to determine which word comes next and to make sure that our message is unfolding on paper in the way we intend it to. In this way, the writing task also becomes a reading task, and the written product becomes a reading resource.

Students have to first be taught that their writing can be read, just like the writing found in books, on the board, or in written notes. They also should be encouraged to read what they have written by using their new skills with voice-print match. And, as their writing becomes more prolific, they will discover that it is necessary to go back and reread as they continue with their ideas. This reading and rereading requires all the same strategic processing that students use while reading leveled texts, and it is often even more demanding than reading leveled books as students tend to write at a higher level than they can read. Because of this, strategic reading is a part of writing, and any instruction or practice in writing is, ultimately, instruction and practice in reading. Every writing opportunity is a reading opportunity.

PROVIDING OPPORTUNITIES FOR INTIMATE CONVERSATION

The time that I spend with students on an individual basis presents an excellent opportunity for me to assess comprehension and support them in thinking more deeply about the books they are reading. Sitting with a student and listening to him or her read allows me to assess the level of comprehension, both indirectly and directly. As the student reads, I closely observe the predicting, cross-checking, and self-correcting that occurs, which provides insight into the child's comprehension. I listen to the student's fluency and expression, both indicators of comprehension. Also, because the setting is comfortable and informal, students tend to talk about the book while they read, either by making comments or asking questions, often without any prompting. My job is to think about these remarks: Are they related to the text? Are they relevant? Do they indicate that the student understands what is happening in the story?

Again, kindergartners do not always realize that a text should make sense and that they should try to understand what they are reading, so it is important to tell them this explicitly. When you see a lack of comprehension, start by reiterating to the student that the book should make sense and that he or she should think while reading, not just about figuring out the words, but also about what the book is actually saying. As with many areas of teaching in kindergarten, it is necessary to be overly explicit about the big picture and to make sure students know the purpose behind what they are doing.

Tell or Retell?

Sometimes I will ask a student to tell me what happened in the book or what the book is about. This more open-ended inquiry allows a reader to respond in a variety of ways that will help demonstrate his or her comprehension. A student may retell the entire story, especially if the text is short, but I rarely use the term *retell* with kindergarten students, and I do not intentionally teach them this skill. If they, by chance, do retell the story, I get one type of insight into their understanding; answering questions or talking more randomly about the text provides me with additional or different information about their comprehension.

Fluency Is a Reflection of Comprehension

All the cognitive processing that happens during reading—processing meaning, language, and print—affects fluency. Fluency is more than just reading quickly, although momentum is definitely an important aspect. Fluency is about reading in phrases, rather than word by word, and involves expression, intonation, and responding to punctuation. You may think that fluency doesn't really apply to the kindergarten level so you won't be addressing it in your instruction. However, Fountas and Pinnell (2006) explain that, for young readers, fluency involves moving the eyes from left to right, returning to the left margin for each new line, voice-print match, the use of space, solving words using letters and sounds, and cross-checking visual information with meaning.

FLUENT READING IS NOT AN IMMEDIATE GOAL IN KINDERGARTEN

When kindergartners are first learning to read, not only is it okay if they read word by word in a somewhat disfluent manner, but it is also desirable and advantageous to their overall learning. I want students pointing to and looking closely at each word as a separate unit. I want them to say each word as they see it independent of the others on the page. As you have read, I teach them to use their finger to hop from one word to the next and discourage the behavior of sliding their finger. I need to know students have mastered voice-print match completely, and I assess this by their ability to read, early on, in a jerky, word-by-word fashion. This is corroborated by Fountas and Pinnell, who say that, for Levels A–C, behaviors should include "reading slowly and carefully with crisp pointing under words" (2006, p. 74). Such disjointed reading does not indicate a lack of comprehension; it is just a natural part of learning to read for kindergartners.

Once students have mastered voice-print match, I still do not worry about disfluent reading. Such reading usually means that students are engaged in serious cognitive processing, such as drawing on their prior knowledge, thinking about and responding to scaffolds and prompts, and cross-checking the three sources of information available to them as they read. Early readers need to do some heavy-duty thinking with almost every word they encounter, and this requires them to linger on each word.

If kindergartners are pushed to read faster or more smoothly too soon, then they will not develop the habit of cross-checking as they read. They will say a word and move on and try to say the next one as quickly as possible without taking the time to monitor what they are saying. This is definitely not what we want to cultivate in young readers. I encourage you to let kindergartners "sit" on words for a few seconds, even if they've read a word correctly. There is a much greater chance that students' comprehension and fluency will be fine in the long run if we allow them time, initially, to read slowly and disfluently while they learn to monitor and make meaning.

TRANSITIONING STUDENTS INTO MORE FLUENT READING

As readers gain experience and less mental processing is required for the reading of each and every word, it will be appropriate to help them transition to reading in phrases with a steady momentum. It will be time to explicitly teach how reading should sound and how readers make their reading more fluent and expressive.

Rereading, which was earlier mentioned as the most important strategy to teach for comprehension, is also the best way to improve fluency. First in the whole-group setting and then during one-on-one instruction, I model how to reread a phrase or sentence to "make it sound more like talking." I then immediately have the student reread it, requesting that he or she make the phrase or sentence sound like talking or like it did when I read it. (The requests are one and the same, but phrasing it one way or the other makes better sense to different students.)

I explicitly introduce the concept of more fluent reading about mid-year, but will not push individual students into rereading text in phrases and focusing on reading faster, smoother, and more expressively until I know that they regularly cross-check all three sources of information while reading. Most students easily transition from seeing and reading words as isolated items to recognizing strings of language as soon as I overtly model it and encourage them to try it.

FLUENT READING IMPROVES STUDENTS' SPEAKING ABILITY

Is it fair to expect students with underdeveloped articulation and expressive language skills to try to read more fluently? When these students are provided with explicit, daily instruction in voice-print match and reading strategies and are then given plenty of opportunities to try the strategies, their oral language skills can do nothing but steadily improve. Reading provides an excellent venue for speaking out loud. Additionally, each attempt at speaking when reading results in the correct use of vocabulary, syntax, and grammar. Early reading provides the chance for students to physically coordinate speech while looking at an accompanying visual.

READ-ALOUD AS A MODEL OF GOOD FLUENCY

There are many reasons to read aloud to students on a daily basis, but one of the most important is that it is a model of fluency in all its aspects. Expressive reading by an adult, especially that which involves dialogue, reiterates to children that reading should sound like talking. Listening to stories on tape or CD, on a computer, or digitally offers more opportunities for students to hear good, fluent reading. I have collected many books on tape or CD, mostly through book orders with acquired bonus points, and let students listen to stories at the Independent Center two or three times each week. I do this more at the beginning of the year when students cannot yet read many books on their own. Once they are able to do some independent reading, having them repeatedly read the same texts is more effective in improving fluency than is listening to stories.

FIVE EFFECTIVE WAYS TO IMPROVE FLUENCY IN KINDERGARTEN

There are five things that you can do to facilitate fluency in kindergarten.

1. **Provide the right level of text.** Fountas and Pinnell remind us that, "When you are reading at 95 to 100 percent accuracy, you have the optimum opportunity to orchestrate many different kinds of information, read with phrasing and fluency, and engage in a minimum amount of on-the-run problem solving while reading for meaning. Little attention needs to be devoted to solving words, so you can concentrate on the meaning (and, if reading aloud, on the way the voice reflects the meaning). An accuracy rate of 95 to 100 percent provides a rich base for fluency" (2006, p. 72).

2. **Teach young readers to rely on the three sources of information.** For the most part, readers should predict the text based on meaning and syntax and then cross-check with the visual information. Focusing too much on the letters and sounds can greatly hinder a reader's reading rate.

3. **Keep instruction light as you teach into students' reading.** Students need to self-monitor and, optimally, self-correct on their own without too many prompts or corrections. If students become accustomed to having you confirm each word they read, they will linger longer on every word, hampering their fluency.

4. **Provide time daily for independent reading with familiar books.** Students need the opportunity to repeatedly read books they know. With each subsequent reading comes improvement in fluency and comprehension.

5. **Teach sight words.** The more sight words a student knows, the easier reading will be. Fluency increases, which in turn enhances comprehension, which positively affects a student's fluency.

Conclusion

The most important thing you can do to develop kindergartners' comprehension is to ensure that they understand what reading is—a message that should make sense and from which they can derive meaning—and then insist that they read for meaning from their very first reading experiences and for each and every one throughout the year. Reading experiences should be managed in a way that ensures that comprehension is occurring. You can achieve this with urgent and intentional teaching based on the balanced-literacy approach. Use shared-reading time to directly and explicitly teach in front of kindergartners' reading experiences and to model and discuss the five critical strategies. Make the time—from day one—to work with students in small groups and then individually, with the right books, to teach into each child's exposures with reading. Use this time to build background knowledge and vocabulary. Prepare students to eventually read independently and to be successful with it by building a network of strategies and teaching them how to choose just-right books. And continue to read aloud to your students daily, building up their language and exposure to different concepts, while demonstrating what fluent and expressive reading sounds like.

References

Abbot, J. (1997). New knowledge about the biological nature of learning. In *Upside down and inside out: A challenge to redesign education systems to fit the needs of a learning society. New Horizons for Learning.* Retrieved September 6, 2011, www.newhorizons.org/trans/abbott2.htm.

Allington, R. (2006). *What really matters for struggling readers: Designing research-based programs.* Boston: Pearson.

Armbruster, B. B., Lehr, F., & Osborn, J. (2003). *Put reading first: The research building blocks for teaching children to read: kindergarten through grade 3.* Jessup: MD: National Institute for Literacy.

Bergen, R. (2008). *Teaching writing in kindergarten: A structured approach to daily writing that helps every child become a confident, capable writer.* New York: Scholastic.

Boushey, G., & Moser, J. (2006). *The daily five: Fostering literacy independence in the elementary grades.* Portland, ME: Stenhouse Publishers.

Bruner, J. (1957). *Going beyond the information given.* New York: Norton.

Bruner, J. S., & Sherwood, V. (1975). Peekaboo and the learning of rule structures. In J. S. Bruner, A. Jolly, & K. Sylva (Eds.), *Play: Its role in development and evolution* (pp. 277–285). Harmondsworth, England: Penguin Books.

Calkins, L. (2001). *The art of teaching reading.* New York: Longman.

Clay, M. (1991). *Becoming literate: The construction of inner control.* Portsmouth, NH: Heinemann.

Clay, M. M. (1993). *Reading recovery: A guidebook for teachers in training.* Portsmouth, NH: Heinemann.

Clay, M. M. (2001). *Change over time in children's literacy development.* Portsmouth, NH: Heinemann.

Clay, M. M. (2006). *An observation survey of early literacy achievement* (2nd ed.). Portsmouth, NH: Heinemann.

Cunningham, P. (2009). *Phonics they use: Words for reading and writing.* Boston: Pearson.

Dorn, L. J., French, C., & Jones, T. (1998). *Apprenticeship in literacy: Transitions across reading and writing.* Portland, ME: Stenhouse Publishers.

Durkin, D. (1966). *Children who read early: Two longitudinal studies.* New York: Teachers College Press.

Durkin, D. (1974–1975). A six-year study of children who learned to read in school at the age of four. *Reading Research Quarterly, 1*, 9–61.

Ellery, V. (2005). *Creating strategic readers*. Newark, DE: International Reading Association.

Fountas, I., & Pinnell. G. S. (1996). *Guided reading: Good first teaching for all children*. Portsmouth, NH: Heinemann.

Fountas, I., & Pinnell, G. L. (2006). *Teaching for comprehension and fluency: Thinking, talking, and writing about reading, K–8*. Portsmouth, NH: Heinemann.

Gentry, J. R. (2006). *Breaking the code: The new science of beginning reading and writing*. Portsmouth, NH: Heinemann.

Johnson, P. (2006). *One child at a time: Making the most of your time with struggling readers, K–6.* Portland, ME: Stenhouse Publishers.

Juel, C. (1988). Learning to read and write: A longitudinal study of 54 children from first through fourth grades. *Journal of Educational Psychology, 80*(4), pp. 437–447.

McGill-Franzen, A. (2006.) *Kindergarten literacy: Matching assessment and instruction in kindergarten*. New York: Scholastic.

National Institute of Child Health and Human Development. (2000). *Report of the National Reading Panel. Teaching children to read: An evidence-based assessment of the scientific research literature on reading and its implications for reading instruction* (NIH Publication No. 00-4769). Washington, D.C.: U.S. Government Printing Office.

Routman, R. (2003). *Reading essentials: The specifics you need to teach reading well*. Portsmouth, NH: Heinemann.

Serafini, F. (2001). *The reading workshop: Creating space for readers*. Portsmouth, NH: Heinemann.

Shaywitz. S. (2003). *Overcoming dyslexia: A new and complete science-based program for reading problems at any level.* New York: Knopf.

Stainthorp, R., & Hughes, D. (2004). An illustrative case study of precocious reading ability. *Gifted Child Quarterly, 48*, 107–120.

Taberski, S. (2000). *On solid ground: Strategies for teaching reading K–3*. Portsmouth, NH: Heinemann.

Vygotsky, L. S. (1978). *Mind in society: The development of higher psychological processes.* Cambridge, MA: Harvard University Press.

Strategic Reading Behaviors and Processes Associated With Each Level of Text

Teaching Points	A–B	3 C	4 D	6 E	8 F	12 G	14 H	16 I	18 J	20 K	24 L	28 M
Book care and handling	▓	▓	▒									
Directionality (read front to back, left to right)	▓	▓	▒									
Where to start (cover, title page, first page, first word on first page)	▓	▓										
Voice-print match (point to each word at the same moment it is said)	▓	▓	▓	▒	▒							
Which finger to use for pointing (index finger of dominant hand, "reading finger")	▓	▓	▒									
Put index finger *under* the words while reading (do not cover the words)	▓	▓	▓	▒	▒							
Skip the finger from word to word while reading (do not slide finger)	▓	▓	▓	▒	▒							
Do a fix-up if you say something that doesn't make sense or sound right	▓	▓	▓	▒	▒	▒	▒	▒	▒	▒	▒	▒
Read it again to do a fix-up	▓	▓	▓	▒	▒	▒	▒	▒	▒	▒	▒	
Terminology: *front, cover, title, beginning, end, letter, word, fix-up*	▓	▓	▒									
Use known sight words to anchor voice-print match	▓	▓	▒	▒								
Find and point to known sight words ("Can you point to the word *see*?")	▓	▓	▒	▒								
Use visual and meaning cues to begin cross-checking	▓	▓	▓	▒	▒	▒	▒					
Listen and watch as the teacher models how to read the first page or two	▓	▓	▒									
Listen to, remember, and use the repeating language patterns in the book	▓	▓	▓	▒								
Look at the picture to predict what the text will say	▓	▓	▒									
Where to start (left-hand page before right-hand page)		▓	▓	▒								

Teaching Points	A–B	3 C	4 D	6 E	8 F	12 G	14 H	16 I	18 J	20 K	24 L	28 M
How to execute a return sweep ("go back and down")		●	○									
Listen to, remember, and use any names that are in the story	●	●	●	○	○	○	○					
Use beginning sounds, along with language patterns and pictures, to read		●	●	○	○	○	○					
Find and point to a certain word and tell how you know what it says (encourage cross-checking, such as, "There's a dog in the picture, and the word *dog* starts with a *d*.")		●	●	○	○	○						
Be sure your reading makes sense; It should sound like talking	●	●	●	○	○	○	○	○	○	○	○	○
Terminology: *title page, first letter, cross-check, "go back and down"*		●	●	○	○	○	○	○				
Use beginning and ending sounds to predict words and cross-check			●	●	○	○	○	○	○	○	○	○
Use language patterns and syntax to read in fluent phrases				●	○	○	○	○	○	○	○	○
Blend individual letter sounds in short words			●	●	○	○	○	○	○	○	○	○
Make comments and ask questions that clarify or reflect comprehension			●	●	○	○	○	○	○	○	○	○
Notice word endings, such as *-ing, -ed, -s*				●	●	○	○	○	○	○	○	○
Cover word endings (*-ing, -ed, -s*) to make words shorter and easier to read				●	●	○	○	○	○	○	○	○
Name and notice different punctuation marks; adjust rate and intonation				●	●	●	○	○	○	○	○	○
Reread to regain meaning, fluency, and to help fix-up mistakes					●	●	●	●	○	○	○	○
Terminology: *fix-up/self-correct, reread, ending, period, question mark, comma, exclamation mark, quotation marks, cross-check*				●	●	●	●	●	●	○	○	○

■ introduce and emphasize

▒ review, reteach, solidify

☐ not usually applicable to this text level

Teaching Points	A–B	3 C	4 D	6 E	8 F	12 G	14 H	16 I	18 J	20 K	24 L	28 M
Notice chunks (*sh, ing, br, -an*) in words; isolate chunks with pointing finger				▓	▓	▓	▓	▓	▓	░	░	░
Blend initial consonants to determine words				▓	▓	▓	▓	▓	▓	░	░	░
Know that *y* says /ē/ on the end of words					▓	▓	▓	▓	▓	░	░	░
Look for small words within large words					▓	▓	▓	▓	▓	▓	▓	▓
Use picture clues and context cues to assign meaning to new vocabulary					▓	▓	▓	▓	▓	▓	▓	▓
Tell about the characters and events in a story					▓	▓	▓	▓	▓	▓	▓	▓
Tell about what you learned after reading nonfiction text					▓	▓	▓	▓	▓	▓	▓	▓
"Twist" sounds in words to ensure meaning					▓	▓	▓	▓	▓	▓	▓	▓
Try different sounds with letters with two or more sounds to determine words					▓	▓	▓	▓	▓	▓	▓	▓
Know long and short vowels and try each to determine words					▓	▓	▓	▓	▓	▓	▓	▓
Notice and think about silent-*e* at the end of words					▓	▓	▓	▓	▓	▓	▓	▓
Slide finger beneath words (rather than hop) or track words with eyes						▓	▓	▓	▓	▓	▓	▓
Make meaningful connections between texts or between text and own life						▓	▓	▓	▓	▓	▓	▓
Self-correct at point of mistake (rather than reread entire sentence)						▓	▓	▓	▓	▓	▓	▓
Read words in chunks rather than by individual letters (*in-vit-ed*)						▓	▓	▓	▓	▓	▓	▓
Read silently						▓	▓	▓	▓	▓	▓	▓
Read on, then go back, to figure out a word							▓	▓	▓	▓	▓	▓
Notice and make note of important words/new vocabulary							▓	▓	▓	▓	▓	▓
Elements of literature: characters, setting, author's purpose, illustrations, point of view, plot, symbols, mood, theme							▓	▓	▓	▓	▓	▓
Retell a story							▓	▓	▓	▓	▓	▓

Tips for Helping Your Child Read

Dear Parents,

At this point, have your child read and reread (and *reread!*) the book that is sent home. Reading each book several times will help your child gain skills, gain confidence, and feel like a reader!

- Read the title to your child because the titles are often much harder than the text inside the book. Have your child read the title back to you and reread it again on the title page, if there is one.

- Get your child started on the book by reading the first page or two to him or her. Students need to know the pattern of the language in the book before they can read it.

- Your child should use his or her index finger to point to the words while reading. Make sure your child is actually looking at each word. Even if your child has the book memorized, a lot of important information about text will still be processed as long as he or she is looking at the words. Your child should "jump" the pointing finger from word to word rather than slide the finger. This helps with the one-to-one voice-print matching. Don't worry if it sounds choppy; this will go away soon.

- If your child has trouble tracking the words or loses his or her concentration, physically move the pointing finger yourself. Or, use your own finger and point along with your child. Remind your child that whatever word he or she is touching is the exact word that should be coming out of his or her mouth. Most students can successfully voice-print match with five words per page at this point.

- If your child makes a mistake, encourage him or her to go back and try it again. Usually, kids will do this on their own. We call this "doing a fix-up," and we applaud all fix-ups with comments like "Wow! You did a fix-up! That's great—that's what good readers do!" The goal is for the child to feel comfortable taking risks, knowing that it is okay if a mistake is made, maybe even good if a mistake is made because then he or she can do a fix-up.

- Understand that most kindergartners are not actually reading yet (though they will be very soon). *Do not expect your child, or ask him or her, to sound out words.* You can talk about the first letter or sound of a word. For example, you might say, "I see that word has a *b*, so it must say *b-b-bunny* and not *r-r-rabbit*."

- You can point out and talk about basic sight words that recur in the book. Choose one or two words per book that you feel your child can or should learn to recognize (also think about the words that have been taught in class). To work on these words and to solidify the concept of what a word is say, "Can you point to the word *red*?" "Can you show me *I*?"

Sincerely,

_____

Take-Home Books

Dear Parents,

Please keep this note in your child's take-home book bag and refer to it as needed. Once you feel you have the hang of things, it's okay to remove it and throw it away.

Your child will bring home two new titles on _____ of each week. For the first few nights, it will be necessary to read the title and the first few pages to your child. After that, your child will probably be able to start reading the books on his or her own. This does not mean that you should go away and let your child read alone. It means to let your child do most of the work and feel like a reader and feel confident. Please supervise your child to make sure he or she is reading correctly. If your child practices at home and makes mistakes and no one notices and assists, then this may actually UNDO what I have taught at school. Reading together should be very rewarding, and it should only take 5–10 minutes each day.

Be sure your child accurately points to the words while reading. If a mistake is made, do not immediately correct it. Instead, ask questions such as these:

1. *Did you look at the picture?*

2. *Did you look at the letters in that word?* What your mouth said doesn't match the letters I see.

3. *Did that make sense?* Most books make sense. It should sound like regular talking.

Try to refrain from asking your child to "sound out" a word. Most students do not yet know how to sound out words, so please do not ask them to. Looking at the key letters and thinking about what makes sense works much better.

Try to manipulate the situation so that your child can self-correct. Then say, "Cool! You did a fix-up." or "Great! You fixed it up. That's what good readers do!" We want children to know that we love it when they fix up their mistakes. This will make them less worried about making mistakes and more inclined to self-correct when they do make a mistake.

Keep books in child's backpack in between reading, so he or she has the books at school each Tuesday!

Sincerely,

_____

Sight Words

Dear Parents,

These are the words that we've been working on in class so far. Ideally, students should be able to read them, spell them out loud, and write them with proper letter formation. Start working on them now so that your child doesn't get behind. The more words a child learns, the easier it is to learn even more words!

Don't have your child "sound out" the words too much. These are "sight" words. Just look at the word and say it.

is	a	I
he	you	she
red	me	it
yes	go	no
my	can	stop
the	see	up

For the word *a,* we make the short-*u* sound, like someone just punched you in the stomach. Making a punching motion is a good hint for your child.

The starts with the "Bad Boys" (*th*; we call them bad because they make us stick our tongue out), so remind your child to see the bad boys (*th*) and stick his or her tongue out for the *th* sound.

Sincerely,

First 100 High-Frequency Words

the	he	be	but	which
of	for	this	what	their
and	was	from	all	said
a	on	I	were	if
to	are	have	when	do
in	as	or	we	will
is	with	by	there	each
you	his	one	can	about
that	they	had	an	how
it	at	not	your	up

out	into	no	made	long
them	has	make	over	little
then	more	than	did	very
she	her	first	down	after
many	two	been	only	words
some	like	its	way	called
so	him	who	find	just
these	see	now	use	where
would	time	people	may	most
other	could	my	water	know

Characteristics of Specific Text Levels
and Exemplar Books for Each Text Level

Levels 1/A and 2/B	
	• 2–5 words per page • 5–8 pages to read • one idea or very simple storyline • very predictable text • print appears on only the left-hand pages or only the right-hand pages • print appears in the same place on every page • print is clearly separated from the pictures • extra space between words • one line of print per page (no return sweep) • repeating language pattern on each page • illustration on each page • repeating high-frequency word(s) • one novel word per page, always in the same position • less common words totally supported by the pictures

Level 3/C	
Dan the Flying Man (Joy Cowley, Wright Group) *I Went Walking* (Sue Williams, Harcourt Brace) *Families* (Brenda Parkes, Newbridge) *How to Make a Mudpie* (Rozanne Lanczak Williams, Creative Teaching Press)	• 4–8 words per page • 5–8 pages to read • simple storyline with familiar topics • longer than 2/B books with either more words per page or more total pages • print generally still appears on only the left-hand pages or only the right-hand pages • placement of print may vary from page to page (top or bottom of page) • print is clearly separated from the pictures • extra space between words • 1–3 lines of text per page • repeating language pattern in the text, but may have different patterns • several high-frequency words per page • less common words supported by the pictures • more difficult vocabulary or concepts than Level 2/B books

Characteristics of Specific Text Levels and Exemplar Books for Each Text Level, continued

Level 4/D	
Mary Wore Her Red Dress (Merle Peek, Clarion) *Who Will Help?* (Creative Teaching Press) *Rules* (Brenda Parkes, Newbridge) *Halloween* (Ann Staman, Educators Publishing Service)	• 2-6 lines of print per page, with more words than previous levels • 8-16 pages in the book • a bit longer and more complex than Level 3/C • print appears on both sides of the book and in different places on the pages • clear print with obvious spacing • repeating language patterns and/or natural sounding language • requires attention to print details, such as beginning sounds • text may contain dialogue • full range of punctuation • more difficult vocabulary or concepts than Level 3/C books • vocabulary contains more inflectional endings (*-ing, -ed, -s*)

Level 6/E	
Mrs. Wishy-Washy (Joy Cowley, Wright Group) *Five Little Monkeys Jumping on the Bed* (Eileen Christelow, Houghton Mifflin) *Tiny's Bath* (Cari Meister, Puffin Easy-to-Read) *The Swim Lesson* (Rozanne Lanczak Williams, Creative Teaching Press)	• the amount of text is gradually increasing; generally 3-8 lines of print per page; up to 15 words per page • 8–20 pages in the book • text placement varies • sentences may continue to the next page • clear print with obvious spacing • supportive illustrations, but the text carries the storyline rather than the pictures • repeating language patterns, if used, vary within the text • text may contain dialogue • full range of punctuation • stories more complex; ideas more subtle • requires word analysis to figure out the text • more difficult—and possibly unfamiliar—concepts than Level 4/D books • new vocabulary helps extend student's known vocabulary • inflectional endings are used (*-ing, -ed, -s*) • the text may appear easy to read but many reading processes and behaviors are required

Level 8/F

Cookie's Week
(Cindy Ward, Putnam)

Rosie's Walk
(Pat Hutchins, Macmillan)

We Need Water
(Helen Frost, Pebble Books)

Grow Little Turnip, Grow Big
(Sterling Publishing)

- texts are slightly longer than Level 6/E and, accordingly, the size of the print is smaller
- generally 3-8 lines of print per page
- 12-24 pages in the book
- text placement varies
- sentences may continue to the next page
- less use of repeating language patterns
- full range of punctuation
- stories more complex; ideas more subtle
- new vocabulary helps extend student's known vocabulary
- inflectional endings are used (*-ing*, *-ed*, *-s*)
- supportive illustrations, but the text carries the storyline rather than the pictures
- literary language may be used in combination with oral language structures
- there may be a sequence of events with an obvious beginning, middle, and end
- there is more variation with the way dialogue is presented and signaled
- the text will provide many opportunities for word analysis

Level 12/G and 14/H

Amy Loves the Snow
(Julia Hoban, Scholastic)

Red Socks and Yellow Socks
(Joy Cowley, Wright Group)

The Three Little Pigs
(retold by Harriet Ziefert, Puffin Easy-to-Read)

My Chickens
(Heather Miller, Children's Press/Scholastic)

Just This Once
(Joy Cowley, Wright Group)

Put Me in the Zoo
(Robert Lopshire, Random House)

Farm
(Angela Leeper, Heinemann Library)

Tarantula
(Edana Eckart, Children's Press/Scholastic)

- the amount of text is gradually increasing; generally 4–8 lines of text per page, but the sentences are longer
- literary language may be intertwined with natural language
- text may introduce students to new experiences rather than be based on completely familiar experiences
- reading vocabulary continues to expand, with new vocabulary introduced
- stories may have more events
- some repetition may be built into the story to support reading

Characteristics of Specific Text Levels and Exemplar Books for Each Text Level, continued

Level 16/I

Are You My Mother? (P.D. Eastman, Random House) *The Little Yellow Chicken* (Joy Cowley, Wright Group) *Go Away Dog* (Joan Nodset, HarperCollins) *Old McDonald's Funny Farm* (Rozanne Lanczak Williams, Creative Teaching Press)	• a variety of text, including some informational books • story structure more complex • varied themes • illustrations extend the text rather than provide support for the text • readers must understand different points of view • new vocabulary may be unusual and challenging • word analysis will only be necessary for unfamiliar words • characters will be memorable

Level 18/J

Green Eggs and Ham (Dr. Seuss, Random House) *Henry and Mudge, The First Book* (Cynthia Rylant, Aladdin) *Mouse Tales* (Arnold Lobel, Harper & Row) *Johnny Appleseed, My Story* (David L. Harrison, Random House)	• variety of text—nonfiction, folktales, realistic stories • stories are longer and more complex but still deal with topics of interest to young children • most concepts and themes are familiar • beginning chapter books (30-60 pages, but short sentences with familiar vocabulary) • new literary styles may be introduced

Level 20/K

Amelia Bedelia (Peggy Parish, Harper & Row) *Arthur's Loose Tooth* (Lillian Hoban, HarperCollins) *Bugs! Bugs! Bugs!* (Jennifer Dussling, DK Publishing) *Making Choices* (Cynthia Martin, Newbridge Educational Publishing)	• variety of text • long stretches of easy text or shorter, more difficult text • stories have many episodes related to the main plot • literary picture books that can be read in a single sitting

Characteristics of Specific Text Levels and Exemplar Books for Each Text Level, continued

Level 24/L	
Cam Jansen (David Adler, Puffin Books) *No Jumping on the Bed!* (Tedd Arnold, Scholastic) *Play Ball, Amelia Bedelia* (Peggy Parish and Wallace Tripp, I Can Read Book 2) *The Bravest Dog Ever: The True Story of Balto* (Natalie Standiford and Donald Cook, Step-Into-Reading)	• longer chapter books with just a few illustrations • great range of genre • more descriptive text • more characters • more detailed information • smaller text size with narrower spacing • story and character details must be retained over several days
Level 28/M	
A Chair for My Mother (Vera B. Williams, Reading Rainbow Books) *Alexander and the Terrible, Horrible, No Good, Very Bad Day* (Judith Viorst, Atheneum) *How Much Is a Million?* (David M. Schwartz, Reading Rainbow Books) *Who Eats What?* (Patricia Lauber, Let's-Read-and-Find-Out Science, Stage 2)	• variety of genre • lots of text per page • smaller print, narrower spacing • complex language structures • sophisticated vocabulary • highly detailed and descriptive • background knowledge required • may include flashbacks • complex plots • character development